Religion and Political
Conflict in Latin America

Sponsored by the Joint Committee on Latin American Studies of the Social Science Research Council and the American Council of Learned Societies

Religion and Political Conflict in Latin America

Edited by Daniel H. Levine

The University of North Carolina Press

Chapel Hill and London

© 1986 The University of North Carolina Press
All rights reserved
Manufactured in the United States of America

92 91 90 89 88 5 4 3 2

Library of Congress Cataloging-in-Publication Data

Main entry under title:
Religion and political conflict in Latin America.
  Bibliography: p.
  Includes index.
  1. Catholic Church—Latin America—History—20th
century—Addresses, essays, lectures. 2. Latin
America—Politics and government—1948—Addresses,
essays, lectures. 3. Latin America—Church history—
Addresses, essays, lectures. I. Levine, Daniel H.
BX1426.2.R44   1986   261.7'098   85-24525

ISBN 0-8078-1689-2
ISBN 0-8078-4150-1 (pbk.)

To John P. Harrison

Contents

Preface

Daniel H. Levine

Scholarship often follows the flag. When massive national (especially security) interests are engaged or threatened, the rush of public and official interest makes for "quick fixes" and a search for instant knowledge on hitherto marginal issues, groups, and areas. But quick fixes and instant scholarship are at best unreliable, at worst prejudicial and misleading. Lagging behind the pace of events, and often far removed from the experiences and motivations of real people, instant analyses distort reality by ignoring the historical roots of current crises and subordinating long-term explanation and understanding to short-term ideological and strategic interests.

For North Americans, the study of religion and politics is a case in point. Events in our own society have converged with sharp conflict in the Third World to cast serious doubt on long-held assumptions about the link between secularization and modernization and the predominance of supposedly "rational" concerns in politics and policy making. Events as distinct as Jonestown and the rise of the Moral Majority, renewed debate over school prayer and in general the resurgence of religious issues in political discourse have together rekindled attention to the continuing links of religion and politics in the United States.[1] In the Third World, developments in different regions and traditions converge, giving urgency to the search for guidance and knowledge. The renewed political salience of Islam has been underscored by growing realization of the emergent radicalism of the Latin American churches. Increased public attention to Latin American Catholicism has been fed by publicity surrounding the 1979 meeting of the region's bishops at Puebla, by the Pope's polemical visits to the region, and above all by the escalating crisis in Central America in which religious themes and actors have played a notable role.

Understanding this process is difficult. It is not that no scholarly work exists. Even setting aside the obvious flaws of instant analysis, we still find a large body of theoretical and empirical work on religion, politics, and their relation. But there are problems. In theoretical terms, much of this work remains wedded to the prejudices of nineteenth-century Marxist and liberal thought, which made religion epiphenomenal, or at best doomed to privatization and slow decline in the face of science and secularization. But this position clearly will not do. Religion is not static, nor is it in visible decline. Indeed, far from dwindling, the links between religion and politics seem to grow in creative and often surprising ways around the globe. The phenomenon is not limited to Latin America, as a glance at Iran, Poland, southern Africa, or the career of the Moral Majority reminds us.

Understanding has also been hampered by the narrowness and parochialism of disciplinary traditions. Anthropologists, for example, have generally taken popular belief and practice as part of a homogeneous world view, rooted in unchanging communities. Sociologists and political scientists, in turn, have focused largely on institutions, examining the church and its stance on issues irrespective of the concerns, practices, and beliefs of the faithful. Neither approach will do. Popular and institutional religion are not well understood if considered apart. Popular religion is not a spontaneous, natural product. Rather, it draws on the stock of resources (material and symbolic) which religious institutions provide to build a coherent explanation of everyday life. Popular groups change as well and, in changing, rework their ties to established structures of power and justification in all spheres of life. Institutional religions are not static either. As we shall see, they change continuously, and in any case, institutional analysis need not be limited to traditional themes of formal structure or legal arrangements. Institutions create and hold loyalties, organize behaviors, and project symbols, meanings, and material resources across time and space. The links of popular to institutional dimensions are thus an empirical question and, as the essays collected here show, are increasingly a matter of conflict and struggle. Neither can be understood alone: it is the intersect that counts.

The standard response to reflections of this sort is to call for more research, preferably interdisciplinary. But it will clearly not be enough to put sociologists, anthropologists, theologians, and political scientists together in a room (or in a volume) and hope for truly interdisciplinary results. Each individual study must transcend disciplinary lines and bring the tools and perspectives of various traditions together. The ideal study should address ideological change while remaining sensitive to the institutional interests and continuities that shape the impact of new ideas. Emergent groups must be recognized and set in the context of the social classes from which they draw. Historical depth is required, with close attention to the way people make sense of their experiences and organize to deal with them. The developing practice of everyday life must be assessed and located in the context of the ideological formations, institutions, and lines of conflict any given social order provides.

To address these concerns, and to stimulate new lines of research and reflection, the Joint Committee on Latin American Studies of the Social Science Research Council sponsored a planning meeting (March 1980) and later a conference (March 1982) on the general topic of popular religion, politics, and culture in Latin America. These meetings laid the basis for this book, and therefore a brief comment seems appropriate here. Planning meetings are used by the Social Science Research Council to outline the state of the art, define central issues, and spur new work in important and hitherto neglected areas. To this end, twelve scholars from different disciplines were invited to submit short statements and then to gather in New York for a day's discussion and debate.[2] Consensus emerged on the need to combine attention to the changing social structure and cultural formation of the *populus* (however defined in a particular society) with analysis of transformations in the institutional churches and in their explicit strategies. The changing uses of religious discourse by popular groups and the links of this process to the developing crisis of authoritarian rule were central to the group's discussions.

After the planning meeting, the Joint Committee authorized Daniel H. Levine and Robert Wasserstrom to organize an interdisciplinary, international conference, which convened in early March 1982 at the Belmont Conference Center in Elkridge, Maryland.[3] Discussions at Belmont followed the lines already noted, with special emphasis on three themes. First, there was broad agreement on the need to join institutional and popular perspectives, linking each to national and international changes in culture, economy, and politics. Second, stress was given to the need to grapple squarely with the content of religious belief and to appreciate the eschatological and transcendental qualities of religion that inform the ways in which people give meaning to experience. After all, to replace Marxist or liberal prejudices with a purely instrumental view of religion would be no advance at all. Finally, developing lines of conflict within religion and politics were addressed, with particular concern for the possibilities of democratization in each.

After the conference, the press of other commitments led some participants to withdraw. But other scholars joined at different stages, and the volume slowly took shape. In the process, the editor has incurred a number of debts, and this is the place for grateful acknowledgment. First, I want to thank the program staff at the Social Science Research Council, whose help was invaluable at each stage of the process. George Reid Andrews and Elizabeth Hansen helped craft the original proposal. Brooke Larsen and Diana Brown helped organize the conference itself and encouraged further work to shape the essays into a volume. Joan Dassin has been most helpful in the later stages of editing and organizing the material for publication.

I am also grateful to the editorial staff at the University of North Carolina Press, particularly to Iris Tillman Hill, whose encouragement and helpful critiques have materially improved the volume. The press's anonymous readers offered comments that stimulated useful revision and reorganization.

Each of the authors acknowledges gratefully the support and assistance that made the individual studies possible. In the name of all the contributors, I want to thank the people we studied for their unfailing generosity and openness to others. I also want to thank the authors for their commitment to this project, now happily concluded. I am grateful for their help and support. I must thank my friends for sticking with me, and in particular I want to thank my family, for reasons they know best. This book is dedicated to a good friend, whose long career materially improved the quality of work in the study of Latin America: John P. Harrison.

Daniel H. Levine
Ann Arbor, Michigan
Princeton, New Jersey

Notes

1. To Sinclair Lewis, this was a deeply rooted theme in American culture, and he had Elmer Gantry see the future in these terms: "He would combine in one association all the moral organizations in America—perhaps later, in the entire world. He would be the executive of that combination; he would be the super-president of the United States, and some day the dictator of the world" (*Elmer Gantry* [New York: New American Library, 1980], p. 393).

2. Those attending were, in alphabetical order, Ralph Della Cava, Shepard Forman (who circulated the initial paper as a basis for the statements submitted), Jean Franco, Manuel Antonio Garretón, Daniel H. Levine, Joyce Riegelhaupt, Jane Schneider, Michael Taussig, Robert Wasserstrom, and Eric Wolf. Elizabeth Hansen organized the meeting for the Joint Committee.

3. Participants presenting papers were Phillip Berryman, Thomas Bruneau, Martín De La Rosa, Rubem Cesar Fernandes, Thomas Kselman, Daniel H. Levine,

Servando Ortoll, Jan Rus, Brian Smith, Michael Taussig, and Robert Wasserstrom. Commentators were Marilena Chaui, Elizabeth Hansen, Charles Reilly, Juan Luis Segundo, and Verena Stolcke. Initial staff work for the Joint Committee was done by George Reid Andrews and Elizabeth Hansen and continued by Diana Brown, who attended in representation of the committee.

Religion and Political Conflict in Latin America

1

Religion, the Poor, and Politics in Latin America Today

Daniel H. Levine

The relation between religion and politics in Latin America today claims our attention and calls us to serious study and reflection. Much has been written in and on this process in recent years, with attention going in more or less equal measure to changes in religion, changes in politics, and the new links between them being created across the region. As a result, we now have many good studies of theology and ideology, the creation of new programs and strategies by the institutional churches, and generally on the dynamic relation of religion (ideas, symbols, groups, and practices) to politics in all its many forms and levels: conservative accommodations, neighborhood movements, military authoritarianism, revolutionary organization, and liberal democracy.[1] These lines of inquiry are now being extended to explore the sources of change at the grass roots and the ways in which transformations in the daily practice of religion and politics are linked to larger structures of power and meaning.

Change has been remarkably rapid and widespread, and the task of understanding its sources and development has absorbed much scholarly attention. But although change has clearly been both deep and far-reaching, change is not irreversible. Moreover, change is not all there is to the process. Significant continuity is visible in the ideas, institutions, and day-to-day routines of both religion and politics. Not surprisingly, the conjunction of intense change with strong pressures for continuity has generated escalating debate and a series of sharp, often bitter and violent conflicts throughout the region.[2]

This book explores this process through a series of case studies that come together around a small set of interrelated issues: changing explanations of poverty (especially its sociological sources and theological significance) and the definition of new roles for the poor within the structures religion and politics provide. These issues take concrete form in struggles to control the beliefs, practices, and organizational expression of what is conventionally known as "popular religion." As we shall see, debates over "the popular" (*lo popular* in Spanish) and struggles to define and control its proper expression have become a central thread of conflict at all levels in cases otherwise as distinct as El Salvador, Nicaragua, Chile, Brazil, Bolivia, or Colombia. The resolution of the issues differs from case to case, in accord with context and circumstances. But the unifying theme in all cases is the same: how to explain poverty and how to provide a role for the poor.

Why this focus on the poor? First, the poor are obviously the majority of the population, and naturally the churches want to reach and orient them in changing and often difficult circumstances. Moreover, the poor have always held a privileged place in Christian thought, and hence attempts to explain poverty in new ways touch contexts of religious significance, which easily become central points of conflict. Further, in situations of economic and political crisis, any attempt to reach, orient, and organize the poor is viewed with fear and suspicion by civil and military authorities. Here, the ability to shape and direct the organizations of the poor and to train and orient those who link the institutional churches to the poor in daily practice (priests, sisters, catechists, and lay leaders—"pastoral agents" of all kinds) is politically explosive and has lately emerged as a central arena of ideological and bureaucratic conflict. As we shall see, in all these cases, change in theology and in sociology are closely intertwined, as new images of the church and its religious mission converge with transformed understandings of the world in which the churches live.

I have stressed conflict so much to reinforce the point that just about every aspect of this field is subject to debate and controversy. This is in no sense a "settled" field, and as we shall see, the issues at stake are highly charged with emotion, meaning, and commitment. The rest of this introduction lays out a broad context and background for the chapters that follow.[3] I do not attempt an exhaustive summary of the field but instead focus on change and continuity around the central themes of poverty and the role of the poor. I begin with a brief analysis of the meanings of poverty and "the popular" in contemporary Latin American debates. I then discuss a few key events in the recent history of these issues, especially the Second Vatican Council (1962–65) and the general meetings of Latin American Catholic bishops held at Medellín

(1968) and Puebla (1979). Particular attention is given to the emergence and significance of grass-roots Christian communities, commonly known as base communities or CEBs (for *comunidades eclesiales de base*), which have often become the focal point of debate and action. Because the contributors to this volume share a few key assumptions about how best to study these issues, I close this introductory chapter with brief comments on theory and method.

One way to put these developments in perspective is to look for a moment through the eyes of those who live the process day to day. In recent work among base communities, I asked about the meaning of the church's "preferential option for the poor," a phrase that will be considered in some detail below. Here is the statement of one Venezuelan peasant, extremely poor, direct, and with a perspective solidly rooted in the Bible he has recently learned to read:

> I believe that here we are nothing, not "church," nothing, if we
> cannot feel for our brother. How can we feel for other things?
> Look, the church tells us that if you love the God you cannot see,
> and you do not love the brother you do see, then you are a faker.
> So I believe that if we cannot feel for our brother, who is right here
> beside us, and we cannot give him a helping hand, then we can't do
> anything. We lose everything. To me, this is how to cooperate as a
> church. Because you are church and I am church. Doing your
> work you are making the church. This is the church we make as we
> work. You go about working not only for yourself but for the com-
> munity. What is the use of this information? To learn about what is
> happening in the world. To get it moving. You are sent because
> someone sends you; there is one who moves you. If not, you can't
> see where you are. He is here with us both, guiding us, and who
> knows where? So this is God's house, and this is the church. For
> me, this is what it is.[4]

Overview: Poverty, the Poor, and "the Popular"

Much of the conflict surrounding the meaning of poverty and the proper place of the poor is summed up in contemporary Latin America in debates over "the popular." The possible meanings of "popular" (as in popular art, religion, music, culture, organizations, and the like) are explored in detail in the studies that follow, and the various dimensions of the popular are brought together in the concluding chapter. Here I simply want to introduce the term with a cautionary note. Caution is needed because the term "popular" has connotations in contemporary Latin America which catch North Americans unawares. Its core meaning rests not on popularity (something favored by many), but rather on a sense of what constitutes the *populus*—the central defining characteristic of the population. At a minimum, "popular" thus involves some notion of subordination and inequality, pointing to "popular" groups or classes. This is accompanied by an explanation of how they came to be poor. As used in Latin America today, "popular" also implies a sense of collective identity, and lately it carries a claim to group autonomy and self-governance. In all these ways, reference to "the popular" directs attention to the ideas, beliefs, practices, and conditions of poor people, however defined, and by extension to the kinds of ties that bind them to institutions of power, privilege, and meaning.

At this point, consensus ends and debate and struggle begin. Conflict starts over the definition of the poor and the proper explanation of poverty itself: who are the poor, why are they poor, and why does poverty grow? Of course, poverty and a concern for the poor are nothing new. After all, the churches (like other major institutions) have always dealt with the poor in some way. But new understandings of poverty can change the stance institutions take and in this way lay the basis for new sorts of relations with the poor in everyday life. The change is deceptively simple. Once attributed largely to *individual* failings, poverty is now increasingly seen as the product of *structural* inequalities. From this point of view, poverty is not a universal, inevitable condition, but rather emerges as the product of certain historically specific structures of power created by human beings and hence changeable. Thus the poor need not be "always" with us, for their condition is contingent on power, and arrangements of power can be challenged and changed.[5]

Note that this is a sociological definition of poverty, which cuts across Catholicism's traditional stress on "the poor in spirit," highlighting instead the need for solidarity with the materially poor. Several important implications flow from this shift to sociological categories. First, as poverty is defined in structural terms, stress is placed on class and on the opposition of classes as a social fact which the church has to recognize. This clearly places the church in the midst of conflict and raises troubling questions for its traditional message of reconciliation.[6] Second, the emphasis on class gains new significance because of the new value given to the experiences and understandings of poor people. Older assumptions about the ignorance of the masses have yielded with remarkably little opposition to a view stressing sharing and solidarity with the poor precisely because their poverty gives them a more authentic and religiously valid perspective.[7]

There are powerful strains of religious populism here, a "going to the people," which is visible in many of the cases in this book. Identification with the poor, born of a desire to share their cause and conditions, has led many priests and sisters to go to the people, much in the style of nineteenth-century Russian populism. Their actions and the religious justifications they create suggest that the poor are no longer to be taken simply as the uninstructed waiting to be led by their betters. Instead, claims to autonomy, self-governance, and independent action are increasingly advanced as legitimate.

What is really new about this process in Latin America is not so much the critique of injustice, or even the repeated clashes of the institutional churches with authoritarian regimes. Although these are indeed sharp, the opposition of religion to political power has ample precedent. But in Latin America today it is clear that the locus of debate and the capacity for sustained action have moved beyond the formal limits of the ecclesiastical institutions to rest, for the first time, with poor people in groups which they themselves take a major hand in running. Here, religious men and women have reworked the meaning of their faith in a context charged with concern for linking religious values to the issues and conflicts of everyday life. As a result, traditional religious symbols, messages, and celebrations have gradually taken on new meanings, spurring and underscoring a new understanding of social life and new commitments for dealing with it. Urgent and difficult questions arise: Is this the way the world must be? Will religion reinforce the existing order or can it lay the foundations for seeing change as both legitimate and possible? Is revolutionary violence legitimate in the Christian scheme of things? Can Catholic groups democratize internally and thus in the long run provide a basis of experience in democracy for the larger society without falling afoul of church and official elites who fear the loss of authority and control? In sum, can poor people work through their religion to less fatalistic understandings of their own situation and in the process use their religion to create structures and paths of action to promote change?

These reflections suggest that much has changed since the days when religion was taken as an unquestioned ally of the established order throughout Latin America. But though change is surely striking, it is important that our concern for change be tempered in two ways. First, we must realize that changes of this magnitude never occur overnight. They have a history, and this history strongly conditions the scope and character of any change undertaken. Second, as noted at the outset, although change is indeed prominent, change is not all there is to the process. Moreover, change is not unidirectional. Change can be reversed, and in any case, important elements of continuity remain to shape and limit the impact of any innovation. The next section traces the history of these changes in detail, through a close look at three landmarks in the process: the Second Vatican Council (Vatican II), Medellín, and Puebla.

Vatican II, Medellín, Puebla, and Beyond

The meetings held at Vatican II, Medellín, and Puebla together constitute a pattern of change, experimentation, accommodation to new perspectives, and, more recently, attempts to restrain change that provide the context of our inquiry. In this section, I will outline briefly the central themes of each meeting, with particular concern for their impact on current struggles over religion, politics, and the popular.

To begin with, the three meetings are linked in many ways. Much of the motive force for recent changes in Latin American Catholicism (as in the church generally) stems from attempts to work out the implications of Vatican II. Indeed, the Medellín conference was convened precisely with the goal of applying Vatican II to Latin America and thus clarifying the church's proper role in the region's continuing transformations.[8] In the same way, Latin American bishops gathered at Puebla eleven years later to weigh the lessons of Medellín, to evaluate past and present experience, and to chart a course for the future. Nor did the process end with Puebla. Subsequent years have been marked by intense debate and conflict, and at the time of writing (early 1985) the Vatican has begun preparations for a major synod to evaluate and clarify the significance of the Second Vatican Council itself and the changes that followed from it.[9]

Vatican II is best seen less as the beginning of change than as the acceptance of new ideas and drives for change hitherto rejected. The council saw far-reaching and as yet not fully absorbed attempts to rethink the nature of the church, the world, and the proper relation between the two. Long predominant models of the church as a perfect, unchanging, and hierarchically ordered institution were complemented by the revival of older models of the church as a "Pilgrim People of God"—a living, changing community of the faithful making its way through history. Viewing the church in these terms opened Catholic thought and action to the legitimation of historical change, both as a simple fact to be accepted and as a source of new, valid values.[10]

The acceptance of change as normal and even desirable freed the church (at least in principle) from identification with existing structures and social arrangements. If all change as a matter of course, none can be identified with God's will. Any social arrangement is historically conditioned and thus can be made over by human action—not simply endured in hopes of a better life to come. Attention to historical change also leads to concern for understanding how societies developed as they did. At Vatican II, this process began with a general interest in sociological analysis, especially with theories of modernization and development. This concern was soon expanded in Latin America to include extensive and controversial borrowing from Marxist ideas, particularly those concerning class, conflict, and violence.

Rethinking the church as a Pilgrim People of God also had a major impact on norms of authority and obedience. The implications were especially notable in three related areas: for relations within the organizations of the church (such as bishop-priest-sister-laity); for the church's stance as an institution toward other institutions; and finally, for the experiences learned in the daily life of church organizations and presumably carried over to other spheres of life. Let me explain.

Within the church, the stress on the historical experience of change moved practice away from a concern with role, rank, and status to a stress on testimony, solidarity, and shared experience as sources of action.[11] The call to identify with the poor as a prerequisite of legitimate leadership is only a small step away. The church's stance toward other institutions is affected by the stress on accepting and even promoting change. Finally, the more general learning about authority from daily practice and experience within church organizations[12] begins to shift in two key ways. First, the expectation of relatively automatic obedience begins to be called into question by clergy, sisters, and laity, who in growing numbers see action (not rank alone) as a central basis of legitimacy. Second, the weight placed on sharing and solidarity has meant the development of greater collegiality and power-sharing among church elites, along with calls for more egalitarian structures of participation in general. As we shall see, the second is considerably more difficult to achieve than the first.

In all these ways, Vatican II combined an open stance to the study and promotion of social change with a commitment to seeing God's role as an active presence in the world. This commitment rests above all on a renewed interest in biblical images, especially those drawn from the Old Testament prophets, who consistently stress God's concern for action and justice over outward conformity and ritual.

Both the opening to sociology and the return to biblical (especially pro-phetic) writings were carried forward powerfully in Latin America after Medellín. I will look closely at Medellín in a moment, but first I want to stress the importance of the turn to the Bible and the tremendous impact of the Old Testament prophets on the ideas of leaders and followers in the Latin American churches. If there is one characteristic that unites all grass-roots Christian groups in the region it is that they read the Bible. They read the Bible regularly, discuss it together, and seek inspiration and guidance from it. *None of this was true on any significant scale before the mid-1960s.* The promo-tion of Bible study, linked to the switch to local languages (Spanish and Portuguese) for ritual and liturgy has had a tremendous impact on the quality of religious life and daily practice. This point is made in almost all the essays in this volume and warrants underscoring here. It is not just that participation grows: it also changes in quality to become more informed, active, and involved. Access to the Bible also changes the link average believers have to authority figures like priests, lessening their dependence. Finally, the general stress on identifying with the poor in any case goes far to demystifying the figure of the priest and sister, who in large numbers now dress in ordinary clothes, live in ordinary houses, and share the day-to-day routines of their congregations in ways that were rare and unusual only decades ago.

But I am ahead of my story, and of course change did not reach so far so quickly. Medellín provides a crucial intermediate step, for at Medellín, the bishops reviewed all aspects of religious life, locating them with specific reference to the history and conditions of Latin America. For our purposes, Medellín is most important for the way in which the bishops dealt with issues of force and violence and with the more general question of social division and class conflict.

Violence has been increasingly central to debates in and on Latin Ameri-can Catholicism in recent years.[13] Pope John Paul II has repeatedly engaged the issue in visits and messages to Latin America. His predecessor, Paul VI, also took a firm position. Speaking to the bishops at Medellín, he strongly supported efforts at social change and denounced injustice and oppression, but he unequivocally ruled out violence as both unchristian and antievangeli-cal. The bishops listened, but their conclusions differed in a subtle and significant way. They stretched the definition of violence beyond individual or even collective acts of physical aggression to embrace the coercion found in the day-to-day operation of unjust and oppressive social orders.

This was called "institutionalized violence," a term now synonymous in many minds with Medellín. The distinction of institutionalized violence from overt aggression was crucial, for it opened the way to legitimating counter-violence—violent acts aimed at overthrowing the institutionalized violence of the established order and replacing it with a more just social and political system. The links to religious obligation were forged through the discussion of sin. At Medellín, conventional notions of sin, rooted in personal morality, were expanded to characterize entire social systems. Unjust societies, marked by vast inequalities and violence of all kinds could thus be seen as "sinful." In this light, political action can be legitimated in terms of liberation from sin, itself clearly a central mission of the church.

Within these general guidelines, Medellín took up the issue of the poor, especially the sources and significance of poverty and the place and proper role of the poor in the structures church and politics provide. The new sociological and biblical orientations noted earlier together produced radically changed views on poverty. In sociological terms, poverty is seen as structural in origin, no longer mainly the product of personal failure or misfortune. This perspective sharply reduces the value given to traditional church concerns for charity and welfare. These are now seen as little more than bandaids, aspirin for a dying man. The misery and injustice of poverty can never be resolved by charity alone. Nor will conversion of the rich quite do. The structures causing poverty must change, and this is a matter of power and political action.[14]

As the predominant explanation of poverty changes, its symbolic meaning also begins to shift, and the imperatives for action grow. The symbolic meaning of poverty no longer lies in passive acceptance and self-sacrifice but in the call for equality and justice. Indeed, after Medellín, the phrase "the poor shall inherit the earth" often assumed very direct, immediate political connotations. In part, this is the product of new sociological categories, identifying the poor above all with the proletariat and peasantry. It also emerged as part of a new, biblically inspired drive to identify with the poor and then take on prophetic leadership roles in the defense of their interests. Finally, the new value given to lay experience (especially the experience of the poor) and the heightened concern for creating more egalitarian structures of participation introduced new elements of organization. Throughout the region, the period since Medellín has seen the elaboration of new rationales for organization, a realization that organization itself is both possible and desirable, and a set of initiatives to promote and protect organization.

In all these areas, the convergence of sociology, theology, ecclesiology (a new sense of the church), and biblical images is crucial. For after Medellín, many initiatives got under way: identifying with the poor, promoting change, challenging structures of power and authority in the name of justice. Not surprisingly, these met with resistance, often violent, and the post-Medellín period was marked by growing radicalization and struggle within the church. Indeed, the intensity of conflict in the decade after Medellín makes greater sense if we realize that Puebla, coming in 1979, was less a high-water mark of commitment than a compromise, an uneasy standoff between those advancing further identification with the cause and condition of the poor and others pursuing consolidation, the reaffirmation of hierarchy, and a withdrawal from exposed and politically risky positions. What happened at Puebla, and what does it mean?

Conflict is perhaps the most notable element surrounding the conference at Puebla and the events that followed. As with Vatican II and Medellín, many issues were discussed at Puebla, and a complete review is impossible here. Instead, I want to stress several themes that together constitute the legacy of Puebla. Three are particularly notable: (1) further refinement of the notion of poverty and the poor; (2) intense concern with the nature of participation within the church, as within any organizations sponsored by or linked to the church in some way; and (3) flowing from these, the beginnings of a sharp debate over the meaning of "the popular" and a related struggle to control and orient popular religion in all its forms.

All the issues noted earlier return to inform these debates at Puebla, with fights over theology, sociology, organization, and action made more acute by the pervasive sense of crisis in the region. Bear in mind that Puebla occurred not long after the overthrow of the socialist government in Chile and just before the Nicaraguan revolution. Moreover, the preparations for Puebla coincided with escalating violence in El Salvador, in which religious groups and church people played a central role.

Puebla is often identified with the phrase "preferential option for the poor." This phrase and the documents that elaborate it represent an extension and deepening of the basic insights laid out at Vatican II and Medellín. The sociological analysis of Puebla is much more concrete and specific, stressing the need to identify with the poor and to see their situation as the result of coercion and structural inequalities.[15] Puebla also carried forward the relationship noted earlier between new sociological explanations and a heightened reliance on biblical models and images.[16]

The issue of participation lay at the heart of Puebla. Here, the bishops and their advisers struggled to understand the meanings and control the consequences of the tremendous expansion in grass-roots organizations (the CEBs noted earlier) since the late 1960s. The issue of participation is complex, and its various aspects must be seen together. First, participation is to be encouraged, but the stress is on informed, active involvement in small groups. Traditional vehicles of mass participation such as pilgrimages, processions, or special events are relatively downplayed in favor of intense, small group experiences. The CEBs received favorable mention at Puebla. Second, the bishops worried about controlling this participation. By "control," they meant to ensure an ideological stance consonant with "official" church teachings (which they defined) and also to shape programs and strategies subject to continuous clerical advice and control. In this vein, praise of CEBs is linked to a stress on their integration with normal parish life.

Ambiguities appear at once, for the concern to ensure obedience and unity around the bishops clashed with the upsurge of autonomous, lay-directed grass-roots groups. As we shall see, the result was intense struggle over the idea of the "popular church" and "the popular" in general. This struggle crystallized in fights to control group agendas, to control the training of lay leaders, and in general to rein in independent initiatives and autonomous actions of any kind.

The years since Puebla have seen only heightened conflict, as most bishops, encouraged and led by the Vatican under Pope John Paul II, strive to reaffirm hierarchy and unity within the institutional church, to downplay class division emphasizing reconciliation instead, and in general to counter what they see as a pervasive and dangerous "temporalization" and excessive "sociologization" of the church's ideas, messages, and organizational expressions.[17] These initiatives are resisted by a smaller group of bishops, by numbers of clergy and religious, as well as by the claims to autonomy and independence advanced by CEBs throughout the region.

In one way or another, these conflicts form the core of each of the case studies collected in this volume. As an empirical matter, conflict often revolves around the control and orientation of the grass-roots Christian communities or CEBs noted earlier. The next section takes a brief look at these issues and notes the parallels between current Latin American experience and that of other historical periods, especially the Puritan sects in the English Revolution.

Base Communities in Perspective

In discussions of Latin American Catholicism the issue of CEBs pops up all the time, and great expectations rest on them. But the evidence is scattered and often contradictory. Wildly varying kinds of groups are lumped together under that general heading, and what passes for a base community in El Salvador or Brazil may bear little or no resemblance to groups of the same name encountered in Colombia, Venezuela, Chile, or Bolivia. There are significant differences within nations as well, arising from competition to control and orient the CEBs. Exploring the history and substance of such groups is the task of many of the essays collected here; an overall review of the evidence is given in the conclusion to the volume. At this point, I want only to set up those discussions by laying out a minimal working definition of the CEBs and pointing to some significant historical parallels.

The task is frustrating, for there is no consensus about the nature of a CEB. Thus it is impossible to come up with any meaningful estimates of how many CEBs exist or to specify some definitive set of programs and activities to which one can point with confidence and say: "*This* is what CEBs do in all cases." All these points are matters of deep, bitter struggle, and conflicting claims abound.

What, then, can be said about the CEBs? It is best to begin with a very skeletal working definition. At a minimum, CEBs are small groups, usually homogeneous in social composition (based on class and neighborhood or village), which gather regularly to read and comment on the Bible. Without exception, CEBs originate in some linkage to the institutional church, a linkage that is maintained through courses, the distribution of mimeographed material, conferences, and periodic visits by clergy and sisters. This bare-bones definition highlights the three elements that make up the name CEB, or "base ecclesial community": a striving for *community* (small, homogeneous); a stress on the *ecclesial* (links to the church); and a sense in which the group is *basic*, either at the base of the church's hierarchical structures or at the base of a social hierarchy, or both. The preceding discussion of poverty and the poor should alert the reader to the sensitive character of this last point.

Many have seen CEBs as seedbeds of a new, democratic culture and social order, providing norms that legitimate equality and the promotion of justice along with practical experience in democracy through the management of independent groups.[18] We may call this the "radical ideal," an ideal well illustrated by some of the experiences in Nicaragua, Chile, El Salvador, or Brazil recounted later in this volume. It is important to realize that groups exemplifying this radical ideal are often few in number. Their significance lies in their centrality, not in their representative character. They may not be typical, but they do clearly occupy a crucial position in the process of religious and political change. They become central by providing a shield for activities prohibited or drastically restricted in society at large and by giving the new ideas emerging in religion a practical medium for expression in everyday life. When political parties are banned and trade unions and similar groups are under heavy pressure, the significance of changes already under way in the CEBs is understandably magnified.

One way to appreciate the significance of what CEBs may represent is to note the way in which they create and nurture a space for the practice of *congregational religion* within contemporary Catholicism and to suggest a parallel between the radical ideal of CEBs and developments central to the experience of Puritans in the English Revolution. Max Weber wrote extensively on this topic, and a brief look at his ideas may help clarify the issues.

To Weber, a religion that is congregational is organized in small, self-managed groups of believers. This structure enhances the dignity of average members and calls them to fuse religion with everyday life through continuous, self-moved ethical practice. Congregational forms of organization underscore the equality of believers, drawing all into participation and encouraging equal access to religious knowledge through a common reliance on the Bible. Through their fusion of congregational form with rigorous ethical doctrine, the Puritan sects shifted the focus of religious practice and undermined the status of traditional religious authorities. The Puritans relied on and read the Bible; they had little use for priests and disdained their magical role as mere chicanery. Indeed, Puritan practice stressed preaching over prayer, discussion and persuasion over ritual, and a disciplined adherence to ethical standards over reliance on divine intercession or priestly absolution.[19]

The experience of many CEBs in Latin America today is obviously parallel. Bible study is stressed, with emphasis on doing justice. The promotion of justice itself is rooted in the core of religious faith, with the example of Jesus and the prophets taking a central role. When these ideas are placed in the context of solidary, reinforcing group structures, the results can be explosive. The legitimacy of the established order is called into question, and new bases for common action are built at the grass roots. Weber's summary comment suggests the way in which changes in religion and politics converge with revolutionary implications. "The more religion became congregational," he wrote, "the more did political circumstances contribute to the transfiguration of the ethics of the subjugated."[20]

Although current CEB experience in line with the radical ideal is parallel to earlier experiences with congregational religion, one key difference remains. These are changes within Catholicism, and Weber dismissed the possibility of such change, pointing to the overwhelming weight of structure and hierarchy in the Catholic church. His reservations ring especially true now, given the concerted counterattack on the radical ideal, mounted with growing force ever since Puebla. What is the likely future? The clearest prospect is surely more and more intense conflict. Conflict is pervasive, bitter, and exceptionally broad-ranging. Disputes over doctrine and theology, clashes over staffing, policies, and programs, and the physical violence of repression and revolution are all tangled together. As the stakes get higher, the pressure on popular groups and their supporters will grow.

In such a situation, popular groups are very vulnerable, and their future is at best cloudy. After all, these are poor people, short on resources and in need of allies. But in the institutional church, prudence and discipline are the current watchwords, and as a result, efforts to control popular groups will surely grow. One anonymous wag hit the mark squarely, describing the future in these terms: "The preferential option for the poor? Well, a little less preferential, a little more optional."

A Note on How to Study This Topic

It is time to draw this already lengthy introduction to a close and let the analyses and data of each contribution stand on their own. As we shall see, despite variations in method and style, the authors share a few basic assumptions about how to study these issues. Indeed, as I noted in the Preface, the book grew from a commitment to rethink the bases of work in the field, and in particular to join the analysis of everyday life and popular religion to the study of institutions in a dynamic and fruitful way. For this reason, before introducing each chapter, it is perhaps appropriate to say a few words about how to study religion and politics.

The transformations in common understandings of the popular noted in these pages call us to serious reflection by forcing us to shed some long-held assumptions about the place of religion and politics in the social order and, further, about the relation of popular groups to elites and institutions in each. Shedding assumptions is difficult and painful, but in this case it is surely overdue. The studies collected here share an approach that rejects three related assumptions long central to studies of religion and politics.

First, they reject the assumption that change and "modernization" have some direct relation to an increase in secularization and a decline in the salience of religion. This premise is set aside, and the assumption of separation as both normal and desirable is replaced by a concern for the vitality of transformations within religion and for the many attempts in contemporary Latin America to create syntheses of religion and politics in response to changing conditions.

Second, they reject the assumption that religious ideas, organizations, and strategies are epiphenomenal, the product of socioeconomic or political interests, which are presumably more rational and "real." All the studies collected here show that "religion" (ideas, groups, practices, and the like) creates interests of its own and, further, that the values and social bonds arising from religion have independent consequences for politics. Thus the issue is not well seen as "religion *or* politics," nor is it well addressed by current concerns over the "politicization of religion." These formulations obscure reality, for the fact is that religion and politics have *always* been related. What is new is not the relationship itself but the specific ideas and organizational forms in which it emerges now.

In any case, the link between religion and politics is genuinely dialectical. Thus belief and behavior cannot be derived in a deductive fashion from either side of the equation. This means that attention to politics and religion must start by respecting the autonomy and validity of each and then exploring the relationships and elective affinities that arise between the two. What exactly does it mean to respect the autonomy and validity of each? At a minimum, this position requires us to see that religious phenomena have a logic and dynamic of their own, that people who belong to religious groups find satisfaction in the very act of participation, just as they may in organizing and carrying out the group's specific activities. As an empirical matter, it is difficult to separate the two. Indeed, very often the fact of membership generates values and experiences of solidarity and self-reliance that have an impact on political interests and capabilities not derivable from the specific programs of the group.

A final assumption rejected in this book holds that the popular is either spontaneous, natural, and somehow "unspoiled" (and hence authentic) *or* is simply the result of ignorance and superstition. The first position ignores the long-term links of popular phenomena to dominant institutions. The second takes the point of view of elites as the only valid one, ignoring the continuous transformation of needs and perspectives in both institutions and popular groups. As an alternative, the authors joined here stress the ways in which popular expression and organization of all kinds are formed historically through their selective, if subordinate, links to institutions.

The point has considerable practical significance, for it reminds us that although elites indeed reach out to control and direct the popular, popular groups are not infinitely malleable. The people and organizations we call popular have needs and interests of their own. They come to the institutions (like the churches) and value the membership, participation, and legitimation these provide. But they do not accept everything that comes their way. Thus full understanding requires us to study both institutions and popular groups, with special concern for points of conflict and variation in each.

The changing issues of religion and politics provide the context, but it is the individuals, movements, and groups that breathe life into the process. Ordinary people have a central role to play, and their ideas are as vital to analysis and understanding as are the more easily documented positions of elites and formal institutions. It is difficult to combine so many kinds and levels of reality, but the task is essential if we are to grasp the process of change in all its richness and achieve durable, reliable understanding. The task is hard but not impossible, and George Eliot's words may serve us as a guide: "We need not shrink from this comparison of small things with great, for does not science tell us that its highest striving is after a unity which shall bind the smallest things with the greatest? In natural science, I have understood, there is nothing petty to the mind that has a large vision of relations, and to which every single object suggests a vast sum of conditions. It is surely the same with the observation of human life."[21]

The Structure of This Book

This book runs from the general to the particular and back again. The first two chapters take a broadly comparative approach. Thomas Kselman starts off with an analysis of the curious career of the concept of "popular religion." He stresses the need to appreciate religion as believed, experienced, and practiced by average people. Only with this as a foundation can scholars grasp the full range of possibilities popular religion offers both for affirming and rejecting the established order. His reflections provide a useful antidote to the simple class-based analysis much favored by radicals, for he shows that it is clearly as false to assume institutional religion supports the established order as it is to see popular religion as necessarily a challenger. These are empirical questions. Kselman outlines various definitions of popular religion and demonstrates how the perspective taken makes for radically different analyses and organizational strategies.

Charles Reilly discusses the popular in terms of the growth of ecclesiastical populism. He draws a useful parallel between the experiences studied in this book and other populist traditions, in Latin America and elsewhere. He gives special stress to the emergence of paraecclesiastical organizations (like the CEBs) and considers their possible role in laying a cultural foundation for long-term political change.

The next two essays look closely at recent Central American experience, with special attention to change at the grass roots and its intersect with the developing economic and political crisis of the area. Phillip Berryman outlines the history of CEBs in Central America and shows how quickly they moved from a limited and religiously conventional set of concerns to an agenda filled with political activism and revolutionary commitment. The change came as the new religious praxis introduced after Medellín came up against escalating repression and official violence. Berryman stresses the close, long-term links between religious transformation and political crisis and notes the intimate ties between institutional and popular levels throughout the process. While considering Central America as a whole, he gives special attention to El Salvador. Michael Dodson explores the parallel (if shorter and sharper) process in Nicaragua. He describes how Christian groups got involved in the anti-Somoza struggle, considers their ties to the Sandinista regime, and clarifies the struggle within the Nicaraguan church to control and orient popular groups. Dodson gives special emphasis to the links between democratization in church and society and to the parallels between contemporary Nicaragua and the religious-political conflicts of the English Revolution.

Two essays on Brazil follow. Brazil is a critical case in Latin America. It has the largest and most progressive hierarchy in the region, and its programs and strategies have for a long time been specifically directed to the promotion of CEBs and similar groups as part of a general challenge to military rule. If there is an ideological continuum in the Latin American church, Brazil surely holds down the left wing. Thomas Bruneau's study looks closely at the development of CEBs, with a detailed case study of their growth and impact in the Amazon region. He notes the central role CEBs played in preserving some openness and opposition during the harshest period of military rule. Like Berryman, Bruneau suggests that even though the actual number of CEBs may be relatively small, they have a significant multiplier role. His Amazon study shows clearly how a church commitment to promote CEBs has a measurable impact on the transformations of religious organization and practice.

Scott Mainwaring looks at the Brazilian experience in an urban setting through an intensive study of one set of strategies and organizations in the industrial city of Nova Iguaçu. He shows how and why the church became committed to these groups, explores their origins and career, and provides valuable insights into the day-to-day experience of internal democratization and self-management. Along with Bruneau, he raises questions about the future of highly politicized CEBs as authoritarian conditions ease. Both authors suggest that under liberalizing circumstances, pressures for the CEBs to withdraw from politics are likely to grow.

The next essay analyzes Chile, and here Brian Smith also documents the direct link between the growth of CEBs and the closure of political space. CEBs expanded tremendously in Chile after the 1973 military coup in a double-edged process. Political activists and activity sought shelter in the churches, just as ecclesiastical elites moved to penetrate and protect popular groups and interests. Smith points to present and likely future conflicts, as pressures for internal democratization and group autonomy clash with institutional traditions of unity, hierarchy, and obedience, reinforced here as elsewhere by powerful pressure from the Vatican.

My chapter on Colombia takes up this process in detail, but from the perspective of Colombia's conservative church hierarchy. Colombia is commonly thought to occupy the right wing of any ideological continuum in Latin American Catholicism, and from the beginning its hierarchy has been determined to preserve authority and unity, reaffirm hierarchy, and thus control and limit popular groups. The result is unrelenting pressure and sustained attacks on internal democratization and radical activism. The experience of various kinds of CEBs (urban and rural) is examined and set in the context of the dominant patterns of Colombian society. Debates over the popular among Colombia's bishops are linked to that church's traditional role in social life, to the parallels between its hierarchical structures and the clientelistic pattern of national politics, and to the bishops' position as leading advocates of Vatican policies throughout Latin America.

Susan Rosales Nelson's study of Bolivia moves our attention away from politics as conventionally understood and to a notion of politics as the construction of power and meaning, embodied in this case in disputes over liturgy and ritual. She notes that "progressive" Catholics in Latin America (like church reformers in other times and places) stress teaching, preaching, and informed participation over more conventional religious celebrations. These are often dismissed as the products of ignorance and dependence, mere reproductions and justifications of the existing social order. She shows what happens when a reforming hierarchy meets up with a clientele with its own agenda to advance. In the process, she clarifies the ties of ritual to shifting power relations in community and society.

Finally, in the concluding chapter, I take up the general threads and review the evidence with particular concern to link democratization in church and society to democracy in the political system. Struggles over the popular tie the two together in contemporary debates, raising similar issues of equality, power, and legitimacy in each. The prospects for a democratization of culture, rooted in greater egalitarianism and democratic practice in the everyday life of the churches are explored, and the implications of this process for the stance of the churches as institutions to democracy in national life are considered.

Notes

1. Among the many important recent works in this field, the following warrant mention here: Phillip Berryman, *The Religious Roots of Rebellion: Christians in the Central American Revolutions* (Maryknoll: Orbis Books, 1984); Thomas C. Bruneau, *The Political Transformation of the Brazilian Catholic Church* (New York: Cambridge University Press, 1974), and also his *The Church in Brazil: The Politics of Religion* (Austin: University of Texas Press, 1982); Daniel H. Levine, *Religion and Politics in Latin America: The Catholic Church in Venezuela and Colombia* (Princeton: Princeton University Press, 1981); Scott Mainwaring, *The Catholic Church and Politics in Brazil, 1916–1985* (Stanford: Stanford University Press, 1985); and Brian H. Smith, *The Church and Politics in Chile: Challenges to Modern Catholicism* (Princeton: Princeton University Press, 1982). I have reviewed the state of the art in the study of religion and politics in Latin America in two recent review essays that give particular attention to Liberation Theology, base communities, and related issues: Daniel H. Levine, "Religion, Society, and Politics: States of the Art," *Latin American Research Review* 16 (1981): 185–209, and "Religion and Politics: Drawing Lines, Understanding Change," *Latin American Research Review* 20 (1985): 185–201. Each of these essays reviews the literature and carries an extensive bibliography. See also Penny Lernoux, *Cry of the People* (New York: Penguin Books, 1982), for a forceful if polemical overview.

2. As we shall see, this struggle is played out in international conferences, national church hierarchies, religious orders and movements, and the daily lives of dioceses, parishes, and base communities. At stake is the ability not only to influence immediate actions but also to shape common understandings of necessary and legitimate behavior and institutions.

3. The general themes laid out in this introduction are taken up once again in the concluding chapter of the volume. There, with the benefit of the intervening case studies, they are considered in sharper and more comparative focus.

4. Interview, 15 January 1983. The biblical reference is to 1 John 4:20–21, which reads as follows: "If anyone says, 'I love God' and hates his brother, he is a liar; for he

who does not love his brother whom he has seen, cannot love God whom he has not seen. And this commandment we have from him, that he who loves God should love his brother also" (Revised Standard Version).

5. This argument was powerfully advanced in words and action by Camilo Torres, who wrote: "When circumstances impede men from devoting themselves to Christ, the priest's proper duty is to combat these circumstances . . . the revolutionary struggle is a christian and priestly struggle" (*Father Camilo Torres: Revolutionary Writings* [New York: Harper & Row, 1972], pp. 264–65). His convictions ultimately led him to join the guerrilla movement in Colombia, where he was killed in 1966. On Camilo Torres see particularly the semifictionalized biography by Walter Broderick, *Camilo Torres* (Garden City: Doubleday, 1975).

6. This point arises particularly in the context of concerns about Marxism, an issue that embraces not only the exchange of ideas but also the possible construction of alliances and the incorporation of Marxist ideas about organization and action into the structures of the church. The hierarchy's fear of Marxist contamination in all these senses underlies recent, growing attacks on Liberation Theology. A leading figure in this attack is Msgr. Alfonso López Trujillo of Colombia, whose ideas are discussed in detail in my contribution on Colombia, elsewhere in this volume. The most recent salvo in the attack is the "Instruction on Certain Aspects of the 'Theology of Liberation,'" issued by the Vatican's Sacred Congregation for the Doctrine of the Faith in August 1984. Most Latin American hierarchies issued formal responses: one response that was strongly supportive of Liberation Theology came from the Peruvian bishops. See "Liberation and the Gospel," *Origins, NC Documentary Service*, 17 January 1985.

7. These changes fit well into the general revaluation of experience that underlay Vatican II's new ideas about authority in the church. See my *Religion and Politics*, chaps. 5 and 6, for a full discussion. Victor Turner suggests that a concern for the meaning of poverty is typical in periods of intense cultural crisis and reorientation. See his *Dramas, Fields, and Metaphors: Symbolic Action in Human Society* (Ithaca: Cornell University Press, 1974), pp. 265–76.

8. The complete title of the Medellín documents is suggestive: CELAM, *The Church in the Present Day Transformation of Latin America in the Light of the Council* (Bogotá: CELAM, 1970).

9. All this activity is something new on a regional scale. This succession of meetings, each preceded by lengthy preparations, reflects the intense concern of church leaders to understand change in the churches they lead and the societies in which they live and then to use this understanding to create an appropriate and effective role in present and future conditions.

10. On models of the church, see Avery Dulles, *Models of the Church* (New York: Doubleday, 1974).

11. On this issue, see Daniel H. Levine, "Authority in Church and Society: Latin American Models," *Comparative Studies in Society and History* 20 (October 1978): 517–44; and Brian Smith and T. H. Sanks, "Liberation Ecclesiology: Praxis, Theory, Praxis," *Theological Studies* 38 (March 1977): 3–38.

12. This is what Juan Luis Segundo refers to as the "hidden messages" of the

church. See his *The Hidden Motives of Pastoral Action: Latin American Reflections* (Maryknoll: Orbis Books, 1978).

13. On the issue of violence, see Daniel H. Levine and Alexander W. Wilde, "The Catholic Church, 'Politics,' and Violence: The Colombian Case," *Review of Politics* 39 (April 1977): 220–39. Phillip Berryman also deals squarely with the thorny implications of violence for the church in Central America in *Religious Roots of Rebellion*, especially chaps. 9–11.

14. These ideas lie at the heart of Liberation Theology, which emerged as a more or less unified body of thought in the years around Medellín.

15. This analysis emerged only after intense debate at Puebla. The issues are discussed in some detail in the conclusion to this volume, but briefly stated, the choice was between a sociology stressing "modernization," which held that poverty and inequality were problems of transition, and a sociology stressing exploitation, which saw the same problems as rooted in structural oppositions of class. The most penetrating account of Puebla, which sets these debates in context, remains Phillip Berryman's "What Happened at Puebla," in Daniel H. Levine, ed., *Churches and Politics in Latin America* (Beverly Hills: Sage, 1980).

16. In his commentary on the Puebla documents, Archbishop Marcos McGrath calls the return to biblical sources a "mighty refreshment" for the church. See his "Introduction and Commentary" to the Puebla texts in John Eagleson and Phillip Scharper, eds., *Puebla and Beyond* (Maryknoll: Orbis Books, 1980), p. 97.

17. The fear of Marxism mentioned in note 6, above, lies at the heart of these concerns.

18. A useful and well-argued example of this line of thought is Rowan Ireland, "Catholic Base Communities, Spiritist Groups, and the Deepening of Democracy in Brazil," Working Paper 131, Latin American Program, Wilson Center (Washington, 1983).

19. The political implications of these changes were apparent to contemporaries. For example, in the period just before the outbreak of the English Revolution, the royalist Duke of Newcastle argued that "there should be more praying and less preaching, for much preaching breeds faction, but much praying causes devotion" (quoted in Christopher Hill, *The Century of Revolution, 1603–1714* [New York: W. W. Norton, 1982] p. 69).

20. *Economy and Society*, Vol. 1 (Berkeley and Los Angeles: University of California Press, 1978), p. 591.

21. *The Mill on the Floss* (New York: Penguin, 1983), p. 287.

2

Ambivalence and Assumption in the Concept of Popular Religion

Thomas A. Kselman

The study of popular religion over the past two decades has forced theologians, historians, and social scientists to reconsider the models and language that had come to dominate the investigation of religion in the modern world. Although popular religion means different things to different people, virtually all those who have worked in this field reject any simple notion that the complex process conveniently labeled "modernization" will inevitably lead to either "secularization" or "dechristianization." Students of religion are now more likely to stress its adaptive and vital elements and to explore the political, social, and theological implications of the beliefs and practices of people whether or not they retain an affiliation with the institutional church. Even those who accept the argument that the forces at work in the modern world contribute to declining levels of orthodox behavior will go on to point out the sustained attachment of the majority to religious rituals that solemnize critical moments in their lives (birth, marriage, and death), the universal acceptance of periodic festivals (Christmas), and in some areas the sustained popularity of the cult of the saints, even among those who reject orthodox Catholicism.

Despite the interest in popular religion, the concept itself remains elusive, for scholars have been unable to agree on what it is intended to describe. François Isambert has called attention to this problem in his valuable study of the history and usage of the term, wherein he labels popular religion an "epistemological object" that has no agreed-upon content.[1] Isambert notes, for example, that some scholars see popular religion as the beliefs and practices of the subordinate classes, both peasants and urban workers, which are contrasted sharply with the religion of the elite. Others see popular religion as a spontaneous and personal relationship between people and the supernatural, which, though it may be stronger in some social groups, can be found throughout the social structure. The first approach to popular religion begins with what Isambert calls a terrain, in this case a particular social class, the second with an object, a certain religious belief.[2] This distinction, one of many illuminated by Isambert, suggests the ambivalence and confusion lurking behind the concept of popular religion.

The problematic nature of the concept should not disillusion those practitioners who desire to continue using it. After all, other concepts—social class, for example—have a similar epistemological status and yet have helped stimulate valuable theoretical and empirical studies. But the utility of the term "popular religion" will depend on a clear understanding of how and why it is used and on distinguishing the different senses in which it is currently applied. The following discussion of how different views on popular religion have emerged and how they still affect current attitudes will, I hope, contribute to a more precise and careful formulation of the concept and a deeper appreciation of the value and significance of the religion of ordinary believers.

Historical Perspectives

Tension between popular religiosity and official Christianity dates from the later days of the Roman Empire, when evangelists battled against pagan beliefs about the powers of local deities by preaching the power of saints and their relics.[3] Although Christianity succeeded in attaching most people in Europe to the sacramental system, the new religion never effaced prior beliefs about the healing properties of sacred fountains and shrines, which were now placed under the protection of the saints. The syncretistic folk religion that emerged in the Early Middle Ages combined elements of Christianity with beliefs and practices that, although suspect, were generally tolerated by the clergy. The Roman church's laxness in the face of "superstition" was an issue in the Reformation of the sixteenth century, and even those who remained Roman Catholics recognized that abuses had occurred. Erasmus, for example, criticized "those who think there is nothing they cannot obtain by relying on the magical prayers and charms thought up by some charlatan." The cult of saints was singled out as especially subject to abuse, for it encouraged people to seek material rather than spiritual benefits and to rely on external ritual rather than internal conversion. The clergy were especially responsible for such practices because, according to Erasmus, "they know it brings in much profit."[4]

In the mid-sixteenth century the Council of Trent responded to criticisms like those of Erasmus by coupling a clear affirmation of the power of the saints with a call to suppress any superstitions that detracted from clerical control of the supernatural. Throughout the seventeenth and eighteenth centuries the church acted to purify popular religion by regulating and sometimes suppressing pilgrimages and by attempting to substitute Eucharistic and Marian devotions for those dedicated to local saints.[5]

The efforts to control popular religion that began during the Counter-Reformation of the sixteenth century led to some of the first systematic investigations of how and why people resorted to supernatural beings for help in their daily lives. One of the best sources for historians of popular religion, for example, is the catalog of practices recorded by Jean-Baptiste Thiers in the late seventeenth century to assist the clergy in rooting out heterodoxical beliefs and rituals.[6] The church's effectiveness in trying to control popular piety is a subject under dispute; the continuation of the struggle against what the clergy believed to be superstitious practices throughout this period suggests that laymen were actively defending their pious traditions.[7] But this confrontation between clergy and laity during the Counter-Reformation has had a major impact on perceptions of popular religiosity.

The sharp distinction between popular and orthodox religion drawn by such authors as Thiers has helped shape all subsequent discussions. The criteria used by Thiers to isolate popular religion were both institutional and theological. According to Thiers, popular religious beliefs were based on an inadequate and naive view of how God works in the world. God is not subject to coercion through the ritual manipulation of words and objects, although he is free to respond to petitions accompanied by prayer and humility. But in Thiers's view, and for the Counter-Reformation clergy generally, priests retained special powers to call on God's active presence in their administration of the sacraments. Most dramatically, the words of consecration at the Mass changed bread and wine into the body and blood of Christ. The Eucharistic devotions promoted by the clergy served to emphasize their supernatural power. Popular cults associated with local saints were discouraged or neglected by the church in part because they encouraged theological naiveté, but the religious ignorance imputed to devotees included both the belief that God could be coerced and their unwillingness to accept that the

Catholic clergy were exclusively endowed with the ability to act as mediators between the supernatural and the natural. The theological critique of popular religion implies the need for educating the populace. Not surprisingly, therefore, the Counter-Reformation church dedicated itself to missions and schools, in both Europe and the New World, which sought to eliminate popular superstitions and replace them with authentic religion.

Historians and ethnographers of Latin America have dealt extensively with the conversion of the Indian populations that took place in the sixteenth and seventeenth centuries.[8] During the same centuries missionaries sought to educate and convert the peasants of western Europe. A number of historians have linked the concerns of both Reformation and Counter-Reformation clergy for religious orthodoxy with the witchcraft trials that spread throughout Europe during this period.[9] The prosecution of witches would bear comparison with the attacks on paganism that were undertaken by the Franciscans in the New World.[10] A normative posture critical of popular religion and an educational program designed to eliminate it are thus implicit in the concept as it has been employed by representatives of the institutional church since the sixteenth century.

It would be misleading, however, to suggest that the relationship between the church and popular religion has been uniformly hostile and that no accommodations have been made. Even during the Counter-Reformation attempts were made to channel as well as to eliminate popular devotions. The example of Our Lady of Guadalupe in Mexico illustrates how the clergy sought to provide Catholic surrogates who would share some of the same attributes and perform some of the same functions as the pagan gods.[11] This sympathetic posture became more pronounced in the nineteenth century, when the church struggled against an intellectual position that denied the importance of the supernatural and a state that sought to eliminate the public role of the church. In an age when secularism and indifference rather than heresy and superstition were perceived as the predominant threats to Christianity, some clergymen looked for allies among those groups of people who remained firmly attached to the supernatural and opposed to the intrusions of state power and the extraction of local resources that followed. The shrines of Our Lady of Lourdes in France and Our Lady of Fátima in Portugal are the most prominent examples of modern cults based on popular religious traditions of healing and prophecy that were used by the church to help defend its intellectual and political programs.[12] But even clergy who were receptive to popular religious traditions strove to retain the distinction between coercion and petition and to insist on the importance of personal commitment and sacramental life among the devotees of church-sponsored cults.

Despite some hostility, then, the Catholic clergy have generally tried to accommodate some forms of popular religiosity. The clergy shared with most laymen a conviction that supernatural intervention in this world was possible and at times necessary, though they disagreed at times about when and how such help should be sought. A more thoroughgoing critique of popular religion emerged in Europe during the seventeenth and eighteenth centuries among the *philosophes*, who regarded religious ritual, including the cult of the saints, as the result of ignorance cultivated by the clergy to maintain their own power. The violent dechristianization undertaken during the French Revolution, in which statues were shot at and beheaded and shrines destroyed, was the work of a minority, but their zeal and effectiveness, for a brief period, suggest a deep-rooted resentment of popular religiosity.[13] The anticlericals who opposed the saints and their shrines were convinced that such devotions sapped the moral and political energy of people. By suggesting that only supernatural intervention could solve their problems, popular religion kept people from using their natural freedom to improve the world. Anticlerical hostility to popular religion survived into the nineteenth century, when it became a commonplace among anticlerical liberals in both Europe and Latin America.[14]

Contemporary Critiques

The critique of popular religion that seeks to channel and purify it through the institutions of the church and the radical position that seeks to eliminate it both continue to influence contemporary attitudes. The Latin American bishops, to judge by the document that resulted from the Puebla conference of 1979, seem in general to accept the need for accommodation. Although they noted several "negative aspects" of popular religion, such as "superstition, magic, fatalism, idolatrous worship of power, fetishism, and ritualism," they also praised as "positive features . . . veneration of the saints as protectors, remembrance of the dead, a feel for pilgrimage as a symbol of human and Christian experience, a capacity for suffering and heroism in withstanding trials and professing the faith."[15] This attempt to distinguish and try to work with the positive elements in popular religion places the Latin American bishops in the mainstream of a long line of church reformers who, though critical of certain beliefs and practices, nevertheless see genuine religious value in traditional devotions.

The more radical position, which rejects cooperation with popular religion, can also be observed in contemporary Latin America, especially among some of the lower clergy. Apparently influenced by the theology of liberation, many priests are critical of the emphasis on individual salvation which is believed to be characteristic of popular religion. Such concerns are believed to detract from the religious obligation to contribute to building the Kingdom of God on earth. The complaints of these critics that otherworldly concerns distract people from improving their lives on earth resemble those made by the anticlericals over the past two centuries.[16]

There is much validity in the theological critique of popular religion that aims at raising the religious and political consciousness of the laity. But it is important to realize that this critical stance toward popular religion based on theological distinctions and judgments informs the language and analysis of many historians and social scientists. In his excellent work on Brazil, for example, Thomas Bruneau sees "popular Catholicism" as a pattern of belief based on vows made to God and the saints, which are frequently rewarded by miraculous intervention. Bruneau's work, which is based on extensive survey research, confirms a relationship between popular Catholicism and "a fatalistic acceptance of the world." According to his findings, "Those in the popular Catholicism pattern are less likely to be aware of the possibilities of change by means of exerting control, making demands, and acting."[17] Similarly, Brian Smith, following Max Weber, has characterized popular piety as "susceptible to magic and superstition, and oriented toward salvation in the next world."[18] But this view of popular religion as encouraging passivity and fatalism can be questioned on the basis of some of the evidence noted by Bruneau and Smith. The vows made to supernatural beings that Bruneau sees as central to popular Catholicism are frequently made in the hope of benefits in this world, including successes in marriage and business. Furthermore, such vows do not necessarily mean the abandonment of more rational methods for achieving desired goals. According to Lisia Nogueria Negrao, a sociologist at the University of Sao Paolo, people who ask the saints of the *macumba* religion of Brazil for help when sick or troubled do so to supplement rather than replace rational techniques.[19] In her review of the work of Keith Thomas, the anthropologist Hildred Geertz has disputed any general association between magic and what she calls "dependent self-deception." According to Geertz, it is equally plausible to argue that "employment of magic implies an attitude of confidence in the taking of personal action. The assumption behind spell-saying might be that one's own efforts will have important effects. In this view, the saying of spell is no less self-reliant than the switching on of an electric light."[20]

The perception of popular religion as concerned primarily with individual salvation may also limit a full appreciation of the complexity of the religious life of the laity. Confusion about the extent to which popular religion encourages fatalism, conservatism, and a concern for otherworldly salvation is to some extent the result of historical changes that have occurred in religious beliefs over the past several centuries. Church-sponsored devotions in which individual believers sought to avoid the punishments of Purgatory and guarantee their individual salvation date from the twelfth century and expanded rapidly during the Counter-Reformation. The assurance of eternal salvation offered by devotions such as those centering on the Rosary and the Scapular resulted in the extensive diffusion of these cults among both the popular classes and religious and lay elites.[21]

To judge by the religious history of Catholic Europe, the concern for personal salvation remained intense during the nineteenth century, when Catholics were able to choose from a constantly expanding market of indulgences that would reduce their time spent in the fires of Purgatory. But during this period the church also made it easier to transfer the benefits of indulgences to friends and family. Devotions aimed at personal salvation were not, then, exclusively selfish. And a belief in the salvation of an eternal soul was not only associated with Catholicism and conservative political ideologies. Some early socialists combined their critique of capitalism and their concern for social justice with a belief in spiritual progress that continued after death, in some cases on the other planets that were being discovered by modern astronomers.[22] Victor Hugo's commitment to social democracy in the herebelow did not prevent him from believing in a spirit-world that was accessible to the living.[23] Scholars and activists alike will have to be cautious and not assume too quickly that there is a clear polarity in which conservative political and social ideologies are aligned with a belief in personal salvation, whereas a commitment to social change is associated with denial of an afterlife. Popular religious belief in previous periods, and perhaps in contemporary Latin America as well, is capable of reconciling what some social scientists see as contradictions.

Is Popular Religion Necessarily Fatalistic?

Along with private devotions, pilgrimages, dances, and vows have been at the center of popular religion. But these rituals are frequently collective acts in which the community calls on God to provide a good harvest, stop an epidemic, or intervene in some other way. Communal rituals designed to invoke God's protection do not imply fatalistic resignation in expectation of a heavenly reward, nor do they obviate the need for activity in this world. After all, the peasants who seek protection for their crops also planted the seeds and cultivated the fields. Collective festivals can, in fact, be seen as a form of action through which communities express solidarity and hope in the face of anxieties about the agricultural cycle and the natural and social disasters that sometimes threaten their existence.[24] They can also be associated with movements that most would agree are politically and socially progressive. The most recent and dramatic evidence of such movements comes from Poland, where the pilgrimage to the Black Madonna at the monastery of Jasna Gora is closely linked with the Solidarity labor union and the cause of Polish independence from the Soviet Union. In Mexico, of course, the image of Our Lady of Guadalupe was of central importance in the war for independence.[25]

Pilgrimages to shrines in which people sought individual and collective help for problems in this world predate Christianity and remain a vital part of popular religiosity throughout much of the Catholic world. Devotions that focus on individual salvation exist alongside these older devotions, which frequently have a collective dimension. Popular religiosity, then, is a complex, historically conditioned set of beliefs that claims to provide remedies for problems in the here-below as well as the hereafter. According to one recent historian, the religious beliefs of ordinary people can be described as "fluid, eclectic, and from the point of view of churchmen or militant unbelievers, incoherent."[26] Characterizations of popular religion that limit themselves to only some of its aspects and stress its fatalism and conservative character must be regarded cautiously. In this vein, historian Natalie Davis notes the dangers students of religious history face when they accept too readily the critical posture toward popular religion derived from theological distinctions and judgments. Such positions may lead to misunderstanding and to under-valuing the religions of the people.[27] Her warning may also be appropriate for scholars who study popular religion in the contemporary world.

The critical views that see popular religion as either inauthentic or socially retrograde are not the only ones available to contemporary scholars. A number of historians and anthropologists use the rituals and myths of popular religiosity to illustrate the existence of social tensions and of values capable of inciting people to initiate social change. Perhaps the most prominent examples of this approach are the studies that relate eschatological hopes to movements of social protest.[28] From the time of the conquest of Latin America by Spain in the sixteenth century, religion has played a major role in provoking and legitimizing resistance against colonial regimes and, later, the centralized states of the nineteenth and twentieth centuries. The revolt of Antonio Conseliheiro in Brazil during the 1890s and the Cristero rebellion in Mexico during the 1920s are just two examples of religiously motivated resistance to the intrusive powers of the state.[29] Implicit in these studies is a belief that popular religion reinforces a sense of social solidarity and human equality at odds with the oppressive structures imposed by modern states and capitalist economies. These feelings are displayed and strengthened at the pilgrimages and festivals that occur regularly in the religious cycle.

Of course, positive assessments of popular religion are also charged with theological and ideological assumptions. For many scholars, the concept of the "popular" is grounded in a class-based interpretation of religious institutions and social structure; when used in this context the word "popular" is frequently linked with grass-roots movements such as the base communities discussed elsewhere in this volume.[30] Scholars who stress the importance of social class in popular religion may at times underplay practices that do not yield a positive impression.[31] Scholars identified with the political right as well as the left have allowed ideology to affect their view of popular religion. Following the liturgical reforms introduced by the Second Vatican Council in the 1960s a favorable interpretation of popular religion was adopted by those who rejected the changes. In their view, the reforms were the result of a misguided effort by a Marxist-inspired clergy to mix religion and politics and to alter the faith of the masses by making them more concerned with political and social progress. This attack, according to the critics of Vatican II, took the form of changes in the liturgical celebrations that traditionally appealed to the people. According to one writer, the council "has succeeded in killing popular religion, which the Council of Trent had been unable to do."[32] In Latin America this position, which combines a defense of traditional piety with a critique of social activism, is maintained by Societies for the Defense of Tradition, Family, and Property.[33] In a sense, this position shares some ground with the attitude of the anticlericals, for in both cases popular religion is understood to be apolitical and to encourage resignation in the face of poverty and oppression. But, unlike the anticlericals, these traditionalists view such attitudes as appropriate and regard any suggestion that religion can be used explicitly to encourage social change as a heretical departure from the true faith.

Redefining the Links of Popular Religion to Society and Politics

Given the complexity of the phenomena in question, it is not surprising that historians, social scientists, and clergymen have adopted a variety of attitudes toward popular religion. But it is important to distinguish these different positions carefully to avoid unnecessary confusion about what a particular writer understands to be the nature and consequences of popular religion. The typology outlined in Table 2.1 summarizes these positions and may help to clarify the different meanings the concept can bear.

Two separate though related theoretical concerns can be isolated among those who have grappled with popular religion. The first has to do with the intrinsic religious value of popular beliefs, which are viewed primarily as a theological problem; the second deals with the impact of popular religion on structures of authority within the Catholic church and, by extension, on other social institutions as well. Three positions can be identified within the religious dimension. There is, first, a group that desires to substitute the beliefs and practices of orthodox Catholicism for those of popular religion, which is understood to be a misguided and pagan view of the ways in which God works in the world. This position, which can be labeled "orthodoxy," contrasts with one that can be called "accommodation," which proposes that popular religion, despite a naive theology, shares certain characteristics and can be reconciled with authentic religion, provided it is controlled by legiti- mate representatives of the institutional church. A third position, "anticleri- calism," rejects the theological distinctions drawn by orthodox and accom- modationist clergy as superficial and irrelevant. According to anticlericals, both popular and institutional religiosity, in either its orthodox or accom- modationist form, are fundamentally flawed by their affirmation of a God whose assistance can be invoked through prayer and ritual. The anticlerical denial of an interventionist God is accompanied by a general unwillingness to affirm specific theological doctrines and a tendency to equate religion with

Table 2.1. Attitudes toward Popular Religion

Religious	Institutional
orthodoxy	traditional
accommodation	progressive
anticlerical	

morality. Anticlericals who acknowledge that God exists see him as the ground of a universal moral standard and judge as religiously positive those actions that accord with their ethical code.

These different categories can perhaps be grasped more easily when related to a specific problem in the history of popular religion. Marian apparitions and the cults they provoked have been an essential element in the popular religion of Latin America and Catholic Europe since the sixteenth century.[34] Orthodox clergy were highly skeptical in responding to reports of such miracles, which they generally interpreted as the work of either the devil or the inflated imagination of the visionary. In addition to trying to discredit the miraculous nature of the apparition, they sought to suppress the shrine that was constructed at the site of the miracle. These actions directed against an emerging popular cult were intended to counter an excessive belief in the power of Mary and the other saints, a power the devotees believed could be invoked directly and easily at the shrine. Accommodationist clergy were also frequently skeptical in the face of initial reports of Marian apparitions. But they were impressed by the popular response and open to the possibility that the miracle was genuine. Thus they sought ways to tolerate or even sanction the new cult, which would be supervised by the clergy. Anticlericals would, of course, deny the apparition as an absurd example of popular ignorance and interpret the cult as the result of a clerical plot designed to keep the populace subservient to the church.

Assessments of popular belief and practice that focus on their theological value carry with them different institutional responses. Thus both orthodox clergy and anticlericals seek to suppress popular religion, though from different motives, and accommodationists look for ways to reconcile it with the institutional church. A second set of theoretical concerns focuses directly on the relationship between popular and institutional religion and on the impact of belief and practice on the structure of authority in the church. According to traditionalists, the beliefs and rituals of popular religion express and reinforce a hierarchical and authoritarian view of the church. Progressives, on the other hand, see popular religion as a cultural construction of the laity, which, by circumventing the sacramental system dominated by the clergy, undermines the ecclesiastical hierarchy. Furthermore, progressives believe that popular religiosity contributes to the formation of values of solidarity and resistance that can lead to political and social reforms.

To continue with the case of Marian apparitions, traditionalists would see them as examples of the strength of popular faith in the ability of the saints, and Mary in particular, to intercede with God. The cults arising from apparitions, assuming they were properly supervised by the clergy, would be seen as enhancing the power of the church, which would profit from the money and the mobilization of the devout by means of organized pilgrimages and devotional confraternities. Progressives, looking at the same evidence, would emphasize the direct relationship between Mary and the visionary, which implied the possibility of contact with the supernatural outside of the sacramental system. They would also note that the visionaries were frequently poor and uneducated and that the cult, especially in its early stages, was the result of the spontaneous support of the lower classes, who had to fight the skepticism of clerical and lay elites.

Traditionalists and progressives could make their case for the ability of Marian apparitions, or some other manifestation of popular religion, either to enhance or to subvert the power of the institutional church with the same evidence. Depending on how it is defined and applied to the evidence, then, the concept of popular religion can yield a broad range of different results, even when the empirical facts under scrutiny are the same. Given the complexity of the concept and the subject matter it seeks to define, it is not surprising that scholars and clergymen tend to waver about the value and consequences of popular religion. The application of these categories to the current debate about popular religion might, however, help illuminate some of the confusion about the concept. The Latin American bishops at Puebla, for example, adopted statements that can be typed generally as accommodationist, but some of their uneasiness with popular religiosity clearly flowed from concerns about its lack of theological orthodoxy. The same evidence that the bishops might use to demonstrate a "positive" feature of popular religion, such as the veneration of saints, might be used by others to reveal a "negative" factor, such as superstition or fetishism. Theologian Bonaventura Kloppenburg, currently the auxiliary bishop of Sao Salvador, Brazil, exemplifies the problem when he asserts that though one must approach popular religion (in this case, the macumba sects of Brazil) with sympathy, there is nevertheless a certain point at which "we have to be intransigent."[35] Finding that point and isolating the theological and institutional concerns that pivot around it has been and continues to be difficult for the Catholic bishops.

The attitude of priests and scholars influenced by Liberation Theology who believe that the church should take an activist role in promoting political and social change is also difficult to type. Theologically, they seem to waver between an anticlerical rejection of popular religion as a misconceived attempt to rely on supernatural beings and a more tolerant view that seeks accommodation. Penny Lernoux, for example, rejects the "fatalism" inherent in popular religion, but nevertheless believes that the church should act to "purify and redirect popular religiosity."[36] An accommodationist posture seems in this case based on a view that popular religion, purified by the church, can be a progressive force.

Popular religion is clearly a problematic concept. There is little agreement about what substantive phenomena it describes, and it is laden with a wide variety of normative postures that range from hostility to admiration, which color the ways popular religion is understood by both scholars and clergymen. Perhaps the problems with the concept are rooted in the several tasks it is called on to perform, for it is at once both an analytical tool used by social scientists and historians and a theological term for clergymen who seek to understand and at times to change the religious beliefs of the laity. François Isambert has noted the advantage of the interplay between theology and the social sciences, which have become more sensitive to the significance of the religious beliefs and practices of ordinary people.[37] Certainly few people would now doubt the need for a better understanding of how religion works to shape political and social values. But the ambivalence and variety of preconceptions uncovered in the concept of popular religion suggest that its utility is, if not exhausted, at least seriously in question. For the concept of "popular religion" to continue to have value, those scholars and clergymen who use it will have to reflect more critically on the values and judgments their use of the term implies.

Notes

1. François Isambert, *Le sens du sacré—Fête et religion populaire* (Paris: Les Editions de Minuit, 1982), p. 15.

2. Ibid., pp. 38–39.

3. For an excellent introduction to the syncretism of the later Roman Empire see Peter Brown, *The Cult of the Saints: Its Rise and Function in Latin Christianity* (Chicago: University of Chicago Press, 1981).

4. From "The Praise of Folly," in *The Essential Erasmus* (New York: Mentor, 1964), pp. 129–31.

5. For a general view of how the Council of Trent affected the church's attitude toward popular religion see Jean Delumeau, *Le catholicisme entre Luther et Voltaire* (Paris: Presses Universitaires de France, 1971). For the status of popular religion in a Protestant religious culture see the fundamental work of Keith Thomas, *Religion and the Decline of Magic* (New York: Scribner's, 1971). More specialized studies include William Christian, Jr., *Local Religion in Sixteenth-Century Spain* (Princeton: Princeton University Press, 1981); William Christian, Jr., *Apparitions in Late Medieval and Renaissance Spain* (Princeton: Princeton University Press, 1981); Dominique Julia, "La réforme post-tridentine en France d'après les procès-verbaux de visites pastorales: Ordre et résistance," in *La società religiosa nell'età moderna* (Naples: Guida Editori, 1973); M. H. Froeschle-Chopard, *La religion populaire en Provence orientale au XVIIIe siècle* (Paris: Beauchesne, 1980); Gabriele de Rosa, "Problemi religiosi della società meridionale nel settecento attraverso le visite pastorali de Angelo Anziani," in Gabriele de Rosa, *Vescovi, popolo e magia nel sud* (Naples: Guida Editori, 1971). For a good selection of articles see James Obelkevich, ed., *Religion and the People, 800–1700* (Chapel Hill: University of North Carolina Press, 1979).

6. For Thiers see François Lebrun, "Le 'Traité des superstitions' de Jean-Baptiste Thiers: Contribution à l'ethnographie de la France du XVIIIe siècle," *Annales de Bretagne* 83 (1976): 443–66. The works of Carlo Ginzburg, now available in English as *The Cheese and the Worms: The Cosmos of a Sixteenth-Century Miller* (New York: Penguin, 1980) and *The Night Battles: Witchcraft and Agrarian Cults in the Sixteenth and Seventeenth Centuries* (New York: Penguin, 1984), exemplify how the records of the Inquisition, which aimed at rooting out popular superstitions, can be used to reconstruct the religious beliefs of ordinary people.

7. For the view that the church effectively suppressed popular religious traditions, see Robert Muchembled, *Culture populaire et culture des élites dans la France moderne* (Paris: Flammarion, 1978). For a more positive assessment of the ability of local religion to adjust to the attempts of the Catholic Reformation see Christian, *Local Religion*, and Julia, "La réforme post-tridentine." The works of Carlo Ginzburg, *The Cheese and the Worms* and *The Night Battles*, exemplify how the Counter-Reformation acted against popular religiosity. For Ginzburg, however, popular religiosity was not suppressed by the church but driven underground.

8. For a selection of articles and a bibliography see Richard Greenleaf, ed., *The Roman Catholic Church in Colonial Latin America* (Tempe: Arizona State University, Center for Latin American Studies, 1977).

9. Thomas, *Religion and the Decline of Magic*; Ginzburg, *The Cheese and the Worms* and *The Night Battles*.

10. For a recent interpretation of some of the clerical excesses see Inga Clendennen, "Disciplining the Indians: Franciscan Ideology and Missionary Violence in Sixteenth-Century Yucatan," *Past and Present*, no. 94 (1982), pp. 27–48.

11. Jacques Lafaye, *Quetzalcoatl and Guadalupe: The Formation of Mexican National Consciousness*, trans. Benjamin Keen (Chicago: University of Chicago Press, 1976).

12. Thomas Kselman, *Miracles and Prophecies in Nineteenth-Century France* (New Brunswick: Rutgers University Press, 1983); William Christian, Jr., "Holy Men in Western Europe," *Comparative Studies in Society and History* 15 (1973): 106–14. For an

example of an attempt to create an American cult modeled on Fatima that combined Marian piety with anticommunism see Thomas Kselman and Steven Avella, "Marian Piety and the Cold War," *Catholic Historical Review* (forthcoming, 1985).

13. For the Enlightenment critique of religion the standard works include Paul Hazard, *The European Mind, 1680–1715* (New York: Meridian, 1963), and Peter Gay, *The Enlightenment,* 2 vols. (New York: Knopf, 1966, 1969). For the dechristianization of the Revolution see Bernard Plongeron, *Conscience religieuse en révolution* (Paris: Ricard, 1969); Michel Vovelle, *Religion et révolution: La déchristianisation de l'an II* (Paris: Hachette, 1976).

14. For a brief overview of anticlericalism in Europe see J. Salwyn Schapiro, *Anticlericalism* (New York: Van Nostrand, 1967). For a recent collection of articles on European anticlericalism in Spain, France, and Italy see *European Studies Review* (1983). The Peruvian liberal Manuel Gonzalez Prada (1848–1918) clearly expressed the anticlerical condemnation of church-sponsored popular religiosity in his speeches and journalism, in which he refers to priests as encouraging "the grossest superstitions." According to Prada, "[Priests] have been the determined oppressors of Humanity, especially of the underprivileged classes. In the past, they did nothing to abolish pauperism and improve the social conditions of the masses; in the present it is the same old story. . . . Catholicism in this country has not gone a step beyond idolatry" (quoted in William Rex Crawford, "Intellectual Opposition to the Tradition of Catholicism," in Frederick Pike, ed., *The Conflict between Church and State in Latin America* [New York: Knopf, 1964], p. 115). For Prada and Peruvian anticlericalism see also Jeffrey L. Klaiber, S.J., *Religion and Revolution in Peru, 1824–1976* (Notre Dame: University of Notre Dame Press, 1977), pp. 24–44. In Mexico the liberal Lorenzo de Zavala criticized church-sponsored shrines at Chalma and Guadalupe; see Charles Hale, *Mexican Liberalism in the Age of Mora, 1821–1853* (New Haven: Yale University Press, 1968), pp. 198–201. The harmful nature of superstitions encouraged by the church was part of the anticlerical critique proposed by the Chilean liberal Miguel Luis Amunategui; see Allen Woll, *A Functional Past: The Uses of History in Nineteenth-Century Chile* (Baton Rouge: Louisiana State University Press, 1982), pp. 168–69.

15. John Eagleson and Phillip Scharper, eds., *Puebla and Beyond* (Maryknoll: Orbis Books, 1980), p. 186.

16. For the divergence between bishops and local clergy, see Brian Smith, *The Church and Politics in Chile: Challenges to Modern Catholicism* (Princeton: Princeton University Press, 1982), p. 50. Juan Luis Segundo, a leading spokesman for the theology of liberation makes this point clearly in the introduction to *The Hidden Motives of Pastoral Action: Latin American Reflections* (Maryknoll: Orbis Books, 1978), p. 1: "The salvation mentioned in the gospel is the progressive, ongoing liberation of people from all the forms of enslavement that now encumber them. . . . No magic in the hereafter will be able to make up for what human beings have failed to do here below." Similarly, according to Gustavo Gutierrez, S.J., another leading representative of the theology of liberation, salvation is "not something otherworldly, in regard to which the present life is merely a test" (quoted in Brian Smith and T. H. Sanks, "Liberation Ecclesiology: Praxis, Theory, Praxis," *Theological Studies* 38 [March 1977]: 13).

17. Thomas C. Bruneau, *The Church in Brazil: The Politics of Religion* (Austin: University of Texas Press, 1982), pp. 30, 116–17. Roger Bastide, in his classic study

The African Religions of Brazil (Baltimore: Johns Hopkins University Press, 1978), p. 341, also falls into this pattern of seeing religion as encouraging resignation, whereas politics encourages rebellion. For a recent assessment of Bastide and several other works concerned with the relations between religion and society, see the review essay by Daniel H. Levine, "Religion, Society, and Politics: States of the Art," *Latin American Research Review* 16 (1981): 185–209.

18. Smith, *Church and Politics*, p. 45.

19. Cited in Warren Hoge, "Macumba: Brazil's Pervasive Cult," *New York Times Magazine*, 31 August 1983. For a discussion of the social composition of Umbanda that demonstrates and discusses its ability to draw in the middle classes, see Diana Brown, "Umbanda and Class Relations in Brazil," in Maxine L. Margolis and William Carter, eds., *Brazil: Anthropological Perspectives* (New York: Columbia University Press, 1979), pp. 270–304. Evidence from the shrine at Lourdes in France indicates that supernatural remedies are sought generally only after secular medicine has failed; see Kselman, *Miracles and Prophecies*, chap. 2. The career of the Peruvian politician Haya de la Torre illustrates how someone who believed in supernatural forces capable of being invoked by an individual was also a "pragmatist and shrewd opportunist, keenly alive to the possibility of influencing the material world through material interests" (Frederick B. Pike, "Vision of Rebirth: The Spiritualist Facet of Peru's Haya de la Torre," *Hispanic American Historical Review* 63 [1983]: 482).

20. Hildred Geertz, "An Anthropology of Religion and Magic, I," *Journal of Interdisciplinary History* 8 (1975): 16. Geertz notes, however, that the argument in favor of associating magic with self-reliance is "equally in error."

21. Jacques Le Goff, *The Birth of Purgatory* (Chicago: University of Chicago Press, 1984); Michel Vovelle and Gaby Vovelle, *Vision de la mort et de l'au-delà en Provence, d'après les autels des âmes du purgatoire, XVIe–XXe siècles* (Paris: Colin, 1970).

22. Michel Nathan, *Le ciel des fourieristes* (Lyons: Presses Universitaires de Lyons, 1981).

23. Maurice Levaillant, *La crise mystique de Victor Hugo* (Paris: José Corti, 1954).

24. Christian, *Local Religion*; Kselman, *Miracles and Prophecies*, pp. 29–31, 62–67, 113–18.

25. The importance of the Black Madonna has been widely noted in newspaper coverage of Solidarity. See, for example, John Kifner, "Mismanagement by Warsaw," *New York Times*, 20 June 1983, p. 16. For the role of Our Lady of Guadalupe in the Mexican war of independence, see Lafaye, *Quetzalcoatl and Guadalupe*; Victor Turner, "Hidalgo: History as Social Drama," in *Dramas, Fields, and Metaphors: Symbolic Action in Human Society* (Ithaca: Cornell University Press, 1974), pp. 98–115. For the use of other shrines in Latin America as national symbols see Penny Lernoux, *Cry of the People* (New York: Penguin, 1982), pp. 378–79.

26. Hugh McLoed, *Religion and the People of Western Europe, 1789–1970* (Oxford: Oxford University Press, 1981), p. 124. Charles Antoine, "La religion populaire en Amerique Latine—fatalisme traditionnel et agression culturelle," in Jean Delumeau, ed., *Histoire vécue du peuple chretien* (Paris: Privat, 1979), 2: 311–35, calls attention to the ambivalence of the concept of popular religion when he proposes it as a label both for personal integration in hostile urban environments and for millennial movements that criticize and attempt to change the social order.

27. Natalie Zemon Davis, "Some Tasks and Some Themes in the Study of Popular

Religion," in Charles Trinkaus and Heiko Obermann, eds., *The Pursuit of Holiness in Late Medieval and Renaissance Religion* (Leiden: E. J. Brill, 1974), pp. 307–36. For a good example of how the study of popular religion freed from any particular theological predisposition can illuminate the social and political values implicit in religious belief and ritual, see Albert Raboteau, *Slave Religion* (New York: Oxford University Press, 1978).

28. Norman Cohn, *The Pursuit of the Millennium*, 2d ed. (New York: Harper & Row, 1961), has played a key role in stimulating research on the relationship between social deprivation, eschatological beliefs, and revolutionary movements. For accounts of such movements in the underdeveloped nations see Vittorio Lantenari, *The Religions of the Oppressed* (New York: Mentor, 1963), and Bryan Wilson, *Magic and the Millennium: A Sociological Study of Religious Movements of Protest among Tribal and Third World People* (London: Heinemann, 1973).

29. Euclides da Cunha, *Rebellion in the Backlands*, trans. Samuel Putman (Chicago: University of Chicago Press, 1944); Jean Meyer, *The Cristero Rebellion: The Mexican People between Church and State, 1926–1929* (Cambridge: Cambridge University Press, 1976). For millennial uprisings see also Steve Stern, *Peru's Indian Peoples and the Challenge of Spanish Conquest: Huamango to 1640* (Madison: University of Wisconsin Press, 1982), and Victoria Bricker, *The Indian Christ, the Indian King* (Austin: University of Texas Press, 1981). Ralph Della Cava, in *Miracle at Joaseiro* (New York: Columbia University Press, 1970), shows how a movement based on popular religiosity provided the impetus for the economic development of an isolated region in northeastern Brazil; see also his "Brazilian Messianism and National Institutions: A Reappraisal of Canudos and Joaseiro," *Hispanic American Historical Review* 48 (1968): 402–20. Among the most sympathetic accounts of popular religiosity is Michael Taussig, who argues in *The Devil and Commodity Fetishism in South America* (Chapel Hill: University of North Carolina Press, 1980), p. xi, that in South America the devil is "a symbol of the alienation experienced by the peasants as they enter the ranks of the proletariat." Another study in which Marxist categories are used to interpret popular religion is Christian Lalive d'Epinay and Jacques Zyllerberg, "Les religions au Chili entre alienation et la prise de conscience," *Social Compass* 21 (1974): 85–100.

30. For a discussion of this understanding of the concept of popular religion see Daniel H. Levine, "Religion and Politics: Dimensions of Renewal," *Thought* 59 (1984): 117–35, and Daniel H. Levine, "Religion and Politics: Drawing Lines, Understanding Change," *Latin American Research Review* 20 (1985): 185–201.

31. Jan Rus, in "Whose Caste War? Indians, Ladinos, and the Chiapas 'Caste War' of 1869," in Murdo MacLeod and Robert Wasserstrom, eds., *Spaniards and Indians in Southeastern Mexico* (Lincoln: University of Nebraska Press, 1983), shows convincingly how a religious movement based on a shrine at Tzajalhemel in Chiapas, Mexico, reflected political and economic pressures being put on the Indians by the ladinos. Rus, however, treats the religious beliefs and practices of the rebels only briefly and never deals with the accusation that on Good Friday in 1868 the devotees at Tzajalhemel crucified a ten-year-old boy. It may be that Rus knows that the ladino historian who is the source for this incident fabricated it to justify the repression of the Indians. But at least two other recent historians treat the report as credible. See Bricker, *The Indian Christ, the Indian King*, p. 121, and Donald Thompson, "Maya

Paganism and Christianity," in *Nativism and Syncretism*, publication 19, Middle American Research Institute (Tulane: Middle American Research Institute, 1960), pp. 19–20.

32. Isambert, *Le sens du sacré*, p. 86.

33. Daniel H. Levine, *Religion and Politics in Latin America: The Catholic Church in Venezuela and Colombia* (Princeton: Princeton University Press, 1981), pp. 28, 49.

34. For the history of Marian apparitions see Christian, *Apparitions in Late Medieval and Renaissance Spain*; Kselman, *Miracles and Prophecies in Nineteenth-Century France*; Kselman and Avella, "Marian Piety and the Cold War."

35. See Hoge, "Macumba," pp. 32–33.

36. For the shifting attitudes of the lower clergy see the remarks of Diego Irrazaval quoted in Smith, *Church and Politics in Chile*, p. 272, and Lernoux, *Cry of the People*, pp. 375–86. For another example of how anticlericalism and accommodation are combined see Phillip Berryman, "Popular Catholicism in Latin America," *Cross Currents* 21 (1971): 284–301. In Berryman's recent work, *The Religious Roots of Rebellion: Christians in the Central American Revolutions* (Maryknoll: Orbis Books, 1984), he notes the power of traditional religious symbols and liturgies and the evolution of the concept of popular religion from its identification with superstition and ignorance to the current tendency to link it with democratic practices within the church, such as the base communities.

37. Isambert, *Le sens du sacré*.

3

Latin America's Religious Populists

Charles A. Reilly

Many countries of Latin America have seen a rebirth of voluntary associations, neighborhood organizations, and combative labor unions. "The people" and "*lo popular*" return or appear for the first time as actors on the political stage now, not as dependent clients but with a broader-based and radically democratic dimension that is new to the continent. It is a new form of populism, its emergence significantly affected by religion, hence "religious populism." This populism is qualitatively very different from the state-heavy, top-down populism of Argentina's Juan Perón or Brazil's Getulio Vargas, or the party-dominated variety in Mexico under and since Lázaro Cárdenas. It also differs from the utopian, elite-dominated Fabian socialist experiment and the romantic Russian "Narodniks" lyricized by Lev Tolstoy. The best historical analogue for today's Latin American populism is found in the societally based, grass-roots, agrarian protest of the late nineteenth-century rural United States.

In most countries of contemporary Latin America, acute financial crisis and austerity are paradoxically accompanied by a trend toward (re)democratization. The military return to their barracks, new political parties appear, meaningful electoral politics occurs, and such trends are welcomed and reinforced by civil society. At the same time, there are similar leveling trends within the churches. Increased identification with the poor, declericalization of leadership, experimentation with new organizational forms, and rejection of rigid hierarchical authority perplex the Pope and some bishops but appear irreversible. I will argue that there is mutual reinforcement in both arenas, that internal church debates about the degree of identification with the poor and appropriate strategies for doing so reinforce trends toward democratization in politics, even as democratic ideals affect the internal operation of the church. If democratization is to deepen and endure in the political sphere, it must be supported in other spheres of society and culture. Authoritarian regimes excluded the masses from political participation, and the churches shifted from compliant support of the regime to an interim role as vehicles for the expression of alternate political values. The churches have even become the source of the democratizing impulse. Democratizing trends within the churches have reinforced and sometimes caused democratizing trends in society.

Religious populism has contributed to democratization in two ways. First, it has offered a theoretical base for organization, a religious world view that includes this world as well as the next, a critique of extant economic and social structures that diminish human opportunity, and a set of communitarian values supportive of popular organization, inspired by the primitive Christian communities. Second, it has provided a practical organizational vehicle for "excluded" sectors of society, most notably the base communities, to organize, to debate, and to mobilize around issues of immediate concern.

To understand this Latin populism, a further look at its organizational forms and ideological content is required. We are all aware that neither state nor church can be adequately assessed by looking simply at its formal institutional structures. Just as "parastate" organizations fill political, military, and economic space, so the gap between institutional churches and popular religion has historically been filled by a panoply of associational forms. The religious base community is one contemporary example of the many paraecclesiastical organizations that have linked churches to the secular sphere. Such organizations may have regressive, preventive, and negative as well as progressive, active, and positive variations. The churches, then, are not just hierarchical organizations and bearers of doctrine; they are also sometimes willing, often reluctant, sponsors of parallel organizations and movements.

Populism is a matter of practical politics and a theory of politics that shapes practical efforts. And if earlier variations of populism reinforced authoritarian tendencies within both church and society, contemporary types may have a very different effect on values, organization, and representation. If the churches buttressed authoritarian regimes for many centuries, even small departures from that norm provoke strong reactions. A revisionist, nonpejorative approach to populism, with elements drawn from industrialized as well as mixed industrialized and developing cases, may help clarify the issues. A reassessment of populism and the social movements and phenomena of today, which I have labeled "religious populism," can contribute both to addressing practical political tasks and to resolving theoretical challenges facing contemporary intellectuals.

We are "theoretical orphans," writes Fernando Henrique Cardoso, because neither liberal pluralist, corporatist, structuralist, nor neo-Marxist paradigms adequately encompass our situation. Weber showed how charism and ethics bridge political and religious categories. Clifford Geertz explicated a positive interpretation of populism. And Antonio Gramsci articulated well the role of "organic intellectuals" within movements for political change. Drawing from Weber as well as Gramsci and Geertz, populism can be reassessed with special attention to its democratizing and demagogic characteristics. If the mechanics and the poetics of religious populist movements captivate us, it is not enough to stop there. The movements and organizations of civil society, as well as the intellectuals who aspire to be organic to them, cannot ignore the state that sets both conditions and ground rules. If democratization is the normative option, the radical democratizing begun in base communities, organizations, and movements must include the state itself. Religious populists, as well as such authors as Michel Foucalt and Manuel Castells, who have heralded the micro and momentary dimensions of power, will do a disservice if they neglect the macro side. The state, like the poor, will be always with us.

Statist versus Societal Populism

Latin American debates on populism usually emphasized but one facet of populist experience—the "state-heavy," strong-man variety of the 1930s, which incorporated the emergent industrial labor class as a political support base. This is not the sole example of populism—an argument that can be clarified through the analysis of other political concepts, especially corporatism. Contemporary discussions of European corporatism distinguish top-down, statist varieties from societal-based ones. This emphasis provides a more useful conceptual and empirical referent for reassessing populism. As Guillermo O'Donnell has pointed out, in Latin America, unike Europe and the United States, the state has shaped the institutions of civil society, not the reverse.[1] Only the churches have been exempt from this rule. In a number of Latin American countries, there is a shift from state-initiated, licensed, structured, and controlled forms of incorporation, to forms anchored more firmly in civil society. The churches have increasingly contributed to this process of (re)democratization in the region. The mutual reinforcement of overlapping membership in ecclesial base community as well as trade union or opposition party in urban Brazil today is the most salient example. Catechists, Catholic Action groups, and leadership formed in church-sponsored cooperatives and associations in Central America are rural examples of the phenomenon. In an important work on corporatism, Philippe Schmitter identified dual strains of corporatism, one originating in the state, the other in civil society.[2] In the former, the state structures, licenses, and channels interest representation, whereas the latter derives its legitimacy, its organizational forms, its very "elan vital" from civil society. Just as corporatist interest representation can follow either state or civil society channels, so too populism can be derived either from the state or strong man of the moment, or it can have its origins in the organizations and movements of civil society.

It is "statist populism" that has received notoriety in Latin American contexts and has been frequently rejected on normative grounds. But there are scholars engaged in reassessing populism today. For example, in a thoughtful essay examining the relationship between national political systems and organized labor in Latin America, David and Ruth Collier make an important revisionist contribution.[3] They distinguish populist movements that derive the impetus for incorporation of labor from party or movement (such as Mexico) from those cases (Chile and Brazil) for which the impetus comes from the state. They then trace the legacies of such incorporation in the 1920s and 1930s to contemporary authoritarian regimes in Latin America. The study confines its assessment of populism to the classic cases of mobilization of the modern labor sector. The Colliers' approach is historically valid but not sufficiently inclusive to embrace rural as well as urban phenomena—the incorporated, adversarial, and even insurgent religious populist cases of today. A different, societally based, and religiously inspired populism exists in contemporary Latin America, whose best historical analogue and antecedent is found in the nineteenth-century United States and for very similar reasons. Some historical examples will illustrate the point.

The prevailing interpretations of Latin American populism are familiar in the twentieth-century literature. Perón in Argentina, Vargas in Brazil, and Cárdenas in Mexico epitomized the political strong men who drew support from emergent urban organizations (and rural ones as well in the Mexican case). Many scholars have stressed the ways in which populism of this kind reinforces the dependence of the membership on elites. Thus, to Torcuato DiTella, such movements have broad support among working classes and/or organized peasantry but do "not result from the autonomous organizational powers of either of these groups."[4] Similarly, Edward Shils and Thomas Skidmore stress the leadership dimension of Latin American populism. Shils notes "the desirability of a direct relationship between leader and led, unmediated by institutions." Skidmore emphasizes "a style of politician produced in a situation where a mass urban electorate is receptive to a colorful leader who relies on direct emotional appeal."[5]

Many Marxists, on the other hand, interpret populism almost exclusively in categories of the Bonapartist stalemate, usually accompanied by the concession that "populism merits a positive assessment in so far as it supersedes oligarchic hegemony."[6] Ernesto Laclau concentrates much more carefully on the populist experience and stresses populism's positive role in counteracting dominant ideologies. He subscribes to the interpretation of Marx and Engels that the Bonapartist (and populist) state mediates between stalemated classes and appeals to "the highest and most radical form of populism—that wherein class interests lead to the suppression of the state as an antagonistic force."[7]

Even the most cursory glance at populist movements over time reveals a persistent elitist strain, despite widely varying views about the proper relations between leaders and led. Thus, despite the Narodniks' goals of identifying with peasants on communitarian farms, they never convinced the Russian peasant of the advantages of their proposed communes. Similarly, the Fabian socialists of England never managed to bridge the elitist gap. Like the Russian case lyricized by Tolstoy, the Fabians' populism was more effective in literature than in life, even after they reluctantly accepted the Labour party.[8] Beatrice and Sydney Webb and George Bernard Shaw ostensibly rejected post-Victorian "haute culture" yet were equally uncomfortable when directly in contact with the common man. And many of them, like populists elsewhere, were vulnerable to the seductions of fascism. They did not succeed in converting political dreams into popular language and effective political instruments.

North American Populists

But there are countervailing examples of populism, more in tune with contemporary Latin America. The best parallel is found in the agrarian revolt led by North American populists of the late nineteenth century in the United States and Canada. This movement had its roots in rural communities; it was nurtured by fundamentalist Christian preachers and encouraged by local, small-town newspaper editors. Unlike top-down, statist varieties of populism, here groups were trying to identify with the people, exercising a *concientización* that originates, not just in the intellectual's vision of what is or what ought to be, but from the experience, diagnosis, and organization of those most affected by the situation. Their rejection of "big banks," "big trusts," and the invading folkways of "back East" was adamant indeed. Although they clearly reacted *against* change and the inroads of "progress" typical of a dramatic moment in capitalist expansion, they were reacting *for* a radically different society with distinct utopian and communitarian overtones. If unsuccessful in obtaining free coinage of gold and silver, one of their prime objectives, their movement did contribute to the public ownership of utilities, a progressive income tax, and increased government support for agriculture and labor. Their Farmers' Alliance provided the organizational base that became the Populist party, translating diffused discontent into a briefly effective political vehicle. Over the twenty-year life of this agrarian revolt (roughly from 1876 to 1896), it introduced a strong regional cooperative program, an amorphous national alliance movement, and a precipitously organized political party that mushroomed and quickly evaporated. (Elements of this legacy survive in current farm belt protest, although this time the mass media determine the thrust and the duration of the complaint.)

This agrarian populism was a mass democratic movement that shaped a distinct political culture, a strong organizational network, and a well-formulated ideological critique. Laurence Goodwyn argues that the "agrarian revolt [was] a mass democratic movement that was organically shaped by its own evolving popular culture of democratic thought" and a "political movement containing its own evolving democratic culture . . . in which people could 'see themselves' and, therefore could aspire for the kind of society conducive to mass human dignity."[9] His account highlights the local organizational mechanisms whereby the National Farmers' Alliance and Industrial Union was formed and briefly sustained. It included the alliance lecturing system of grass-roots discussion and education groups that operated in twelve states, serving as cooperative and bargaining organizations to counter exploitive "capital lien" agricultural credit mechanisms that held farmers in practical bondage, as well as cooperative alliance exchange efforts, which briefly delayed more centralized transport, concentrated landownership, and a monetary system that were permanently changing the U.S. agricultural structure.

On the ideational level, the alliance articulated a radical critique of the society, economy, and polity taking shape at that crossroads in U.S. history. It appealed for a different role for the state, insisted on structural reform, and proposed a utopian "cooperative commonwealth." The movement tried, albeit unsuccessfully, to originate an alliance between farmers and labor and took up the unfinished Civil War question of incorporating the Negro into U.S. society.

Ultimately, the movement failed. Goodwyn reluctantly wrote its epitaph: "As reformers of any era quickly discover, social energy is a highly perishable ingredient; it burns, if at all, with consuming heat and then flickers out abruptly." He poses a challenge to the religious neopopulists of today, namely, the need "to understand the failure of this society's sole previous mainstream attempt to bring democratic structural reform to a triumphant industrial system. Such an inquiry would, of course, also seek to understand something about the forces and values that prevailed over populist objections to shape American social and political relations in the twentieth century. The issues of Populism were large, they dominate our world."[10]

This populism provides a useful analogue to contemporary Latin American movements. *Concientización* efforts in various Latin American nations in recent decades resemble the agrarian populist interlude of North America. The elements common to both mass movements include local-level organizations perceived as desirable and possible; intermediate and regional organizations to surmount isolation and project the image (if not the reality) of power; an intellectual leadership with vehicles for communicating societal critique and alternatives; and legitimating, value-based organizations capable of drawing on shared religious themes, symbols, and world view.

The contemporary Latin American movement has most of these elements. Much of Latin American Catholic and Protestant social involvement grew out of the "neopopulist," conscientization philosophy and small group discussion of Paulo Freire's politicizing literacy and adult education methods. These small discussion groups were prototypes for the ecclesial base communities and the setting for a new effort at defining mass and elite relationships. As Emmanuel De Kadt summarized his perceptions of the early Catholic radicals in Brazil, "These intellectuals have a deep-seated horror of the manipulation of the people—their central credo is that solution to the problems lived by the people must ultimately come from the people themselves, that their own ideas and visions, developed in a wholly different milieu, may at most serve as a sounding board, but never as signposts to the people."[11] Freire's humanist philosophy and *concientización* programs were subsequently enriched by the theology of liberation and ecclesiastically legitimated through the Latin American Bishops' Conference (Conferencia Episcopal Latinoamericana, CELAM) and its regional meetings at Medellín and Puebla. Christians began to speak of their "preferential option for the poor." Some churchmen and women suffered persecution and repression—an experience that melded middle-class clerics with peasants and workers in a fashion seldom achieved before. Intermediate associations or institutions, such as the ecclesial base communities, cells, and small groups, have infused religious and political vitality into these neopopulist organizations rooted in civil society. They do not resemble the statist variety typified in Getulio Vargas or the syndical variety of a Juan Perón. What, then, are the organizational forms of the religious populists, and whence their political dynamism?

Paraecclesiastical Organizations: Ideal Types and Stereotypes

In contemporary Latin America's religious populism, between institutional church and popular religious groups, there is a third category, which I will label "paraecclesiastical organizations." Such intermediate organizations are not new to the church. Indeed, papal social teaching has persistently favored mediating institutions for linking levels within the church and for bridging religion and politics. As a matter of empirical fact, despite its image as a monolithic bureaucracy, the church has been surprisingly pluralist in organizational forms and often inclusive even in doctrinal and ideological preferences. Thus there are many sources of parallel power to countermand formal lines of authority. Direct links from Pope to national hierarchies and territorial bishops are crosscut by the transnational character and relative autonomy of religious orders, for example.

Church history is, in fact, replete with the creation of paraecclesiastical organizations. The classical religious orders of the Middle Ages and the many charitable and educational institutions in the eighteenth and nineteenth centuries maintained their distance from national hierarchies. The church as an institution did not cease evolving as states multiplied social welfare functions. Indeed, with new stages of capital formation and industrialization, churches began to accompany the mobile pool of labor. Immigrant churches were spawned, and programs multiplied for retaining clientele, providing services, and maintaining familiar, old-country institutions and cultural practices for extended periods of time in alien settings. European migrants formed many such organizations and networks in North and South America (and many of them served as the basis for "machine" and populist politics of that era).

In the twentieth century, the Latin American church became an institutional innovator within Roman Catholicism. National bishops' conferences were organized and functioned there prior to Pope John XXIII, and the Vatican Council's legitimation of innovation was not limited to elite initiatives or to change within the ecclesiastical institution. Significant change also emerged at the mass level, in the form of the ecclesial base community or CEB (with similar groups in many of the Protestant and Evangelical churches of the continent). Though clearly linked to the institutional church, the base communities show considerable autonomy both in their organizational forms and their manner of dealing with the secular context. Especially in the political arena, the institutional church has sought to maintain a buffer zone between direct, partisan political activity and indirect influence on political life. Clerics are frequently reminded to maintain distance from partisan political activity. (Indeed, many of the recent tensions between the papacy and Latin American clerics, especially in Central America, arose, on the one hand, from clerical unwillingness to rely on such buffers and, on the other, from projection by the Pope of Polish church survival tactics on the Latin American church.) The contemporary base community permits "deniability" while at the same time extending church influence.

Besides the ebb and flow of paraecclesiastical organizations, adapting to changing times and circumstances, there has been a similar flux in the doctrinal and ideological tolerance of the church. George Orwell observed that in both Catholicism and Communism, "only the educated are orthodox."[12] The history of heresy in the church indicates the boundaries of tolerable paraecclesiastical ventures. Though ostensibly focused on dogma, censure is more frequently incurred for "discipline," that is, organizational and institutional variations that might threaten the mainline national church in its relations with Rome or, not infrequently, with the state. Millennial movements, the "prepolitical convulsions" described by Eric Hobsbawm, frequently had renegade clerical leadership, and the cultural organizations of immigrant churches in northern America were usually clerical-dominated. Throughout the nineteenth and early twentieth centuries, in the North American church, there was the threat and occasionally the schismatic separation of "national churches"—mainly East European in origin—which split from the Irish-dominated U.S. hierarchy (who were in turn at pains to assure Rome of complete orthodoxy). "Americanism" was a short-lived and overpublicized trend at separatism and accommodation to the Protestant milieu of the New World.

The Latin American experience has been quite different. The initial blend of cross and crown, subsequent anticlericalism, scarcity of clerics, and syncretistic adaptation of both native American and African religious traditions are just a few of the salient internal differences.

But if in Latin America progressive or radical tendencies within the church have gained international notoriety, in many countries conservative and reactionary paraecclesiastical organizations still support the social, economic, and political status quo. *Opus Dei* and "Country, Tradition, and Liberty" continue to play significant, if less bloody, roles among economic and social elites than did the Cristeros and Sinarquistas several decades ago in Mexico.

Paraecclesiastical organizations today have become sources and surrogates for political activity as well as mediators between ecclesiastical institutions and the faithful. Formerly, such intermediate organizations linked church to society through charitable and welfare functions. Just as the state has become more pervasive in society, so has the political, often oppositional quality of church organizations increased. Catholic hierarchies such as the Brazilian or Chilean face new dilemmas when they choose to extricate themselves from politics. They may very well so choose, and in some cases, church influence and involvement will continue indirectly through the paraecclesiasticals. In other instances, groups and individuals will simply leave the church and seek political involvement independent of hierarchical preferences.

The Changing Church-State Arena

There are many facets to Latin America—different regimes, different societies, different development processes. Indeed, there are many Latin Americas and, within each country, considerable regional variation. Protracted violence occurred in some countries early in this century, not to be repeated. Elsewhere, violence has been endemic. Sometimes, heady periods of economic "boom and miracle" were followed by abrupt crashes. The same decades witnessed substantial change within the churches and in their manner of insertion into sociopolitical contexts. Without exhausting the variation in church-state relationships in the region, I will emphasize the main characteristics of three model patterns, exemplified in a number of states in the region. First, there are the cases where religious populism has served as both source and surrogate for political activity in authoritarian regimes (Brazil and Chile); second, cases where the populist thrust reinforces insurrection (Central America); and third, stalemated cases, exemplified in Mexico and Colombia, where the institutional churches remain relatively unchanged, where marginal groups within the church radicalize, and where the processes of liberalization, if they occur, receive no impetus and usually result in persons leaving the institution. Variation among the cases can be observed in the organizational relationships between hierarchy and quasi-autonomous organizations of socially committed Christians and can be explained according to the past- or future-oriented world view of the organized groups.

Elsewhere, I have written on the new ways in which religious organizations have served both as surrogates and wellsprings of political identification and activity, especially in authoritarian and repressive regimes.[13] Commentators generally agree on the extraordinarily increased involvement of the state both in the economy and the polity. The phenomenon is not exclusive to Latin America; indeed, political scientists in the United States are showing increased concern with the dilutions of representation as political functionaries play an increasing role in the establishment of policy. A similar shift has occurred in the churches of Latin America.

More than two decades ago, Ivan Vallier characterized Latin American Catholic bishops as "pluralists, politicians, papists, or pastors" according to their emphasis on internal ecclesiastical affairs or the way their activities went beyond sacramental and evangelical functions to include social, political, and economic activities.[14] Happily, the category of "populists" adds yet another "p" to his list. Vallier's static interpretation, however, concentrated on the hierarchy, neglecting the many layers of syncretistic, "popular" Catholicism that lay beneath the surface independent of clerical intrusion. Since 1970, both social science research and daily newspapers attest to institutional and popular responses ranging from national conferences of bishops to both progressive and regressive parallel organizations—whether base communities linked to a militant labor party or anticommunist crusades by pot-banging housewives. Individual bishops such as Dom Helder Camara and Archbishop Oscar Romero took "prophetic" stands. The many faces of "popular Catholicism" with millennial and anarchistic tendencies have been increasingly studied. Changes occurred in the church because of the state, and vice versa.

As the 1960s gave way to the 1970s, analysts began to isolate characteristics of late capitalist development in Europe, then in Latin America, as import-substitution strategies waned and the military adopted a caretaker role in many countries. Authoritarianism became a topic of inquiry, and its military and bureaucratic modes were dissected. The national security state was recognized. The churches had to adapt once again—in some cases to bureaucratic-authoritarian rule, elsewhere to outright repressive situations that sometimes provoked insurrectional responses. Finally, in many cases, surprisingly enough, serious church-state confrontation never occurred and stalemated situations prevailed. I suggest here a few elements for situating religious populists in three different Latin American political contexts.

The Bureaucratic-Authoritarian Situation: Brazil and Chile

Brazil and Chile have been prototypical cases of bureaucratic authoritarianism, and the church in both countries has played a significant role at hierarchical and popular levels. The bureaucratic-authoritarian regime is known for excluding previously organized political actors (especially urban labor) from political participation. The churches partially filled this vacuum, speaking against abuses of human rights, delegitimizing regime activities, initiating economic and social development programs, and providing a protective umbrella for alternative organizations. In many cases, this meant, in practice, offering a radical democratizing alternative at the grassroots and community levels. And this alternative frequently became an organized opposition. The Brazilian hierarchy, through its independent newspapers, pulpits, and national-level religious organizations such as the Justice and Peace groups, provided significant leadership to civil society throughout the 1960s and early 1970s until other Brazilian professional and political organizations of journalists, lawyers, professors, students, and the like began to take up the slack. Even as the political "opening" and liberalization process advanced, the Brazilian church retained a political representational role. Within the churches, one can identify markedly different postures at different moments, according to the amount of representational space, level of repression, and ability of civil society to assert itself before the state. If the courageous stand of the cardinal of Santiago, Chile, in the early years of the Pinochet regime offered a surrogate for political identification and activity, the latter half of the decade indicates his withdrawal or extrication from that role. The Brazilian church, on the other hand, has sustained a representational support role even as the political opening or democratization process continues. (See the chapters by Thomas Bruneau and Scott Mainwaring in this volume.)

Insurrectional Situations

If Brazil and Chile demonstrate dynamic ties between institutional and popular religion, which create alternatives and strengthen opposition forces at the institutional, informal, and ideological levels, the Central American scenario is quite different. In Nicaragua, Guatemala, or El Salvador, it is not the Episcopal Conference or strong minority groups among the bishops, but rather individual hierarchs, scattered religious and clergy, and, surprisingly, large numbers of base communities and catechists who have emerged to lead the struggle against repression and injustice and who have frequently been killed for their efforts. (See the chapters by Phillip Berryman and Michael Dodson in this volume.)

Decades of frustrated reform, much of it triggered by "pastors and pluralists," by Peace Corps volunteers, and by cooperative specialists from the United States, have prompted significant numbers of peasants and Indians to abandon community development, cooperative production, or land reform efforts and resort to armed rebellion. From the frustration of blocked reform emerged the conversion of many such persons to insurgency. In Central America, it is not the hierarchy but popular religious groups, a few clergy and religious, and mostly lay leaders, who, fortified by Liberation Theology and still more by Old Testament and peasant-inspired justice and exasperation, have opted for rebellion. As a corporate group, the hierarchy has been silent or has pleaded for peace. If it has criticized government excesses, it has cast similar blame on the left and sought a perhaps impossible role as mediator between extremely polarized sides. The tragedy of protracted fratricidal religious warfare is very likely. If Vietnam has been the dominant metaphor for U.S. involvement in Central America, both religious and imperial dimensions of conflict there suggest that Ulster may be more appropriate. The United States is the external power that presumes to arbitrate here and manages to prolong the agony. Ireland was Britain's first colony and is destined to be its last. And who gets Central America?

Stalemate: Mexico and Colombia

Another cluster of Latin American cases includes countries that experienced exceptionally violent social upheaval during the first half of this century and are characterized by relatively stalemated relationships between church hierarchy and state. The hierarchy is generally very conservative, church-state relationships are cool and cautious, social involvement by the church is more charitable than promotional, and a frequent result is the radicalization of more progressive church members and consequent internal polarization within the church. (See the chapter on Colombia by Daniel Levine.) How does one explain the extraordinary social influence of both institutional and popular forms of religiosity in some countries and its social quiescence in others? Clearly, religious and fratricidal wars of earlier decades have left their legacy, as have constitutional arrangements, tacit social pacts, anticlerical feelings, and the peculiar legacies of co-optation in each country. "*Coronelismo*" and "*Caciquismo*," the Latin variants of political clientelism, have vied with clerical paternalism for hegemony at the local level. Clearly, the church's instinct for survival is a constant. The proportion of foreign-born versus national clergy is yet another significant variable.

Although these explanations are plausible, I believe that a fuller understanding of variation rests on the relationships between popular religion and the hierarchy and whether that relationship leads to the creation of socially relevant paraecclesiastical organizations. Besides organization, ideology is crucial. As Geertz notes, "The beliefs contained in populist ideology have the dual functions of 'solutions to critical dilemmas' and 'mobilizing agents.'"[15] He emphasizes the *past* orientation of the "solution" school and the *future* thrust of "mobilizing agents." The stalemated hierarchies of Mexico and Colombia do indeed look back to "la violencia." In the Brazilian, Chilean, and (at least at the base community level) Central American cases, base communities and hierarchy have functioned as future-oriented mobilization agents. A change in this ideology and increased political space will encourage extrication from politics in the former cases, whereas exhaustion from civil war may occasion changed postures and increased political involvement by Central American bishops. This dual, reinforcing role of ideology explains the presence or absence of church organizations as sources and surrogates for political activity in critical periods of social and political change. Whether the religious populists can sustain "social energy" over the long haul will, in considerable measure, depend on their willingness to enter social pacts and on the depth and quality of the intellectual/people relationship.

Populism, Romanticism, and Intellectual Fad

Perhaps the cynical proposition that populism is an ideology of intellectuals who purport to speak for the masses is an overstatement; nonetheless, there is room to question whether intellectuals (populist politicians or Latin American clerics) overly romanticize the "people" and the "popular." After all, intellectual fashion regarding the people has been notably fickle. The negative connotations of "masses," the widely held suspicion of "mass politics" that was current in Europe and the United States as well as among the intelligentsia of Latin America during the 1930s and 1940s, was deeply influenced by European fascist experiments, Latin American "integralist" offshoots, and Stalinist totalitarian tragedies. Such fears may have receded in some quarters, replaced by different attitudes to "things popular." It appears that the old populism is dead. Political strong men no longer manipulate urban masses to confront traditional rural oligarchs and embark on modernization adventures in Latin America.

Especially in South America today, intellectuals are enthused by the effervescence of civil society; by the social movements whereby minority groups, ethnic, racial, feminist, or religious, reenter the public scene. There is a welcome and timely regard for the poetics of power—the role of culture, of religion, of symbol as both source and surrogate for political activity, especially in liberalizing or democratizing authoritarian regimes. Repressed and dormant civil society comes to life. But the mechanics of power—the use (legitimate or not) of force, the expanding role of the state—cannot casually be overlooked. As Fernando Henrique Cardoso has written, "It's understandable and healthy that in countries such as Brazil—with its elitist political tradition and conservative, state-centric political thought—there is a political reassessment of social movements and an attitude of solidarity with the bases. But it is theoretically unsatisfactory and politically ineffective to imagine a politics of social transformation which does not say what to do with and in the state, to give it a direction which benefits the majority. . . . The real point is not to downplay the significance of the base nor to restrict mobilization or 'assemblyism' . . . but to create the necessary mechanisms to pressure and control nuclei of decision-making and power."[16]

Religious populism, one element in a rejuvenated civil society, cannot abstract from the state, either theoretically or politically. Religious populism, operating through paraecclesiastical organizations in some Latin American countries, is less vulnerable before the state and can help create alternatives. The religious populist experiment of nineteenth-century North America closely parallels the current Latin variant. Both express a radical critique of society during a period of profound economic and political transformation. Both pose a leveling, democratic vision of what those societies should and should not become. The North American effort hastily tried to mount a political party capable of stemming the modernizing tide of capitalist concentration. It won some skirmishes and concessions but lost the war. Religious populists and paraecclesiastical organizations in some Latin American countries today contribute to the depth, perseverance, and political efficacy of the fragile democratization trends in the region. The issues of populism are indeed large. They still dominate our world.

Notes

1. Guillermo O'Donnell, "Comparative Historical Formations of the State Apparatus," *International Social Science Journal* 32 (1981): 717.
2. Philippe Schmitter, "Still the Century of Corporatism?" *Review of Politics* 36 (January 1974): 85–131.
3. David Collier and Ruth Collier, "Populism and Populist Legacies in Latin America" (paper prepared for Rutgers Conference on Populism, 1979).
4. Torcuato DiTella, "Populism," in Claudio Veliz, ed., *Obstacles to Change in Latin America* (New York: Oxford University Press, 1965), p. 47.
5. Edward Shils, *The Torment of Secrecy* (London: Heinemann, 1956), p. 98; Thomas Skidmore, *Politics in Brazil* (New York: Oxford University Press, 1967), p. 7.
6. Juan Carolos Portantiero and Emilio de Ipola, "Lo nacional-popular y los populismos realmente existentes" (mimeo, Mexico, 1981).
7. Ernesto Laclau, *Politics and Ideology in Marxist Theory* (London: NLB, 1977).
8. The following works were referred to in my review of populism: Margaret Canavan, *Populism* (New York: Harcourt Brace Jovanovich, 1981); Robert W. Cherny, *Populism, Progressivism, and the Transformation of Nebraska Politics* (Lincoln: University of Nebraska Press, 1981); Michael L. Conniff, *Urban Politics in Brazil: The Rise of Populism, 1925–1945* (Pittsburgh: University of Pittsburgh Press, 1981); Otavio Ianni, *A formacão do estado populista na America Latina* (Rio: Paz e Terra, 1979); Ghita Ionescu and Ernest Gellner, *Populism* (London: Weidenfeld and Nicholson, 1969); Norman MacKenzie and Jeanne MacKenzie, *The Fabians* (New York: Simon and Schuster, 1977); Norman Pollack, *The Populist Mind* (New York: Bobbs-Merrill, 1967); Francisco Weffort, *O populismo na politica Brasileira* (Rio: Paz e Terra, 1978); and Laurence Goodwyn, *Democratic Promise: The Populist Movement in America* (New York: Oxford University Press, 1976).
9. Goodwyn, *Democratic Promise*, pp. 601, 604.
10. Ibid., pp. xxii, xxiii.
11. Emmanuel De Kadt, *Catholic Radicals in Brazil* (New York: Oxford University Press, 1970).
12. George Orwell, *The Road to Wigan Pier* (New York: Harcourt Brace, 1937).
13. Charles Reilly, "Cultural Movements in Latin America," in Myron Aranoff, ed., *Culture and Political Change* (New Brunswick: Transaction Books, 1983); Charles Reilly and Martín Dela Rosa, eds., *Religión y política en Mexico* (Mexico: Siglo XXI Editores, 1985).
14. Ivan Vallier, *Catholicism, Social Control, and Modernization in Latin America* (Englewood Cliffs, N.J.: Prentice-Hall, 1970).
15. Clifford Geertz, "Ideology as a Cultural System," in David Apter, *Ideology and Discontent* (Glencoe: Free Press, 1964), p. 64.
16. Fernando Henrique Cardoso, "Regime politico e mudanca social," *Revista de Cultura e Politica* 3 (November–December 1981): 7–26.

4

El Salvador:
From Evangelization to Insurrection

Phillip Berryman

Today. . . more than ever I believe in the mass organizations. . . .
I believe that the mass organizations are the social forces that are
going to push and pressure, that are going to achieve a genuine
society with social justice and freedom.

Archbishop Oscar Romero,
interviewed in February 1980, six weeks before being murdered

The church's role in Central American conflicts is well known. Most attention has been focused on public controversies involving the hierarchies, such
as the presence of priests in the Sandinista government. The murders of four
American churchwomen and of Archbishop Oscar Romero in El Salvador in
1980 drew attention to the violence against church people. In Guatemala and
El Salvador about two dozen priests were murdered between 1977 and 1982,
as well as some sisters and Protestant pastors and hundreds of active lay
people.

That violence reflected the conviction of the landholding oligarchy and the
military that the church's pastoral work was responsible for the rise of
militant organizations during the 1970s. This essay seeks to describe how
pastoral work, particularly in the CEBs (*comunidades eclesiales de base,* "grass-
roots Christian communities"), intersected with the rise and growth of those
movements. The focus will be on El Salvador and especially on the work of a
group of Jesuits in the parish of Aguilares. Some references will be made to
similar phenomena in Nicaragua and Guatemala. Although the cases de-

scribed here cannot be said to have been the norm, they were crucial to the rise of the militant mass organizations that were central to the emerging struggle in Central America.

First Stirrings of Change

As was the case elsewhere, the pre–Vatican II Catholic church in Central America was a strongly conservative force. In the 1920s, for example, the Nicaraguan bishops paid little attention to the struggle of Augusto Cesar Sandino except to urge his followers to abandon their "sterile struggle" and return to family, work, and religion; in 1942 the archbishop of Managua crowned President Anastasio Somoza's daughter Queen of the Army in a ceremony in the national stadium, using a crown from the statue of the virgin of Candelaria;[1] and in 1954 Archbishop Mariano Rossell of Guatemala City organized nationwide processions with a popular "black Christ" to stir up anticommunist sentiments and cooperated with the U.S. embassy in the CIA overthrow of the Arbenz government. More important than these overt actions, however, was the day-to-day reinforcement of a fatalistic world view through popular religiosity in which the image of God resembles a celestial hacienda owner. As has frequently been stated, the church was one of the three pillars of society, the other two being the landholding oligarchy and the military.

For the Catholic church as a whole, the Second Vatican Council (1962–65) represented an acceptance of the results of the Reformation, the Enlightenment, democracy, and the modern world in general. In the Third World, the church endorsed development. One expression of developmentalism in Central America was parish promotion of peasant cooperatives. Another expression was Christian Democrat parties, although they had no formal links with the hierarchy or clergy. But the ink was scarcely dry on the council documents when Latin Americans began to speak pejoratively of developmentalism. Just as Latin American social scientists were unveiling dependency theory, theologians and others in the church were developing critiques of imported ideas and models of pastoral work and asserting that the Latin American church needed its own frameworks and methods. An early expression of these thoughts came in the meeting of Latin American bishops at Medellín in 1968. Soon there was a new theological-pastoral framework (Liberation Theology) and a new pastoral methodology (evangelization in lay-led *comunidades de base*).

These currents reached Central America at the end of the decade. Nationwide "pastoral weeks" were held in Guatemala (1968), Nicaragua (1969), and El Salvador (1970). In all countries, regional training centers were set up at which lay leaders could receive intensive formation. In the late 1960s and early 1970s, there were occasional public confrontations between groups in power and church people: the "Melville case," when American Maryknoll missionaries had to leave Guatemala when it was discovered that they were joining a guerrilla organization (1967); public letters from groups of priests denouncing the Somoza dictatorship and occupations of the cathedral in protest in Nicaragua; the kidnapping of a priest in El Salvador. For the most part, however, these were years of quiet work during which the new *comunidades de base* model was increasingly used. Let us now look at one example of such work.

Aguilares

The town of Aguilares sits just off a main highway about twenty-five miles north of San Salvador. Surrounded by sugarcane fields held by large landholders and, more distantly, by hills where peasants cultivate corn and beans, it could be viewed as a microcosm of El Salvador. In September 1972, Father Rutilio Grande arrived with other Jesuits in the Aguilares parish and immediately put into motion a pastoral plan. That plan was based on Grande's studies and observations in South America and the conclusions other members of the team had drawn from their participation in other CEB pastoral work in El Salvador. Because of this methodical approach and because the Aguilares team had more members than a typical parish, the pastoral plan unfolded more rapidly than would be normal elsewhere.

The priests and students set out to organize two-week "missions" in each area of the parish. Team members would live with the people of the area, systematically visiting each family to get to know them (for example, eating each meal at a different house). Through conversation they would get a sense of how people viewed their lives and their problems. These observations were recorded in a card file, which enabled team members to grasp recurring images, words, ideas, and patterns in people's thinking and culture.

In the evenings the people would gather for sessions at which Bible passages were read, interspersed with commentaries and questions. They would then break into groups to discuss the passages and return at the end to present their conclusions. Then a team member would summarize what had been said, using the people's own wording but drawing out the main themes. The essence of this method was for the people to use Scripture to confront their lives. The team consciously chose to take traditional religiosity as its starting point, for example, challenging the notion that it is God's will that some be rich while others are desperately poor by asking whether the Genesis text means that the Lord made the earth for the landholders. People came to grasp the rudiments of a new biblical version of their lives. More than content, however, they received method: a way of reading the Scriptures that emphasized human dignity and responsibility for the world and saw their own strivings for unity at the local level as part of God's plan for forming one human family.

At the same time they were forming an initial local community with their own chosen leadership (several people rather than one individual to make the leadership collective). In less than a year there were thirty-seven such communities with some three hundred leaders, who continued to meet regularly in their villages and in the neighborhoods of the town of Aguilares. Because there were about thirty thousand people in the parish, these CEBs by no means reached everyone. During the period after the initial establishment of these communities, the team estimated than an average of 673 people attended weekly CEB meetings. The circle of those influenced by the gospel was considerably larger, from two to five thousand people.[2]

The Aguilares team was able to build on the experience of other groups in El Salvador and Central America. Many parishes undertaking the CEB model of pastoral work were initially inspired by what Father Leo Mahon and a group of Chicago priests had done in San Miguielito, a district on the outskirts of Panama City, starting in 1963. Mahon had worked out a course held in small groups meeting in homes. Trained lay leaders led discussions on basic human experiences (injustice, community, sexual love, human dignity, unity/disunity) with a family analogy (God is Father, Christ is Brother, we are brothers in the family of the church). Parishes in Nicaragua, Guatemala, and El Salvador initially borrowed this course, but many eventually came to regard it as too church-centered because it did not directly address the structural roots of injustice. At that point they began to use the dialogue and Scripture method to consider more critically issues such as inequities in landholdings. The CEB model of pastoral work was widely adopted in rural parishes of the archdiocese of San Salvador (where today the FPL [Fuerzas Populares de Liberación Farabundo Martí, Farabundo Martí Popular Liberation Forces] guerrillas are active), but was found much less in the eastern part of the country (Morazan, where ERP [Ejército Revolucionario del

Pueblo] guerrillas are strong). In Nicaragua, such work was widely pursued in some rural areas, especially by American Capuchin priests in the sparsely populated Atlantic region. Sacred Heart priests used a similar method with Indians in the Quiché region of Guatemala, although there it was called Catholic Action, and Belgian priests in the agroexport belt of the southern coast also formed CEBs.

An observer in the early 1970s would find few differences in ideas, language, approach, aims, and aspirations between pastoral agents doing CEB work in Central America and those engaged in similar work elsewhere in Latin America. From the late 1960s until the early 1970s, the mood in Latin America had been one of excitement and belief that change could be effected. But with increasing militarization and repression (symbolized by the 1973 Chilean coup), people throughout the continent saw "liberation" as a goal increasingly far away, perhaps for one's grandchildren.

Why the Crisis in Central America?

The upsurge of revolutionary organization and action in Central America caught most observers by surprise. As one respected Central American social scientist has noted, "At the beginning of the 1970's, neither the popular forces nor the vanguard, nor least of all the social scientists of the region, would have been able to predict the dimensions of the crisis that would so deeply shake Central American society some years later."[3]

To make sense of the situation, it may be helpful to note the considerable similarities between the Central American cases studied by Eric R. Wolf in his *Peasant Wars of the Twentieth Century*. In his analysis of Guatemala, Shelton Davis draws on Wolf and points out that modern peasant wars have occurred where traditional peasants are dislocated by the expansion of modern capitalist relations of production; where population growth increases the problems of peasant agricultural production; where the state loses its control over the peasantry; and, where peasants form links with urban social classes and with revolutionary political parties.[4] The Wolf-Davis framework is useful for placing developments in Central America in a larger context.

It is commonplace in discussions of Central America to speak of the small agroexport elites whose original fortunes were made a century ago in the first coffee boom after they had taken the peasants' lands. The expansion of agroexport into new crops after World War II has received less notice. The new crops (sugar, cotton, and beef) required large extensions of flat land.

Davis notes that between 1961 and 1973, in Guatemala, arable land for export crops increased by 6.5 percent a year, but new arable land for food production increased by only 1.7 to 2 percent a year. There was little new agricultural land for the growing peasant population. The average size of farm units for Indians in the Guatemalan highlands decreased from 1.3 hectares per person in 1950 to less than .85 hectares per person in 1975.[5]

A similar process was taking place in El Salvador, where perhaps the most noticeable effect was an increase in the numbers of landless peasants from about 11 percent of the rural population in 1961 to 40 percent in 1975. Some of the landless are renters or sharecroppers; others must depend on day labor, which is highly seasonal. One study showed that in the mid-1970s the average such laborer in El Salvador could get only 141 days of work a year.

John A. Booth found that real working-class income declined in Nicaragua, El Salvador, and Guatemala during the 1970s. His research reinforces the general impression of grass-roots activists, including church workers, that the "crisis" began to be felt in the early 1970s. This idea contradicts the more conventional view, as exemplified in the Kissinger Commission Report (1984), which sees the crisis as the product of the world economic recession beginning in the late 1970s.[6] It is not accidental that living conditions for many, if not most, people worsened even though overall growth rates remained near 6 percent: the same model of development—agroexport expansion and relatively capital-intensive industrialization through the Central American Common Market—led to both outcomes.

These are some indicators of the first two elements in Davis's summary above: a breakdown in the existing way of life caused by the expansion of capitalist agriculture (new export crops) aggravated by demographic growth. To these objective aspects are added the subjective reaction of people, expressed in Davis's final two conditions, which will be treated in the rest of this essay.

Two additional characteristics of Nicaragua, El Salvador, and Guatemala undoubtedly help explain the outbreak of revolutionary movements. First, these are small countries (Nicaragua's population under 3 million; Guatemala's no more than 7 million). In the large or medium-sized Latin American countries they would be no more than provinces. Smallness and relative homogeneity easily result in local conflicts becoming national crises; the same conflicts in large countries such as Brazil, Mexico, or even Colombia would remain local and could be handled accordingly. Second, each of these countries shows the ongoing effects of a kind of "original sin" that left the country in the hands of oligarchical military elites: in Nicaragua, the Somoza dictatorship, which grew out of occupation by U.S. Marines; in El Salvador fifty years of military rule following the 1932 massacre of as many as thirty thousand peasants; in Guatemala a brutal military rule that emerged from the CIA-financed coup that overthrew the Arbenz government in 1954. The narrow elites felt no need to carry out or even permit any economic or political reforms.

The ruling groups were well aware of pressure on the social system. For example, during the 1960s the Salvadorean military, with U.S. advisers and a counterinsurgency ideology, set up ORDEN (Organización Democrática Nacionalista, Democratic Nationalist Organization) as a paramilitary and spy network.

In 1969, pressured by peasant movements, the Honduran military government decreed a land reform. To acquire lands, it began to expel Salvadoreans, some of whom had been farming for many years. The Salvadorean elites, fearful of the impact of tens or even hundreds of thousands of peasants adding to demographic pressure, drummed up war fever (especially on the occasion of soccer games between the two countries) and in June launched an attack on Honduras. Several thousand people, mainly Honduran peasants, were killed before a cease-fire could be arranged. The international press called it a "soccer war," but it was in fact a manifestation of latent tensions over land tenure.

Such, then, was the context—*la realidad nacional*—in which the CEB pastoral work unfolded in the 1970s.

CEBs and Popular Organizations

How does pastoral work lead, in practice, to political activism? To begin with, small group evangelization in CEBs often brings a sense of enthusiasm and hope. People emerge from a passive world view and begin to feel that their action can make a difference, that indeed God is on their side as he was with the Israelites in their Exodus. People gain a growing sense of their own dignity, and they feel their efforts to unite in their local community are part of a much larger movement toward unity. They may experience some improvements by attending literacy classes or pressuring the government bureaucracy to build a school or a health center, or to send a teacher, or dig a well. But soon they run up against the limits of this stage of *concientización* and realize they must take the next step: organization.

As noted above, declining living conditions made people receptive to a new

form of organization. In El Salvador, peasants increasingly saw that significant change could not occur under the existing political system, even when
politicians were honest and well-intentioned. The electoral fraud against the
Christian Democrat–led reform coalition reinforced that impression. People
began looking for more militant forms of action and expressed their desperation in the slogan, "Better to die of a bullet than of hunger."

One of the organizations able to profit from this readiness was FECCAS
(Federación de Campesinos Cristianos de El Salvador, Federation of Christian Peasants of El Salvador), which had been started by Christian Demo-
crats in the 1960s. In the early 1970s a new leadership turned FECCAS in a
more militant direction. FECCAS organizers arriving in villages could begin
their efforts with CEB members, who joined FECCAS believing it a direct
outgrowth of the process started by church people.

The confluence of these organizing efforts and others soon became a
national movement. In the region of Suchitoto (a town not far from Aguilares, where some of the first CEB work had begun in 1969), a government
hydroelectric project already under way would soon be flooding farmland
and displacing some fifteen thousand peasants. Their cause became a ral-
lying point. Out of a series of meetings in 1974 involving grass-roots organizers, political party leaders, university professors, church people, and others
there emerged an umbrella organization called FAPU (Frente de Acción
Popular Unificada, United Popular Action Front). This "first FAPU" (to be
distinguished from a subsequent popular organization with the same name)
was hindered by divisions, but it exemplified the tendency for local struggles
to become national.

In November 1976 in La Cayetana, San Vicente, government troops
attacked a group of peasants who had occupied unused land, hoping to rent
it. Attacking with tanks and bazookas, the soldiers killed six peasants and
arrested twenty-six, and thirteen disappeared. This incident is particularly
significant because those affected belonged to no particular peasant organization; instead, their action (the first such land occupation in El Salvador)
arose from discussions and out of a decision in their CEB. After they had
been thrown off the land the people formed the UTC (Union de Trabajadores del Campo, Rural Workers Union), which later linked up with
FECCAS.

As grass-roots Christian groups evolved to greater activism, guerrilla
organization also began reaching out to build alliances with them. Shortly
after the San Vicente attack, the FPL, a guerrilla group formed in 1970, sent
a letter to Christians, commenting on these events and inviting them to

become involved in the struggle. This letter indicates that the guerrilla organizations were already involved in some of the grass-roots work. In other words, the popular organizations emerged in part because of the political work of the guerrillas.

In June 1975 another army attack on peasants in a place called Las Tres Calles inspired a protest by university students and FAPU on 30 July. Government troops attacked the marchers, trapping them as they crossed a bridge; at least twenty were killed. A group of priests and sisters invited the march organizers to bring some of the bodies to the cathedral for a funeral. The cathedral was then closed and occupied. Inside the cathedral leaders of the nascent popular organizations engaged in sharp ideological debate. When the cathedral occupation ended on 6 August, a large group had split from the FAPU umbrella to form the BPR (Bloque Popular Revolucionario, Revolutionary Peoples Bloc), initially composed largely of FECCAS and UTC members along with the national teachers' organization. FAPU and other popular organizations were formed subsequently.

At this point, these organizations may be broadly characterized as grassroots groups with a strong peasant base. Their militancy reflected a conviction that traditional organizations, and especially political parties, were impotent to effect basic changes. Their framework of analysis was Marxist, and indeed later events showed that they were linked to the guerrilla organizations, although in the mid-1970s these were small and carried out very few actions. It is important to be clear about these links because the record shows that the popular organizations cannot be viewed simply as tools of Marxist-Leninist groups. Rather, they were an autonomous expression of peasant desperation, and at the local level they acted autonomously. The BPR in particular was closely connected to church people. It would not be excessive to call it a spinoff of the CEBs in the sense that at the village level, ordinary peasants viewed their militancy in FECCAS as a logical and direct outgrowth of their formation in the gospel through the CEBs. The peasants saw a direct continuity between their "awakening" through the Scriptures and their participation in mass-based organizations that the landholders called "communist."

Some church workers, including priests, were close to and participated in the process that led to formation of the popular organizations. Others found them problematic and were not sure what their relationship with the CEBs should be. Rutilio Grande, the pastor of Aguilares, for example, did not participate in the 1975 cathedral occupation. He followed official church teaching in the belief that political options are for the laity and that the priest as a minister of unity in the community should not take a partisan position. He did recognize the legitimacy of these organizations, however, and denounced the oppression that provoked them. Such a position leads to problems in practical application. One example arose in late 1975, when FECCAS was preparing its first public demonstration. Some of the leaders (who were also parish "delegates of the Word") asked for a special mass. After some discussion, the Jesuit parish team compromised, offering to celebrate a special "peasant Christmas" but without any organizational placards or slogan-chanting in the church.

The question would continue to reappear. One could argue that the proper role of priests and sisters was simply consciousness-raising and evangelization and that the people were making political options on their own. But that might seem as though the church's pastoral agents were abandoning people when evangelization led to risk and danger. Did not pastoral commitment imply a duty to stay with people and accompany them throughout their journey? If so, what were the implications for the relationship between the church (pastoral agents and CEBs) and the popular organizations? The resolution of this issue was critical to the character of CEB work in El Salvador and Guatemala. The next section explores in detail the conflict that developed around these issues and brings us back to El Salvador and specifically to Aguilares.

CEB pastoral work was the dominant model in rural parishes of the archdiocese of San Salvador during the early and mid-1970s. Some of the parishes using it were Suchitoto, Aguilares, Rosario Mora, Guazapa, Quetzaitepeque, Zacatecoluca, Tecoluca, Arcato, and Cojutepeque, virtually all of which have been sites of major battles between the insurgents and the army in recent years. CEB work was less common in the western and eastern parts of the country.

In Nicaragua under Somoza, there was no similar movement toward mass peasant organizations, although CEPA (Centro de Educación y Promoción Agrícola, Center for Agricultural Education and Training) was begun by Jesuits and trained local lay leaders. By the mid-1970s a network existed of hundreds of peasants it had trained. Although this network was not a popular organization, CEPA provided critical peasant structure when a mass anti-Somoza movement developed in the late 1970s.

In Guatemala the equivalent of FECCAS-UTC was CUC (Comité de Unidad Campesina, Committee for Peasant Unity), which emerged in 1978. CUC may well have consciously studied and applied lessons from peasant organizing in El Salvador. In any case, it often built upon previous work done by church people, such as starting with local CEB leaders. CUC also rapidly became a national movement.

The popular organizations in El Salvador and Guatemala built toward having a broad array of organizations, representing many sectors: peasants, labor unions, shantytown dwellers, students, teachers, professional people, church groups, and the like. It is important to realize, nevertheless, that these organizations started with peasants, many of whom had become involved through the pastoral approach of the CEBs.

Growing Conflict

To this point I have discussed how the popular organizations largely grew out of pastoral work in a context of crisis and deteriorating living conditions and people's efforts to organize. From 1975 to 1980 El Salvador was like a stage on which the major protagonists, the oligarchy and the military on one side and the popular organizations—and by implication, people in the Catholic church—on the other, acted out the conflict.

Occasionally hints of reformist tendencies appeared among the elites. One such sign came in 1976, when the military-dominated government proposed a mild land reform, more like a pilot project to begin in two provinces. Most left sectors, including the BPR, denounced it as a "Yankee" plot to defuse growing peasant militancy; the oligarchy, for its part, unleashed a strident publicity campaign in the newspapers and lobbied among the military. Within a few months the plan had been shelved. Having blocked the land reform, the oligarchy, through organizations representing landholders and private sector interests, seems to have decided that the moment had come to deal with the popular organizations and those sectors of the church close to them. An incident in December 1976 offered the pretext.

Some FECCAS peasants in the Aguilares area were being expelled from land as the waters rose because of the hydroelectric project mentioned earlier. They organized a march to the home of the Orellana family, who owned the land, hoping to pressure them into helping them acquire land elsewhere (the peasants had been on the hacienda for fifty years). The confrontation became angry, there was some confusion, shots were fired, and Eduardo Orellana was killed (probably shot accidentally by his brother, Francisco).

The landholders' organizations immediately began to portray Orellana as a martyr at the hands of "murderous hordes" and placed newspaper ads denouncing FECCAS, the Jesuits, other priests, and even Archbishop Luis Chavez y Gonzalez. Within days the government was arresting, torturing, and deporting priests. By mid-1977 more than twenty priests had been subjected to this treatment.

The opening attack on the church and the popular organizations coincided with the final weeks of the electoral campaign in which the reformist coalition, UNO (Unión Nacional Opositora, National Opposition Union), was facing the official party. When the official party won through massive fraud, UNO staged a week-long rally that was ended only when official troops attacked it, beating hundreds and killing twenty or more. The blood was firehosed off the street.

That attack took place on 28 February 1977. On 12 March, as he was driving through cane fields to say Saturday evening mass, the pastor of Aguilares, Rutilio Grande, was machine-gunned to death, along with two passengers. The immediate spark for the murder may have been the finding of the body of Roberto Poma, the head of the government tourist agency, the previous day. Poma had been kidnapped by a guerrilla organization, and the murder of Grande may have reflected an "eye for an eye" mentality. But in a larger sense, his murder was simply one element in the several attacks being mounted on the church and the popular organizations. In response, the newly installed Archbishop Oscar Romero closed the Catholic schools for three days and organized one large outdoor mass the following Sunday (suppressing regular parish masses) as an extraordinary measure of protest.

But the violence continued. In May, after another upper-class figure was kidnapped and killed by guerrillas, Father Alfonso Navarro was murdered in his parish house by a paramilitary group called the White Warriors Union (generally believed to be directed by Major Roberto D'Aubuisson). The army and security forces then undertook a military sweep of the Aguilares area, using helicopters and tanks. After first moving through the countryside, they came down to the town, attacking the parish house and church in the predawn hours, beating priests and other people there, and shooting and killing a man who had gone into the bell tower to alert the town. During the day, troops went from house to house beating people. Some were carried off simply because they had pictures of Rutilio Grande—indeed, the attack was called Operation Rutilio. Troops occupied the church and turned it into a barracks. Perhaps fifty were killed and hundreds were arrested. It is important to recall that this full military operation was unleashed not against guerrillas but against popular organizations and church leaders.

Finally, in June the White Warriors Union announced that the Jesuits had thirty days to leave the country; otherwise they would be murdered, one by one. The bizarre nature of this threat with its "countdown" finally drew international attention to El Salvador, which became recognized as a place where human rights were massively violated with impunity. When General Humberto Romero became president in July, the dizzying pace of events slowed somewhat. The deadline passed, and the White Warriors Union did not carry out its threat. But by this point, it was clear that the oligarchy and the military linked popular organizations with the church. A parish like Aguilares or a priest like Grande took on a symbolic importance.

The popular organizations continued to expand throughout the country. FAPU became increasingly prominent from 1977 on and was well represented among urban unions. It did not have strong connections to CEBs, although at a later period it would occupy churches as a tactic. In the countryside FECCAS-UTC organized strikes, and on a national level it sought to present peasant demands such as seeking to raise the minimum wage (approximately U.S. $2 a day) and guarantee proper working conditions (for example, by requiring the hacienda to provide a particular number of tortillas and beans at meals). At the same time, open conflict and violence intensified.

During Holy Week 1978, ORDEN and government troops carried out a major attack on FECCAS in the area of San Pedro Perulapán, a few miles from San Salvador. Six FECCAS members were murdered and sixty-eight disappeared. The newspapers portrayed FECCAS as the aggressor, but an archdiocesan bulletin presented a documented account showing the opposite to be true. It was experiences such as these that led the Catholic archdiocese of San Salvador to begin systematically to collect and publish data on human rights violations. The new archbishop, Oscar Romero, began to speak out on the nature of the popular organization and to address directly the issue of the church's proper role in the national crisis.

In August 1978, Romero published a pastoral letter called "The Church and the Popular Organizations." His very issuance of a letter on this topic was remarkable; its content was even more remarkable. In the context of El Salvador the government and oligarchy regarded these organizations as "communist." This view was reinforced by El Salvador's other bishops, who issued a "Declaration" during the same period that judged the popular organizations essentially as "Marxist." Romero took a different line and laid down a series of criteria, which may be summarized as follows:

1. It is normal and natural that there be a relationship between the church

and organizations that spring from it (meaning, presumably, FECCAS and UTC).

2. Faith and politics are united in the Christian, but they are not identified; there should be a synthesis, but particular programs of political organizations should not replace the contents of the faith.

3. The autonomy of both the church and the organizations should be respected; no one should expect the church or its symbols to be used on behalf of an organization.

4. There may be tensions between loyalty to the faith and to an organization.

5. Christians in the organizations should keep their faith explicit. It should be their "ultimate frame of reference"; those who have lost their faith should not use the faith for political purposes.

6. Not all Christians have a political vocation, and no one should be compelled to join an organization.

7. It is natural that priests should feel sympathies for popular organizations and be asked to work with them; their role, however, should be as "stimulators and guides in the faith and in the justice which faith demands." Only in exceptional cases, in consultation with the bishop, and after practicing discernment, should a priest become involved in political tasks.[7]

Archbishop Romero was not seeking to show a positive relationship between the church and the popular organizations. Instead, he wanted to insist that the two not be fused and that people recognize the autonomy of the church and of faith. This view reflected a recognition that at the village level (and particularly for the individual peasant member) the church and popular organizations might be identical, with the CEB and the FECCAS meeting under the same roof and having the same leader. In fact, Romero recommended that the same individual not lead the CEB and a peasant organization at the same time. Here, as in other letters and actions, Archbishop Romero emerged as a defender of human rights, a "voice of the voiceless." In his sermons and other public statements, he stood up to the government and denounced violation of human rights. He spoke not primarily as an individual but as a representative of priests and sisters who worked with the people and the many peasants and poor people who approached him directly. He knew personally some of the FECCAS leaders and spoke with affection of some who were murdered.

Conflicts multiplied during 1979 as the overthrow of Somoza gave many Salvadoreans a "we're next" feeling. In their street demonstrations the popular organizations chanted "*Romero y Somoza, son la misma cosa*" ([President Humberto] Romero and Somoza are the same thing). The level of violence was also rising: whereas in previous years those killed or who disappeared numbered in the dozens, by mid-October 1979, the figure for that year had reached 580.

The coup of 15 October 1979 was clearly intended to preempt a mass insurrection such as had occurred in Nicaragua. Immediately after the coup, however, troops attacked demonstrations and used violence against striking workers. In December alone 281 people were killed; for example, on 18 December hundreds of troops attacked two haciendas and a slaughterhouse where workers were on strike and killed at least 35 people. Thus, although the junta proclaimed reform intentions, it practiced increased killing and repression.

The year 1980 may be viewed as a long, slow-motion slide toward the war that most people felt was inevitable. On 3 January, most of the respected politicians and professional people who had entered the postcoup government resigned and soon joined the emerging FDR (Frente Democrático Revolucionario, Revolutionary Democratic Front). This was the political wing of the guerrilla organizations, which had also recently united. The popular organizations were in effect part of the political front of the insurrection. In June 1980 alone, 1,028 civilians were victims of murder. The popular organizations still sought to organize strikes and some demonstrations, but increasingly efficient violence from the government made such activity impossible.

Throughout this period, attacks against church people continued. By October 1980 there had been dozens of acts of violence against the church, including the murder of about a dozen priests and many lay leaders, as well as arbitrary arrests, torture, and acts of intimidation such as machine-gunning church institutions. Thus for Salvadorans the rape and murder of the four American churchwomen (a few days after the torture and murder of five top FDR leaders) was no surprise but merely one more instance of a now familiar pattern.

Although guerrilla organizations had been active since the mid-1970s it was only in mid-1980 that they began to move toward combat and overcame their long-standing rivalries sufficiently to act in coordination. The long-expected move toward guerrilla war began with the "general" or "final" offensive of January 1981. With that offensive and the onset of guerrilla war the popular organizations receded in importance. For four or five years they have been the protagonists on the stage, dramatizing the plight of the country's poor, and particularly the peasants and the landless, and their struggles, waged in a nonviolent way, were met with violence. Now the protagonist became the FMLN (Frente Farabundo Martí de Liberación Nacional, Farabundo Martí National Liberation Front) and the army. Some members of the popular organizations passed into the related guerrilla organization, for example, those from the BPR into the FPL. Those who had been militant members of the organizations often had to leave their villages and became refugees.

Just as the large-scale killing of civilians in 1980 signaled the end of a public role for the popular organizations, the public role of the Catholic church changed during this same period. On 24 March, Archbishop Romero was shot to death while he was saying mass. Certainly his defense of the legitimacy of the popular organizations made him enemies. His successor, Archbishop Arturo Rivera y Damas, repeatedly insisted on the need for "dialogue," meaning a negotiated approach to ending the war. CEBs continued to exist, functioning as spaces wherein people could renew their hope and faith, but they did not have a protagonist role in the struggle.

The involvement of church people in the revolutionary struggles in Nicaragua and Guatemala has been as intense as in El Salvador. Some of the characteristics of that involvement during the phases equivalent to the 1975–80 period in El Salvador are instructive. In Nicaragua, although Somoza's notorious profiteering had caused increasing discontent with his dictatorship as early as the December 1972 earthquake, the actual process of the overthrow was brief in comparison to events in El Salvador. Starting with a partially abortive Sandinista offensive in October 1977, and mass indignation over the murder of journalist Pedro Joaquín Chamorro in January 1978, events moved rapidly. There were major military confrontations in five cities in September 1978, and by the following 19 July, Somoza was gone. Throughout most of this period the general anti-Somoza sentiment obscured the disagreement over the nature of his replacement. The Sandinistas and their sympathizers wanted a deep social revolution; opposition political parties and business groups hoped for an essentially reform government in which the existing elites would retain their power and privilege. The Catholic church institutionally straddled these differences with the hierarchy making clear its opposition to the Sandinistas until the final weeks, when all sectors were united. Grass-roots elements in the church did not play a separate role. Nonetheless, CEPA, the training center for rural lay leaders, came to function as a network allied with the Sandinistas, and it evolved into the ATC (Asociación de Trabajadores del Campo, Association of Rural Workers), which is today the official Sandinista farmworker union. Similarly, in practice, Catholic parishes, both those with CEBs and others, often ended up aiding Sandinistas and those involved in the insurrection. As one priest later explained, "Everyone was Christian and everyone was Sandinista." Many Protestant pastors and congregations also collaborated in the struggle.

Under Somoza the church as such was seldom directly attacked. Members of CEBs and particularly leaders were sometimes killed by the National Guard if they were judged to be linked to the Sandinistas. In general, however, it would seem that the church institutionally was not attacked, just as Somoza used little violence against his middle-class opposition.

Consequently, the nature of a post-Somoza Nicaragua was unclear: would a thorough social revolution ensue (which would inevitably erode upper- and middle-class power and privilege) or would some elements of reform be introduced? For brief weeks and months after the fall of Somoza, there was a kind of "honeymoon" in which the anti-Somoza elites and the Sandinistas seemed to be in agreement, but at a certain point (symbolized by the resignation of businessman Alfonso Robelo from the junta in April 1980) the honeymoon ended. Just as Nicaraguan society became polarized between the elites and the Sandinista-led poor, so did the Catholic church. Those who had gone through the CEB process saw the ongoing Sandinista revolution as an embodiment of gospel values, whereas the Catholic hierarchy reflected a sensitivity and used a language similar to that of the disenchanted elites, as reflected, for example, in the newspaper *La Prensa*.

The experience of Guatemala has been closer to that of El Salvador. The level of violence, however, has been much higher. Ever since the 1966–68 period, when they killed an estimated six to eight thousand peasants to put down a guerrilla movement that never had more than three hundred combatants, the Guatemalan army and police had been in a state of permanent "counterinsurgency," expressed primarily in the hundreds of political murders a year throughout the 1970s.

Because of the level of repression, there was much less space on the political stage than in El Salvador. Hence there was no period such as 1975–80 in El Salvador, when the popular organizations were on center stage. Events were much more compressed; CUC and other popular organizations appeared in 1978, and by 1979 the Democratic Front against Repression was operating as a protopolitical front, while during the same year the guerrilla organizations were carrying out large-scale propaganda actions, such as occupying dozens of villages and towns and even engaging in direct combat with the Guatemalan army. By 1980 events such as the Sandinista victory in

Nicaragua, the coup and growing conflict in El Salvador, and the January 1980 police attack on the Spanish embassy (which had been occupied by CUC), starting a fire in which thirty-nine people, occupiers and embassy personnel alike, were burned alive, all reinforced a widespread belief in the inevitability of insurrection, soon.

As we have seen, the CEBs had fed into the popular organizations, especially the CUC. A unique feature in Guatemala was the Justice and Peace Commission, which was launched in April 1978. It was organized originally out of a sense of frustration on the part of some pastoral agents over the institutional church's almost complete silence about government repression. (By manipulation of the church bureaucracy, Cardinal Mario Casariego of Guatemala City had been able to nullify efforts of other bishops.) In its original conception it seemed to be following a human rights commission model, but it soon became a new network of church people, priests, sisters, pastors, and lay people around the country, holding courses and denouncing violations of human rights. It could thus be seen as linking many CEBs together. When the Democratic Front against Repression was formed, the Justice and Peace Commission became a member. This network of church activists thereby became a popular organization alongside peasant organizations, labor unions, student organizations, shantytown dwellers, and the like. Through the Justice and Peace Commission, church groups became protagonists on such space as existed on the political stage in Guatemala.

There was no clear point in Guatemala at which the phase of popular organizations ended and that of guerrilla struggle began (as January 1981 in El Salvador). Rather, the available space continued to shrink, and government intelligence and repression became more effective and more ruthless. By late 1981, more than one hundred church workers, most of them connected with the Justice and Peace Commission, had fled Guatemala. At that point, much pastoral work with CEBs had become virtually clandestine.

A coup in March 1982 brought General Efraín Ríos Montt to power. His "bullets and beans" counterinsurgency strategy against the Indian highlands is well known. Essentially, it amounted to selective massacre of villages or groups of villagers considered to have guerrilla links and concentration of others in controlled areas. Estimates of the numbers killed during 1982 vary from three to five thousand to eight thousand or more, almost all Indians. The salience of the church and of church-related organizations is especially visible in a case like that of Quiché province, where the army occupied a number of convents and churches (abandoned in June 1980, when all church personnel left after two priests were killed and the bishop narrowly escaped an ambush) and turned them into garrisons. At the same time evangelical sects with their otherworldly theology were welcomed, Ríos Montt being himself an elder of the Church of the Word. The army's counterinsurgency strategy clearly viewed CEB pastoral work, such popular organizations as CUC, and the guerrillas as one single target. The August 1983 coup that overthrew Ríos Montt and replaced him with General Oscar Mejía Víctores reduced the explicitly religious aspect but brought no major change in policy.

This essay has highlighted key aspects of the links between CEBs and the revolutionary struggles now taking place in Central America. I have focused particularly on the experience of El Salvador and on the parish in Aguilares and have noted parallels to other cases in the region.

Clearly, CEB work in Central America was similar in its origins to developments elsewhere in Latin America. The methodology and message of the CEBs were part of a general movement of change in the Latin American church. The critical differences for Central America arose from the accelerating impoverishment of the mass of the population, made concrete in growing landlessness, lack of work, and hunger. In such a context, it is not surprising that the push for *concientización* in CEBs should have led people to feel a need for organization, to create organizations, and to learn leadership skills within them. Notable instances are FECCAS-UTC in El Salvador, CUC in Guatemala, and the CEPA network in Nicaragua. The nascent popular organizations' nonviolent struggles for people's rights were met with violent repression, directed not only at the organizations but at church pastoral agents and, to some degree, at the church itself as an institution. When the struggles reached the level of open guerrilla warfare, the role of the popular organizations—and of the CEBs—was correspondingly diminished.

To some extent those who blamed the church for fomenting Marxism were right—the popular organizations often seemed to spring out of CEBs. For the people at the village level it seemed hard (and perhaps not important) to distinguish between the CEB and the organization. Hence Archbishop Romero felt that he had to insist on the differences between the two, while nonetheless stressing the positive relationship. This symbiotic relationship posed new problems, especially for pastoral workers: should priests and sisters simply defend people's rights to organize, or should they accompany them in their struggle, even joining the organizations?

Clearly, something new was happening here, something that went beyond earlier "Christian-Marxist dialogue" or "Christians for Socialism," which, even at their most developed level, remained largely a matter for intellectuals or at best a coalition of existing organizations. The situation in Central America is new. How important is this phenomenon? Can it be measured? From the figures noted in the case of Aguilares, it is clear that even the most thorough and systematic CEB work actively incorporates only a minority of the people in an area. Although the CEB model predominated among pastoral workers in some rural areas of El Salvador in the 1970s, it was less common in other parts of the country. Only a minority of parishes in Nicaragua and Guatemala used a CEB-style pastoral approach.

But it is a mistake to focus on quantitative considerations alone. The popular organizations became large, and many of their members saw their participation as motivated in part by religious principles. That is, even though they themselves had not gone from being CEB members to joining an organization, they were aware of that religious connection. When they listened to radio broadcasts of Archbishop Oscar Romero's Sunday homilies—sermons lasting well over an hour, in which he commented on the biblical texts of the day but also spoke of specific conflicts in El Salvador—they could feel that he was legitimating and supporting their own militancy. What is crucial is the central tendency of events, not numbers alone. The central tendency is clearly to change the uses of religion by transforming the context of religious practice and thereby to create new possibilities for involvement in social change. People's struggle takes on religious legitimation.

To take but one example, which itself is of great significance, many people give an explicitly Christian interpretation to the life-and-death aspect of their struggle. They know that many have already died and many others—possibly including themselves—may have to die. They explicitly connect that fact and possibility to the death of Jesus, who was executed by the powerful of his time because his message was found to be threatening, but who was also vindicated by God, who raised him up. Just as out of his death came life, so out of the deaths of people today new life will emerge, including the new life of a society that is more just and where infants will not die of easily preventable gastrointestinal diseases while a few accumulate and enjoy fortunes. Archbishop Romero's widely quoted statement, "If I die, I will arise in the Salvadorean people," epitomizes this interpretation.

The evolution of CEBs and popular organizations provides a good example of how Liberation Theology works in practice. Experience clearly plays a major role. When they began, church workers such as Rutilio Grande and the Jesuit team in Aguilares did not have clear answers to what the relationship of pastoral work to political action should be because the phenomenon was indeed new. Archbishop Romero's pastoral letter, the outgrowth of several years of experience and written in consultation with theologians, at least outlined the parameters of the question. He noted that despite the positive relationship between the CEBs and the organizations, care should be taken not to confuse the two, but rather to safeguard the autonomy of the church and of Christian faith. The entire experience led to a deeper insight into the meaning of the church, and at the same time theological reflection was an aid for greater clarity in pastoral work.

These events are simply one chapter of a much larger story—the story of the struggle of people in Latin America and elsewhere for the recognition of their elemental rights and the role of religion in that struggle. An understanding of these events is essential for an adequate view of the depth of the struggle in Central America today and may prove relevant for analogous situations elsewhere.

Notes

1. Jorge E. Arellano, *Breve historia de la iglesia en Nicaragua (1523–1979)* (Managua: N.p., 1980), pp. 85–86, 90.

2. UCA (Universidad Centroamericana José Simeon Canas), *Rutilio Grande: Mártir de la evangelización rural* (San Salvador: UCA Editores, 1978).

3. Edelberto Torres-Rivas, "Seven Keys to Understanding the Central American Crisis," *Contemporary Marxism*, no. 3 (1981), pp. 49–61.

4. Shelton Davis, "State Violence and Agrarian Crisis in Guatemala" (Paper presented at the Latin American Studies Association National Meeting, Washington, D.C., February 1982), p. 6; Eric R. Wolf, *Peasant Wars of the Twentieth Century* (New York: Harper & Row, 1969).

5. Davis, "State Violence," p. 6.

6. John A. Booth, "Toward Explaining Regional Crisis in Central America: Socioeconomic and Political Roots of Rebellion" (revised version of paper given at Fortyfourth International Congress of Americanists, Manchester, England, September 1982); see also *Report of the National Bipartisan Commission on Central America* (Washington, D.C.: U.S. Government Printing Office, 1984).

7. Phillip Berryman, *The Religious Roots of Rebellion: Christians in the Central American Revolutions* (Maryknoll: Orbis Books, 1984), pp. 338–39. The texts of Archbishop Romero's four pastoral letters, along with other major speeches and letters, have been published in translation. See *Archbishop Oscar Romero, Voice of the Voiceless* (Maryknoll: Orbis Books, 1985).

5

Nicaragua:
The Struggle for the Church

Michael Dodson

> We ought to be humble. That is a beautiful Christian virtue that
> ought to be practiced by revolutionaries. We should exercise
> revolutionary criticism. Christians talk about confession. Criti-
> cism is a type of confession. We should be the continuous object
> of criticism because the leaders of a revolution ought to be . . .
> under the critical gaze of all the people and subject to the
> revolutionary vigilance of all the people. . . . The work of the
> Sandinistas cannot be completed without the participation of
> Christians. . . . Christians and Sandinistas . . . should form a true
> integration . . . in order to move this revolution forward.
>
> *Tomas Borge,* minister of interior, *El Nuevo Diario,* 27 May 1981

Contemporary Nicaragua offers a rare opportunity to observe and assess the
profound involvement of religious institutions and groups in a revolutionary
process. The Catholic church has participated actively in the Sandinist
revolution, and Nicaraguans, a people widely known for their religiosity, take
obvious pride in its involvement. It has been demonstrated that thousands of
church people, many acting explicitly out of religious motivation and with the
support of their Christian communities, made direct and substantial contributions to the popular insurrection against *Somocismo.*[1] The story of the
church's role in the popular insurrection will be summarized only briefly here
to lay a groundwork for examining the church's struggle to find an appropriate role in revolutionary Nicaragua.

Religion and revolution do not mesh easily, as has been demonstrated in nearly four years of the revolutionary process. The effort to adapt to the new revolutionary environment has created numerous schisms within the church and has generated new tensions between church and government. All groups in revolutionary Nicaragua seem to appreciate the church's importance in the society and its potential utility in suport of or in opposition to Sandinist programs. Consequently, there is an intense struggle in Nicaragua today in which diverse groups compete to capture the church's resources, especially its moral and symbolic authority, often for conflicting secular ends. For this reason, an important dimension of the Nicaraguan revolution is the politicization of religion. Although such politicization is nothing new, seldom can it be observed in a society that is at the same time deeply religious and militantly revolutionary.

Religious opposition to the social upheaval that accompanies revolutionary movements is common and familiar; it is much less common to find religion positively associated with a revolution in the political order for the obvious reason that religious traditions do not normally countenance the violence inherent in revolution. In the Western Christian tradition one can trace back at least as far as St. Augustine the view that the city of God owes a healthy respect to the city of man for the order and safety it provides to assure a peaceful environment in which the faithful can worship God and practice the moral principles taught by their religion. Less obviously and somewhat more skeptically, it can be argued that institutionalized religion opposes revolution and supports the status quo when it has made its own peace with the prevailing political order and enjoys benefits it does not wish to lose. Marx made this view well known by suggesting that religion was a form of false consciousness, an opiate that distracted workers from the causes of their misery, thereby deflecting their revolutionary energies into harmless channels.

There are times, however, when religion becomes a source of political revolution. In Iran today, for example, the revolution is conservative and the religious role correspondingly "fundamentalist." The Ayatollah Khomeini and his followers are revolutionizing the political order to restore an original religious vision of society. Or, in Poland, where Catholicism appears to be a fertile source of opposition to authoritarian rule, the religious challenge is radical. The political authorities in Poland certainly see a revolutionary threat in the church's sponsorship of such democratic values as participation and the freedom to organize independent trade unions.

Central America presents a third possibility, wherein religion has become a source of revolution because it has itself undergone a revolution. Such a situation was exemplified by the Puritan Revolution in seventeenth-century England. By revolutionizing Christianity theologically and organizationally, this religious event was a rich source of ideas and incentives for the democratization of European politics that began at that time.[2] Latin American Catholicism has been undergoing its own theological and organizational revolution since the influence of the Second Vatican Council began to penetrate the continent in the mid-1960s. Guerrilla priests made dramatic appearances in several countries, and radical movements by priests challenged authoritarian governments and conservative hierarchies, attracting much publicity throughout Latin America between 1966 and 1974.[3] Also, a new theology of liberation was created (and is still being created), reaching into every level of the church throughout the region. To be sure, the degree of its acceptance varies from country to country and among the various elements that make up the church in a given country. For instance, the Brazilian bishops display a greater commitment to Liberation Theology than do their Colombian or Mexican counterparts. Yet to some degree the new theology has taken hold in virtually every national hierarchy.

At the grass-roots level, Christian base communities (CEBs) have appeared all over Latin America. These groups represent both a theological and an organizational revolution for they reflect a democratization of the religious institution. In CEBs peasants and workers take charge of their own religious nurture in the context of their immediate social and political environment. Religious practice thus becomes the fruit of direct interplay between religious values and political events. Where those political events are conspicuously marked by the struggle against oppression, religion is likely to become an influential source of political revolution, as it has in Nicaragua.

Any discussion of the role of the church in the Nicaraguan revolution must pay careful attention to this unique convergence of revolutionary change in church and polity. When the Latin American bishops, assembled at Puebla, Mexico, in January 1979, gave official confirmation to the Catholic church's "preferential option for the poor," it may have seemed to the casual observer like a mere ratification of the church's steady revolutionary transformation over a decade and a half. Even as the Puebla meetings concluded, the Nicaraguans were readying their final offensive against Somoza. Was the church prepared to embrace this revolution with its clear preferential option for the poor? To raise this question is to realize that before the Sandinist revolution the church had not had to respond to a full-scale revolution anywhere in Latin America in the post-Vatican II era.[4] It had come close to doing so in Chile during the Allende period, but the Chilean experiment was cut short by a military coup before the church was fully tested. Nicaragua, then, presents a unique situation for the changing church in Latin America, with its emphasis on serving the poor and oppressed.

The following discussion distinguishes between the insurrectionary phase of the Nicaraguan revolution and the post-triumph phase of national reconstruction. The distinction is extremely important to understanding conflict within the church as well as between church and state. It may be helpful to enunciate briefly the questions that inform the discussion. First, I ask how, why, and to what degree the church took an active part in the popular insurrection. The answers to this question will reveal that the church must be understood as composed of multiple levels and diverse groups whose faith experiences, pastoral practices, and political loyalties vary considerably. In this sense, one must be cautious when speaking of the church and the revolution, for different groups within the church saw the insurrection differently, just as they now take different views of the Sandinist government and its programs. Only a brief and summary answer is given to this first question in the present essay.

Much more attention will be given to a second broad question and the corollary questions that grow out of it. What elements of the church have actively embraced the revolution under Sandinist leadership, and what elements have stood apart from it and, perhaps, actively opposed it? I will try to show that the answer to this question has come to focus on issues of a "parallel magisterium," a "popular church," the proper role of Christian base communities in a revolutionary society, and the concept of nonpartisan pastoral action. Although it involves incorporating a political concept into discussion of a religious institution, it may be helpful to associate each of these issues with a single, overriding issue: the simultaneous democratization of church and polity. Do the converging religious and political paths of revolution portend increased democratization for Nicaragua?

The Church in the Popular Insurrection

The roots of church involvement in the insurrection go back to the late 1960s. Here I attempt only a brief summary of key events, attempting to specify their analytic significance for understanding the conflict that surrounds the church in the present revolutionary stage.

Before the Latin American Bishops' Conference at Medellín, Colombia, in 1968, the Nicaraguan church was traditional and socially conservative. It was weak in resources and therefore not firmly established among the people at the grass-roots level. Heavily dependent on foreign clergy, foreign funds, and clerical training in foreign seminaries, the church did not cultivate dynamic ties with the faithful, particularly among the poor.[5] Medellín, however, encouraged an atmosphere of creativity, and in Nicaragua an infusion of new personnel into the church after 1968 fostered experimentation and change. Among the most notable changes were the naming of a new archbishop of Managua, Monseñor Miguel Obando y Bravo, the inauguration of national pastoral meetings to examine the national situation in light of Medellín, and the appearance of new priests in Nicaragua trained in the spirit of Vatican II. Under their tutelage a small number of Christian base communities were formed, first in Managua and later in other cities and in the countryside. Through their work with high school and university students, they encouraged a growing social activism among Catholic youth.

By 1970 a stage was set for serious church confrontation with the Somoza regime. The new clergy and the activist youth began to engage in a variety of protest activities such as the occupation of the cathedral, hunger strikes, and marches. Some members of the hierarchy, including Archbishop Obando, gave tentative support to such actions. Moreover, this activism attracted the attention of the Sandinist Front of National Liberation (Frente Sandinista de Liberación Nacional, FSLN), and significant contacts were made between the FSLN and some priests and student leaders.[6] In other words, grass-roots work that laid a basis for church collaboration in the insurrection took place even before 1972. Clergy, hierarchy, and lay activists came into open conflict with the regime on the basis of religious concerns that intruded into the political arena, the hierarchy took some steps to back away from a traditional posture of automatic support for the government, and, at the grass-roots, the FSLN made direct contact with the church.

The 1972 earthquake was a turning point in the country's political history and in the political role of the church. The now-familiar story of *Somocista* corruption that exploited and distorted the recovery effort drove a powerful wedge between the church and the regime. Priests, religious, and lay people working at the base level through Christian communities (as CEBs tend to be called in Nicaragua) experienced the systemic corruption and violence of *Somocismo* and thus had a concrete reference for what the bishops at Medellín called "structural sin." As a consequence, their pastoral work increasingly became geared to the political reality, assuming the cast of political opposition.

Popular discontent with *Somocismo* deepened and solidified in the years following the earthquake, as exemplified by negative reaction to the 1974 election that returned Somoza to the presidency. This fraudulent election led to the formation of the Democratic Union for Liberation (UDEL), a popular front of opposition groups. For its part, the church moved into direct opposition to Somoza on two levels. The hierarchy began to issue statements that indirectly criticized the government, especially Somoza's personal use of the National Guard and the near monopoly held by the Liberal party in the political arena. The hierarchy also spoke out for the right of dissent within the country. At the base level, there was significant identification with the FSLN and some degree of active collaboration. The FSLN capture of *Somocista* officials at a Christmas party in December 1974 served to heighten this identification. As one Maryknoll sister put it, listening to news of the capture and the FSLN declarations that were broadcast throughout the country "was like listening to our own salvation history." Numerous young people from Christian communities in the poor neighborhoods of Managua began to join the FSLN, and many others were in active sympathy.[7]

When our view is broadened to take account of events outside Managua and especially in the countryside, we find that church innovation at this time included the creation of two important religious programs of long-term political importance. These were the Delegates of the Word and the Evangelical Committee for Agrarian Advancement (Comité Evangelico de Promoción Agraria, CEPA). The two are closely related.

CEPA was created in 1969 by Jesuits in Nicaragua to provide training for peasant leaders. Originally based in the western zone of the country, in the coffee-growing regions of Carazo and Masaya, CEPA eventually expanded northward to León and Estelí. Over a period of several years, as it became clear that peasants could not improve their economic situation without organizing, the CEPA program came to center more and more on creating peasant organizations that could engage in political action. For Christians working in CEPA this was a radicalizing process, theologically and politically. It led some into active sympathy with the FSLN long before the first insurrection broke out in September 1978. Some joined the armed struggle, while others took leadership roles in the FSLN-sponsored Association of Rural Workers (Asociación de Trabajadores del Campo, ATC), which was set up in 1977. As with the CEBs, this grass-roots activity of priests and lay Catholics working with peasants flourished outside direct supervision and control of the bishops. When the bishops perceived that they could not contain CEPA to activities they regarded as appropriately religious and nonpolitical, they attempted to pressure the organization and restrict its activities. By the time of the insurrection, CEPA had cut its formal ties with the church and regarded itself as an independent Christian organization. At the triumph it was closely allied with the FSLN.[8]

CEPA evolved out of a broader church program called Delegates of the Word, which provided for a lay leadership in rural areas not regularly served by a priest. The delegates were trained to provide worship as well as some literacy training and health services for peasants. As with the Christian communities in the urban areas, religious services led by delegates generally consisted of dialogues, keyed to biblical texts, that dealt with the immediate economic and social problems of the community. Not surprisingly, the delegates tended to become leaders of CEBs in the rural areas. For this reason they frequently were targets of National Guard repression, and a number of them were killed. This violence served to push the institutional church into opposition to Somoza, while pushing the delegates and the CEBs they represented into support of the FSLN.

These programs provided a rich experience of innovation at the grass roots that depended heavily on the laity or, in some instances, on foreign clergy and religious. The programs responded directly to local conditions and often, although not always, were only weakly tied to the institutional church through direct hierarchical supervision and control. CEBs became numerous in some rural areas of Nicaragua. They tended to concentrate in zones where fighting was most intense and resistance most effective during the popular insurrection.[9]

The popular insurrection that overthrew Somoza is generally dated from the uprising in Monimbó in September 1978. But even in 1977 the regime looked vulnerable, and popular hostility to it was more and more openly expressed. The FSLN took a more offensive posture at this time, launching attacks on the National Guard in several cities. Several members of the Solentiname religious community participated in one such attack on a National Guard post at San Carlos, near the Costa Rican border. Immediately afterward the leader of the community, Ernesto Cardenal, declared his allegiance to the FSLN. In retaliation, the National Guard attacked Solentiname and burned it to the ground.

In fairly rapid sequence, the following events took place to deepen church involvement in the nascent insurrection. First, the opposition group Los Doce, or the Twelve, announced its opposition to Somoza. This group, which symbolized the breadth and depth of anti-Somoza sentiment, included two priests, Fernando Cardenal and Miguel D'Escoto. Second, the formation of the Twelve seemed to catalyze deeper official church involvement in the opposition. Several bishops, including Archbishop Obando, soon were active in mediation efforts. Third, Gaspar Garcia Laviana, a Sacred Heart priest, joined the FSLN as an armed combatant on Christmas day 1977. Shortly thereafter, on 6 January 1978, the bishops issued a pastoral letter denouncing a wide range of fundamental abuses by the regime. But even as this document was made public the pivotal event in the anti-Somoza struggle occurred, the assassination of Pedro Joaquin Chamorro, editor of *La Prensa* and focal point of the moderate opposition. In the wake of his death, all hope of moderate solutions seemed lost. Henceforth, the hierarchy came increasingly into open support of the forces seeking Somoza's resignation.

Meanwhile, at the level of CEBs many church people moved into open and direct support of the FSLN. Their support was clearly a valuable resource to the FSLN, which found the work of organizing people in the insurrection to be much easier in areas where CEBs were firmly rooted. These institutions of religious inspiration were, in short, effective vehicles of grass-roots political action in the revolutionary setting of the popular insurrection.

The FSLN triumph on 19 July 1979 was greeted with immense enthusiasm by the Nicaraguan people. Most people in the church shared in this enthusiasm and saw the FSLN as a liberating army. There were, however, some within the church who were cautious about a Sandinist revolution, and a few actively opposed it. The broad problem facing the church, one that has become extremely complex and vexing, was how it should accompany the revolutionary process. The strong church presence in the insurrection foreshadowed significant church presence in the reconstruction, but defining the nature and limits of that presence has led to constant struggle in the church as well as to frequent conflict between church and state.

Anticipating the arguments to follow, we may say that the Nicaraguan church, and particularly the episcopal hierarchy, had some genuine basis for concern about the place the church would occupy in a revolutionary society. First, despite the theological revolution precipitated in Latin America by Vatican II and Medellín, the church had little practical experience with social and political revolution. Indeed, historically the Central American church had identified with tradition and stability. The cases of Chile and especially Cuba seemed to suggest that revolution was inherently threatening to the church and to the spirituality of the people.[10] Hence the bishops feared that the church might be pushed to the sidelines by the revolution with a consequent loss or diminution of religious identity. Second, the making of a revolution against *Somocismo* called forth much experimentation within the church. Dynamic new religious organizations were created, such as the Christian base communities, CEPA, and the Antonio Valdivieso Center, which had considerable or even total independence from the bishops. Much of the church's energy was now absorbed in these organizations, whose loyalty to the revolution might be not only greater than that of the bishops, but indeed whose commitment to the revolution might exceed their commitment to the church itself as the bishops understood it. Against this backdrop the maintenance of church unity became a paramount goal for the hierarchy, whereas freedom to experiment and innovate in concert with the revolution has been the goal for Christians at lower levels of the church.

Democratization of Church and Polity since the Triumph

In the euphoria that surrounded the triumph of the popular insurrection, all elements of the Nicaraguan church (excepting a small group of die-hard *Somocistas*) seemed to accept the legitimacy of the revolution and to accept, if not embrace, the leadership of the FSLN. Masses were celebrated in parishes all over the country in honor of the triumph, and Archbishop Obando even presided over such a mass. In June the hierarchy had issued a statement that seemed to endorse the insurrection by contending that the Somoza regime had lost all basis of legitimacy. Later, in a famous and widely discussed pastoral letter released in November 1979, the bishops went so far as to endorse certain aspects of socialism (although in a carefully qualified way) and seemed to offer general, if somewhat vague, support to the new Sandinist government. Meanwhile, at the grass roots intense activity was under way to cultivate ties between church programs and organizations and the revolutionary government.[11]

Beneath this facade of unity lay the seed of deep division within the church and between church and regime. A decade of experimentation within the church that matured in the context of a popular uprising gave grass-roots religious groups and organizations unprecedented autonomy. Formed in the seedbed of a revolutionary society and nurtured in an atmosphere of theological innovation, these grass-roots elements of the church entered the post-triumph era with postures of independence and theological perspectives that quickly raised a challenge to hierarchical control.

Some of these groups faced conflicting loyalties that soon threatened to become mutually exclusive: whether to work in concert with the revolution, which they had helped to make, or to work in harmony with the bishops to restore church unity. The emergence of a parallel church embodied a direct challenge to ecclesiastical authority and required the imposition of hierarchically sponsored strategies of nonpartisan pastoral action. The hierarchy's felt need to reinstitute control ran directly against the experiential history of grass-roots elements. As we have seen, it also reflected a different theology. The struggle to resolve these differences has involved all sectors of Nicaraguan society and has placed the church at the center of the struggle to define the revolution in the post-triumph phase. A more detailed analysis of this struggle for the church must begin with a discussion of the Christian base communities.

The Christian base community is an experiment with church structures and pastoral practices that typifies the post-Vatican II emphasis in Latin America on a church of the poor. The CEB received the blessing of Pope Paul VI and Pope John Paul II and of the Latin American bishops at both Medellín and Puebla. In fact, at Puebla, although the bishops were cautious at first and sought to stress the evangelical nature of the CEBs, they also showered much favorable attention on them as "an expression of the Church's preferential love for the poor."[12] CEBs vary greatly throughout Latin America, however, in part because of widely differing social contexts and political histories. We must therefore examine the context in which CEBs arose in Nicaragua to understand why they have been viewed with suspicion and mistrusted by at least some of the bishops of that country, particularly in the highly charged post-triumph atmosphere.

This dilemma was most evident among the priests serving in the government. For such priests as the Jesuit Fernando Cardenal and Maryknoll father Miguel D'Escoto, who were members of Los Doce and had played key roles in the overthrow of Somoza (both had spoken out in the United States against the dictatorship), serving as ministers in the Sandinist government was a logical extension of their earlier role. Moreover, the post-Medellín theology that they embraced seemed to justify their roles in public policy making. In the eyes of the bishops, however, such roles were solely political and excluded the pastoral. They also implicated the church in the political program of the revolution to a degree that made the bishops, who were skeptical about the revolution, quite uncomfortable. Tension between the bishops and priests in government was a constant that waxed and waned in the political dialogue in the country for much of the first five years of the revolution. For Cardenal the issue came to a head in December 1984, when he was compelled by the Jesuit Order to choose between staying in the order and accepting an appointment as minister of education. He elected to take the government post and so was required to leave the Jesuit order.

The dilemma also arose in the CEBs that were served by priests and religious who had supported the FSLN during the insurrection. Particularly within the Managua archdiocese they were increasingly pressured not to get involved in the political tasks of reconstruction. For the priests and religious such demands meant forsaking activities that had strong theological and pastoral justification. But from the archbishop's point of view these church leaders and their parishioners in the CEBs were a "popular church" that threatened to become a "parallel church."[13]

We can begin by broadly defining the central characteristics of CEBs. Following Bruneau, we can draw up a useful portrait by touching on each of the three terms that make up the name. The CEBs are first of all *communities* that bring together several groups of people from the same social class and neighborhood to talk, exchange ideas, provide mutual support, and work together toward common ends. Second, the communities are *ecclesial* and understand themselves as having a religious origin and bonding. Ordinarily priests or religious have taken the initiative to form the community, and the Bible serves as the primary instrument of reflection around which the community functions. As an ecclesial community, the CEB is closely tied to the church. Finally, this community is located at the *base* of both church and society. The CEBs are almost universally communities of the poor wherein people come together to discuss the concrete problems they face and to understand the guidance Christian faith offers in confronting those problems. This activity reorients the church and opens up the possibility of redefining its mission. In practice, this can mean pressuring the church from below to take sides in social conflict, and it tends to highlight the class nature of society. The CEB can also represent a considerable broadening of the locus of authority within the church, depending on the degree of hierarchical direction and control.

In such countries as Brazil and Chile the church hierarchy has initiated and encouraged the development of CEBs; in other countries, including Nicaragua, CEBs originally developed independent of the hierarchy. This reality can cause tension and conflict within the church, especially when uncertainty and change are the order of the day as they are in revolutionary Nicaragua. Phillip Berryman has suggested a fourfold schema for illustrating the contexts in which CEBs in Latin America may be understood. First, we can visualize those countries "in which the power structure does not need to employ widespread and extreme repression, even though most of the people are poor and the economic structure works against them"; examples are Mexico, Venezuela, and Costa Rica. Second, there are countries in which significant repression exists and no opposition favoring the poor is tolerated; all the countries of southern Latin America, including Brazil, Argentina, and Chile, are in this category. Third are countries in which "serious revolutionaries are struggling to take power," as illustrated by El Salvador. And fourth is a country that already is in revolutionary transformation, such as Cuba and Nicaragua.[14]

To understand the Nicaraguan church it is necessary to apply this schema to the entire time frame under review here. The Nicaraguan context under Somoza was clearly of the second type, extreme repression. Although Somoza tried to avoid conflict with the church hierarchy, his regime did visit systematic repression upon the poor. Emerging in this repressive context, Nicaraguan CEBs became an important resource of the Sandinist revolution. But their personal journey to revolution came about independently of hierarchical direction. As a result, the CEBs stood in some tension and estrangement from the bishops at the outset of the post-triumph period: many CEBs were strongly committed to the revolution, but the bishops were uncertain and tentative.

By the summer of 1981, two years after the FSLN triumph, the CEBs had become deeply embroiled in the political struggles of the reconstruction. As one editorialist expressed it in *El Nuevo Diario*, "Here in Nicaragua, an authentic manipulation is being carried out, implemented at a Latin American level, to separate the Church, especially the pastors, from the poor and their project of liberation."[15] The editorial refers to the prolific writing on the role of religion in the revolution that appears in the press, to numerous intrachurch quarrels over such matters as the removal of priests and religious serving in poor barrios, which has itself received much publicity, and to the fate of priests who hold positions in the Government of National Reconstruction. It also refers to the widespread rumors in Nicaragua about CELAM interventions in the religious affairs of the nation, particularly attempts to win Archbishop Obando y Bravo over to a hard-line conservative position. I will take up all but the last of these issues below.

For the moment, let us look at the reaction of the CEBs in Managua, which published a joint statement on 9 September: "The CEBs were born in Managua during the 60s and 70s in a very normal manner from the pastoral and liturgical renewal of the Second Vatican Council through the archdiocesan parochial life with our pastors. The Word of God brought us little by little to feel with the heart of Christ the sufferings of our people. With our whole church, we joined the struggle of the people against the Somoza dictatorship in the Insurrection."[16]

This direct and simple statement makes it clear, first, that CEBs were created through a process of religious renewal that was carried out in close association with priests at a parish level. Moreover, specifically religious practices within the structure of CEBs led to identification with the revolutionary struggle. At the same time, the statement obscures an important point that has already been raised. The clergy with whom they worked were not necessarily acting in close concert with the hierarchy. Indeed, they often enjoyed only tacit approval, at best sometimes tacit disapproval, and only rarely active cooperation. Therefore, what parish priests and CEB members now see as a natural evolution of religious and political commitment, the bishops see as an alarming level of autonomy or even co-optation of the CEBs by political factions. For example, when CEBs engage in active cooperation with the Sandinist Defense Committee (widespread in the first year of the revolution), the 19 of July Sandinist Youth, or the Association of Rural Workers, the Nicaraguan bishops are likely to see what James Madison called the "spirit of faction" in such activities. They regard them as excessively partisan, representing an undue politicization of the church. In their strong reaction to this perceived threat lies one major source of conflict involving the church.

Active participants in the CEBs are sensitive to this problem. They stress religious motivations, underscore the deep spiritual roots of their work, and emphasize their ties to the church. They meet with their pastors on a weekly basis and repeatedly invite the bishops to their meetings and religious celebrations. Much of their time together is spent in prayer and reflection on the Bible. But prayer and Bible study are dedicated to active involvement in the revolutionary process: "We know well that Medellín, Puebla, Paul VI and the whole Magisterium of the church set conditions in order that the CEBs be authentically 'ecclesial' and do not disintegrate into sects or simply political groups. We demonstrate it by telling how we live, what we struggle for and what we believe in."[17] They insist they are aware that the Nicaraguan revolution can err and is not synonymous with the Kingdom of God. This is all the more reason, they assert, for Christians to be active in the revolutionary process so that they can criticize it from within as well as humanize it.

But if we look at the Nicaraguan church as a whole, considering some of the major subdivisions that compose it, we find a complex picture of innovation at the base level and of relations between base and hierarchy and between church and government. This innovation can be illustrated by briefly contrasting the Atlantic Coast region and the northern diocese of Estelí with the Managua archdiocese. Zelaya, the easternmost province of Nicaragua, which includes the Atlantic Coast region, has long been relatively isolated and neglected in national affairs. On the Atlantic Coast the CEBs have been in place for fifteen years and the role of lay leaders, or Delegates of the Word, is familiar and accepted. A typical CEB will enroll between sixty and one hundred families, and lay leaders provide most, if not all, pastoral services. The bishop of the diocese has strongly endorsed the program as the only way to provide a church presence where there are few priests. In mid-1984 a new bishop was added to this diocese. Like his colleague, Bishop Salvador Schleafer, Bishop Pablo Schmidt is a Capuchin and a North American. In other words, the CEBs are an integral part of the pastoral plan of this diocese, and therefore the issue of a parallel church has not arisen in Zelaya. The same is true of Estelí in northern Nicaragua, but for different reasons. There Bishop López Ardón was openly supportive of the CEBs before the triumph, although they were not created at his initiative. In recent years, as pressure to close ranks within the Bishops' Conference has increased, the bishop has shown less interest in the CEBs and more in the charismatic movement, but he has done little to oppose the CEBs publicly.

Of course, it does not necessarily follow that where CEBs are well established they work closely in concert with the revolution. Although they appear to do so in Managua and in parts of the western zone of the country, in Zelaya the CEBs have come into conflict with the Sandinists. An illustration will serve to make the point. The Sandinists have taken more interest in the Atlantic Coast than the Somoza regime ever did. They have sent agricultural experts there as well as literary *brigadistas*. But however well intentioned they may have been, these experts from Managua have been inexperienced and often insensitive to the needs of indigenous people as they themselves see them. A result has been friction with the church because the CEBs had already established agricultural programs, literacy training, and health care. Sandinist efforts seemed heavy-handed when they either ignored or discounted the effectiveness of these church programs.[18]

To summarize, the picture of church experimentation at the base level in Nicaragua is complex, with interactions between base and hierarchy, or between church and government, varying from region to region. The existence of a parallel church is a nonissue on the Atlantic Coast and an insignificant one in Estelí, but it is fiercely contested in the Managua archdiocese.

Issue of a Parallel Church
in the Managua Archdiocese

In some dioceses, then, the democratization of the church has proceeded with the tacit approval or active collaboration of the bishop, and CEBs function without any perceived threat to the integrity of the church. This has not been the case in the archdiocese of Managua, where the issue of a parallel church has generated a conflict of growing proportions and intensity. Although this conflict appears in some respects to be peculiar to Managua, it has been treated by many as a microcosm of the church in the Nicaraguan revolution. I will attempt to show that this view overgeneralizes, although the intrachurch conflict in Managua is of crucial significance to the long-term relations of church and regime within the context of the Nicaraguan revolution.

When the role of the church in the Nicaraguan revolution is viewed from the Managua archdiocese, the role of CEBs is seen to be part and parcel of other issues, including the role of foreign clergy and religious, the role of independent religious orders, most notably the Jesuits and Maryknoll, and the role of the Antonio Valdivieso Center and the Historical Institute of the Jesuit Central American University. To this list we must add the presence of priests in the Government of National Reconstruction. Outside the country this last problem undoubtedly received the most attention in the media. Within the country it is seen as but one of the constellation of problems set out above. In the following analysis, therefore, I will attempt to assess these issues by treating them together in terms of both intrachurch conflict and church-state conflict.

Beginning with the uprising in Monimbó in September 1978, the struggle against the Somoza dictatorship involved the CEBs of the Managua archdiocese in intensive political activity that deepened their ties to the FSLN over the next ten months. In the fighting that broke out in Masaya, Chinandega, León, Matagalpa, Estelí, the eastern barrios of Managua, and Open Tres (now Ciudad Sandino), a poor barrio on the outskirts of the capital, FSLN success was greatly facilitated by the existence and cooperation of CEB organizations. Indeed, the CEBs provided intelligence, communication links, food, safe houses, medical aid, and combatants. It is important to appreciate that many of the combatants, including a significant number of the *muchachos* martyred in the fighting, were not guerrillas but young Christians who joined the struggle (some did take up arms) out of sympathy for and identification with the FSLN. The actions in some of the cities were not initiated by the

FSLN but were carried out by the residents of the communities themselves. Fernando Cardenal, until December 1984 a Jesuit priest and presently minister of education, has spoken of what the experience of this insurrectionary period meant to those Christians who formed the Revolutionary Christian Movement. This movement, organized as early as 1972, consisted of a few priests and Christian youth from the Jesuit University and the poor barrios of eastern Managua. Their numbers grew over the years and, according to Cardenal, as many as four hundred young people went into the Sandinist front from this movement.[19] The experience appears to have been widespread enough to say that at the grass-roots level the insurrectionary period led many Christians to a deep sense of spiritual identification with the Sandinist movement. Their strong identification with the revolution stands in sharp contrast to the cautious and tentative posture of the hierarchy. It comes as little surprise, then, that one group of Christians at the base would seek their future within the revolution. For instance, in the words of one of its founders, the Antonio Valdivieso Center was established "to gather together and channel the rich experience of our people [in the revolutionary struggle] and to combat the tremendous counterrevolution that is appearing [in the country]."[20]

This view, and the experience on which it rests, may be contrasted with that of the bishops. In June 1979, shortly before the triumph, they issued a statement that seemed to endorse the insurrection, arguing that the Somoza government had lost any basis of legitimacy. But their statement also contained a warning that political pluralism must be maintained and that after Somoza the Nicaraguan people should seek to transcend political partisanship. Fernando Cardenal has also pointed out that before this declaration, which came at the final stage of the insurrection, the Theological Reflection Group that had formed around the bishops was seeking a peaceful solution to the problem of *Somocismo*, even as fighting raged throughout the country.[21]

The bishops' caution was visible in another declaration, issued soon after the Sandinist victory, which warned against the dangers of "massification" and "state idolatries." This declaration insisted that belief in God be encouraged as part of the task of national reconstruction. But the most notable statement of the hierarchy's views came in the pastoral letter of 17 November 1979. Though supporting the government in a general way and even embracing some aspects of socialism, the document also made clear the bishops' concern over the creation and consolidation of Sandinist popular organizations. It speaks of the "risks" and "dangers" of the revolutionary process and urges criticism and the protection of "Christian liberty." It is apparent that the liberty the bishops stress exists in considerable tension with the unity of the church in relation to the revolutionary process they also seek. Even as they spoke, other groups within the church were actively collaborating with, even directly participating in, the Sandinist government.

The Antonio Valdivieso Center was established by Catholic and Protestant clergy in August 1979 to promote dialogue and cooperation with the government and active Christian participation in the revolution. In September the Central American University hosted a conference on the role of Christians in the Sandinist revolution, which attracted priests, religious, lay participants in the CEBs, and both Christian and non-Christian members of the government.

The Historical Institute, headed by the Jesuit priest Alvaro Arguello, resolved to assist the work of the Valdivieso Center and to initiate an oral history of the Christian role in the revolution.[22] Meanwhile, a number of prominent clergy were accepting significant leadership positions in the Sandinist government. At the same time, the government, aware that the church's role in the revolution was a matter of intense debate and controversy, sought to clarify its own view of the matter.

The result was an official communication of the National Directorate of the FSLN on religion, published in *Barricada* on 7 October 1980. The FSLN statement had several goals. First, it sought to acknowledge the Christian presence in the revolution. Thus the document recounts the courageous activities of the Delegates of the Word in the struggle against Somoza in the countryside and names many Christian martyrs. It also mentions the institutional church and specifically praises the bishops of Managua and León, who "valiantly denounced the dictatorship's crimes." The Sandinists' conclusion is that "Christians have been an integral part of our revolutionary history to a degree without precedence in any other revolutionary movement of Latin America and possibly the world."[23]

Second, the communiqué sought to reassure the church that religious freedom would be guaranteed in Nicaragua: "Freedom to prefer a religious faith is an unalienable human right which the Revolutionary Government fully guarantees." Interestingly, the government's statement explicitly rejects a Marxist interpretation of religion in society: "Our experience has shown that it is possible to be a believer and a committed revolutionary at the same time and that there is no irreconcilable contradiction between the two." Ironically, such statements may well have had the effect of increasing the anxiety of the church hierarchy, for their reaction was to prepare a detailed reply criticizing the official pronouncement. In it they worried about the dangers of a one-party state, about atheistic ideologies, and about popular mobilization through Sandinist-led mass organizations.[24]

Finally, the document attempted to affirm and support religious celebrations and festivals, which have always been an important part of Nicaraguan life. The document adds a warning, however, that if "political parties or individuals should try to convert popular religious festivals and activities into political acts against the revolution . . . the FSLN would declare its right to defend the people and the Revolution." Again, the bishops' response was to worry about government intrusion into religious festivals, perhaps fearing co-optation for revolutionary purposes, and to reject the government's authority to determine whether religious activities were being converted into political events of a counterrevolutionary nature.[25]

What, then, is the proper role of the CEBs in revolutionary Nicaragua? What danger, if any, is posed to the religious integrity of the church by the activities of CEBs insofar as they are geared to active support of the revolution? Reflecting on these questions leads one to compare the sense given to the phrase "popular church" in Nicaragua and neighboring El Salvador. In El Salvador, the term is proudly and positively applied by church people to the CEBs, whose opposition to an unpopular regime is seen to be part and parcel of an authentic spiritual role. To the degree that Salvadoran bishops do not support such a role, they are seen as reactionary.[26] In Nicaragua CEBs avoid using the term "popular church" to describe themselves so as not to aggravate tensions within the church or provoke the charge of playing a political rather than a religious role in society. In short, the term denies religious authenticity in Nicaragua, though it affirms that same authenticity in El Salvador. This point underscores the profound difference between the pre- and post-triumph stages of the revolutionary process.

The Latin American bishops at Puebla did not endorse a popular church model for Latin America. Yet they did endorse the CEB as an appropriate pastoral method of carrying out the church's preferential option for the poor. How can the CEBs respond to the needs of the poor while remaining aloof from partisan political action? Alexander Wilde has suggested that it will not be possible for the CEBs to do so in the context of authoritarian societies.[27] Study of Nicaragua strongly confirms this suggestion, for it is clear that by virtue of their birth in *Somocista* Nicaragua, CEBs were strongly politicized through repressive attacks by the government. Indeed, the process of creating and activating CEBs helped politicize the entire church. But politics is not a one-way street, and the point holds just as true in a revolutionary setting. The openness of the Nicaraguan revolution has invited the repoliticization of religion in the struggle over the fate of the Sandinist revolution. CEBs born in the revolutionary process see their pastoral work as authentic only if it takes account of and seeks to support the transformation of Nicaraguan society. The bishops, however, see this as unwarranted partisanship, a challenge to hierarchical authority, and a rupture in church unity.[28]

The conflict is captured neatly in a model put forward by Daniel H. Levine, who writes of two contrasting models of the church.[29] The bishops' model, as in Nicaragua, stresses control from above, obedience to hierarchical authority, the transmittal of truth and hope from the church to the world, and an overall emphasis on the rechristianization of society. Each of these points is sensitive and conflictual in Nicaragua today for the Christian communities at the grass roots by and large embrace a second model, that of the church as a "historical community of believers." In this view a solidarity among bishops, priests, and laity replaces a centralized chain of command from top to bottom. In place of strict obedience to hierarchical dicta, it stresses dialogue and shared experience. And it views the church as a pluralistic body encompassing a broad distribution of authority and power that accords a significant pastoral role to the laity. This model seeks to change society rather than impose a new version of Christendom. The creation and evolution of CEBs in Nicaragua strikingly illustrates the emergence of this second model. Viewing the popular church through this model helps to explain why conflict both within and about the church in the Nicaraguan revolution is so intense in the present stage.

Working for the Revolution

The mistrust between hierarchy and government is vividly illustrated by the continuing controversy over the role of priests serving in the Sandinist government. This controversy also demonstrates the diversity of groups within the church and their widely differing points of view about the interrelation of faith and politics. For present purposes, a brief summary of the issue will suffice.

Public debate centers on four priests who have served in the Sandinist government since it came to power. They are Miguel D'Escoto, M.M., who is foreign minister, Ernesto Cardenal, minister of culture, Fernando Cardenal, who has headed the Literacy Campaign and the Sandinist Youth Organization and now is minister of education, and Edgard Parrales, a Franciscan, who has been minister of social welfare and is now Nicaraguan ambassador to the Organization of American States. Other priests have positions in the Council of State, and numerous lay Catholics hold important positions in the government, but our attention is focused on the four priests most prominently mentioned in the media.

Initially the hierarchy acceded to the priests serving in government on the grounds that a national emergency required their service. But less than a year after the triumph they concluded that the emergency had passed, and on 13 May 1980, without consulting the affected priests, called upon them to resign their offices. On 20 May nine priests responded by urging dialogue with the bishops and, in effect, refusing to resign. An impasse was created and tension mounted as the conflict went unresolved. The government became involved by designating the president of the Supreme Court to head a special mission to the Vatican to seek its judgment in the matter. In October, he reported that, in the Vatican's view, "it is the bishops who have to resolve the situation."[30] In January 1981 the priests asked the bishops for face-to-face dialogue but were informed that they no longer had the episcopacy's approval to participate in the government. In May, Archbishop Obando told an interviewer that the Nicaraguan hierarchy had done all it could and had sent details to the Vatican for a final resolution, which only the Pope could provide.

Then, on 1 June 1981, the bishops issued another pastoral letter. Stating that they had "total backing and authorization to proceed" from the Holy See, they insisted that the priests leave their government posts forthwith: "We declare that if the priests who are occupying political office and exercising partisan functions do not leave those responsibilities as soon as possible . . . we will consider them in an attitude of open rebellion and formal disobedience to legitimate ecclesiastical authority and subject to the sanctions provided by the laws of the church."[31] With this declaration, the level of conflict rose sharply. Although issued in the name of unity, the bishops' action triggered a new round of intense public controversy. This initiative not only demanded resignations, it also went out of its way to declare CEPA, the Valdivieso Center, and the Historical Institute not to be official church organizations and to "have neither the approval nor the recommendation of the Episcopal Conference." Again, the priests refused to resign under these pressures, insisting on "our unshakable commitment to the Sandinist Popular Revolution, in faithfulness to our people, which is to say, in faithfulness to the will of God."[32]

This conflict is obviously more than a clash of wills. It is a clash of theologies and of pastoral strategies that has put pressure on traditional church authority. Its roots lie in the democratizing experience of the popular struggle that gave diverse groups within the church great latitude to develop their own pastoral options. The involvement of priests in the struggle nurtured a strong identification with the FSLN at the grass roots and helped to authenticate a pastoral option for the poor. In the post-triumph period, the government has had frequent occasion to recall and to laud the Christian presence in the insurrection. For those in the church who fear the drift of Sandinist policy, such testimonials seem to be efforts to co-opt groups within the church and therefore are taken as a challenge to church unity and hierarchical authority.

The CEBs and clergy who strongly support the Sandinist revolution, of course, take a different view. They see no incompatibility between the priestly vocation and working to realize the goals of the revolution, and they strongly reject the bishops' contention that the state of emergency has ended. They see the efforts to remove the priests as highly complementary to the plans of those who oppose the Sandinist government. From a strictly intrachurch point of view, priests working at the base level are preoccupied because in their religiosity the Nicaraguan people generally respect the authority of the bishops. At the same time, because many have developed very strong loyalties to the priests, sisters, and lay leaders who work with them at the base, intense public conflict between the bishops and priests has caused confusion and stress among the laity.

Calling themselves "Christian revolutionaries," representatives of Managua CEBs responded publicly to the bishops' demand for resignation of the priests in government. They described Father D'Escoto as projecting "the Christian image of Nicaragua before the other peoples of the world." They noted that Ernesto Cardenal, in establishing the Ministry of Culture, created a public agency "dedicated to the redemption of the cultural values of our people within a profoundly Christian perspective." In this spirit they argued that removal of the priests from the government would be a severe loss both for the revolution and for the church. They warned that the church would be harmed by removing the hierarchy "from the liberating process": "The active participation of the church in politics is known by everyone . . . from historic times to the present. But now those who are serving their people are threatened with sanctions. There is a contradiction between what the communiqué says are its desires not to be interpreted politically and the real consequences that this action has in the political development of the country."[33]

Does this strong position reflect the thinking of most CEBs or of most poor people in urban barrios or in the Christian communities of the countryside? Observations from a firsthand account of a CEB meeting in Ciudad Sandino, near Managua, will illustrate the answer. The meeting, attended by thirteen or fourteen people, opens with Scripture reading and discussion. After half an hour, discussion turns to community problems, including Christian participation in barrio politics and the removal by the bishops of priests and religious working in the popular barrios. The key issue turns out to be whether the newly built chapel is to be used for a Sandinist Defense Committee (Comité de Defensa Sandinista, CDS) zone meeting. Some members balk at this prospect. They are not sure this use is proper, and they do not know if they can justify it to neighbors who will oppose it. Though they reach agreement to permit the CDS meeting to be held in the chapel, they clearly have diverse views, levels of understanding, and theological perspectives. Some remain traditional in their religious conceptions, even though they may use such slogans as "Christianity and revolution, there is no contradiction." These include Christians who took an active part in the insurrection, the justification for which they could see clearly. The work of reconstruction is more ambiguous, and it is slow and difficult.[34]

Against this backdrop of a single CEB, one must see the entire barrio of Ciudad Sandino, home to about seventy thousand people, many of them deeply religious. Although most are Catholic, small evangelical Protestant groups are numerous and active. Most of these emphasize spirituality and focus relatively little attention on social issues and hence on the problems of reconstruction. But this difference is seen in the Catholic church itself. There are priests and religious in the barrio who are totally committed to the revolution. At the same time, there are so-called "new Catechumenate" priests serving there who are organizing spiritually oriented communities that reflect a tepid and declining commitment to and involvement in the revolution. In short, the reality of the church at the base level, as exemplified in Ciudad Sandino, is one of rich diversity and complexity. A small part of it ignores the revolution, another part hesitantly embraces the revolution, and still another part embraces it with enthusiasm and dedication. What takes place at this level—diverse pastoral tendencies of equal authenticity—is grist for the mill at another, more broadly political level of the revolutionary process.

It is clear that the clash of competing views and pastoral options has propelled the church into the broader political struggle that grips Nicaragua. The archbishop of Managua, Monseñor Obando y Bravo, who acquired great prestige for his courageous opposition to Somoza, has contributed to this involvement not only by pushing insistently and publicly for the resignation of the four priests but by interfering in the pastoral work of priests and religious working in the poor barrios of his diocese. Those affected have worked in open concert with the revolutionary process. He has asked the superiors of a North American sister of St. Agnes, who worked with CEPA, to transfer her out of the country. A similar action was taken against the Sisters of the Assumption who worked in the barrio of San Judas in the eastern zone of Managua. One of the most celebrated cases was that of Father Manuel Batalla, O.P., who served the Sacred Heart parish in the barrio of Monseñor Lezcano. This priest had encouraged his parishioners to take part in the popular organizations being created by the Sandinist government. The curia asked his superiors to remove him, but his parishioners, together with other CEBs in Managua, mobilized to support him. In response, the curia claimed that it was solely the decision of the Dominican Order to remove the priests, a claim subsequently refuted in public by the Dominicans. Yet another such incident took place in the barrio of Santa Rosa, when Obando transferred Father Arias Caldera, who was extremely popular, from his parish, which was closely identified with the revolution, to a more middle-class parish.

Some of these clashes have resulted in standoffs, some in victories for the CEBs. In other actions, several Jesuits have been successfully dismissed from their parishes through intervention by the curia. Other foreign priests and religious have not been allowed to return to Nicaragua after having left the country. There is considerable irony in these actions. In other parts of Central and South America clergy are expelled from a country or refused entrance by regimes that have political objections to their pastoral work. In Nicaragua they are removed from their parishes or expelled from the country by the church hierarchy that has religious objections to their pastoral work, which it regards as excessively political. When there are popular protests against these actions, the priests and religious involved are accused of politicizing the people.

Events surrounding the Sandinist triumph in Nicaragua provide an exceptional opportunity to observe what happens when a rapidly changing religious institution finds itself caught up in political revolution. The Nicaraguan case certainly confirms one's expectation that a socially consequential church would find itself deeply embroiled in the processes of a political revolution. In Nicaragua, the church has been both cause and objective of revolutionary struggle. In that context, three broad conclusions can be drawn from the earlier discussion.

First, although religious renewal in Nicaragua was stimulated to a significant degree by changes in the international church following Vatican II, the course of that renewal was substantially shaped by the popular struggle against *Somocismo*. The experimentation with new pastoral options focused on the poor and, centered in such programs as the Delegates of the Word, the CEBs, and CEPA, gave the church vibrant new life but also made manifest the fact that the church exists and functions on many levels. For many poor people in Nicaragua today the CEB is the church. This is not to say, of course, that they reject the authority of the bishops, but merely to underline that their experience of the church is strong and active within the CEB. In such dioceses as Zelaya and Estelí no problems arise because the levels of the church are acknowledged and in Zelaya they are well integrated, whereas in Estelí they are strong in their autonomy. In Managua, by contrast, this reality is extremely problematic for the very reason that the levels are not integrated.

The conflict in the Managua archdiocese can also be viewed in a more explicitly political way, which reveals a core problem in the institutional church's preferential option for the poor, not just in Nicaragua but throughout Latin America. Following Puebla's lead, the Nicaraguan hierarchy insist on political pluralism and on being a church that transcends class allegiances, thereby avoiding the taint of political partisanship. The church is not seen as a class-based institution, and therefore it cannot countenance pastoral strategies that presuppose a class division of society. How, then, can it allow free rein to CEBs that are loyal to the revolution? Formed in the Nicaraguan revolutionary process, these CEBs, by contrast, have assumed a class basis to social conflict. Moreover, they are loyal to a revolution that is committed to a course of public policy that is inherently partisan along social class lines. Conflict between hierarchy and base is thus inevitable and lends itself easily to manipulation by secular political groups.

A second conclusion is closely related to the first and helps make clear why the conflict between hierarchy and base is so readily manipulated for political purposes. The different levels of the church embrace different models of decision making and authority. The bishops maintain a traditional view of centralized authority with decisions emanating from the top down. Such a model does not adapt well to the reality of CEBs operating with significant autonomy. Moreover, underlying the differing perspectives on authority are two different theologies. The theology that animates the most dynamic CEBs, especially in Managua, places great emphasis on concrete works to change society in behalf of the poor. It is a theology with political implications and, in revolutionary Nicaragua, with concrete political options. The coupling of this political theology and CEB autonomy raises a more or less direct challenge to the hierarchy's view of the church and its essentially spiritual mission. The resulting rift between hierarchy and base is fertile ground for those who see the church as an important ally either for or against the revolution.

Finally, the pluralism and the conflict described in this essay are by-products of what I would call a profound experiment in the democratization of Nicaraguan society. Historically, church and regime were mirror images of each other from the standpoint of authority and decision making. Neither required, or permitted, the active participation of the people, and above all of the poor, in determining the direction of polity or church. But recent Nicaraguan history reflects the confluence of strongly democratizing trends in both church and politics. For some this is a fearful prospect. For others it is a source of inspiration and commitment, both religiously and politically. For the church at the grass-roots level there may be danger in this trend. The CEBs, upon which this essay has focused, can scarcely separate their history from that of insurrectionary struggle and the creation of Sandinist popular organizations. Their fate has gone hand in hand with that of popular political organizations. Does their long-term fate then depend on those political organizations? Will they flourish only if their secular counterparts flourish? There is a sobering question here about the ability of CEBs to retain a viable separate identity over time. With the revolution only five years old, it is too soon to predict the fate of the CEBs. It is clear, however, that the popular church and, indeed, the church as a whole is likely to remain at the center of political controversy in the Nicaraguan revolution.

Notes

1. Some recent sources on this topic are Phillip Berryman, *The Religious Roots of Rebellion: Christians in the Central American Revolutions* (Maryknoll: Orbis Books, 1984); Michael Dodson and Tommie Sue Montgomery, "The Churches in the Nicaraguan Revolution," in Thomas Walker, ed., *Nicaragua in Revolution* (New York: Praeger, 1981); and the entire issue of *Nicarauac* 2 (April–June 1981).

2. See Christopher Hill, *The World Turned Upside Down: Radical Ideas during the English Revolution* (New York: Penguin, 1982).

3. For a recent study of these politically radical clerical movements see Michael Dodson, "The Christian Left in Latin American Politics," in Daniel H. Levine, ed., *The Church and Politics in Latin America* (Beverly Hills: Sage, 1980), pp. 111–34.

4. The Cuban revolution occurred several years before the convening of Vatican II. The church did not support Castro's guerrilla forces and viewed the revolutionary

change they brought to the country with fear and hostility. In turn, Castro and his followers held an orthodox Marxist view that religion and the church represented counterrevolutionary forces. As a result, religion played an insignificant role in the changing of Cuban society after 1959.

5. "The Catholic Church in Nicaragua," Report of the U.S. Catholic Press Association, 1963, p. 18.

6. "Climate of Violence Hits Nicaragua," *NC News Service* (Washington, D.C.: U.S. Catholic Conference, 1 October 1970), p. 2.

7. Interview with Peggy Dillon, M.M., Ciudad Sandino, Nicaragua, 29 July 1980.

8. Philip Wheaton and Yvonne Dilling, *Nicaragua: A Peoples' Revolution* (Washington, D.C., 1980), pp. 23–24.

9. One Nicaraguan pastor described the vitality of the CEBs and delegate programs by noting that their influence has reached even the most remote northern regions of the country. He had traveled three hundred kilometers north from Managua by car and then walked twelve hours to meet with peasants, who themselves had walked two days to take part in religious assemblies. Such assemblies had a high level of participation, focused on current events in the revolution, and treated them from a biblical perspective. By his estimate there were twelve hundred CEBs in Chinandega and four hundred in Matagalpa. A Capuchin superior estimated that there were eight hundred CEBs in Zelaya, the largest rural province in Nicaragua and the most remote. He also suggested that some seventeen hundred Delegates of the Word were actively functioning in the CEBs of Zelaya in 1981.

10. The case of Cuba has been mentioned in note 4. That of Chile differed in that the election of Allende and the Unidad Popular coalition took place shortly after the CELAM meeting at Medellín. The period was characterized by the enthusiastic commitment of some clergy to left-wing politics. Their high political profile greatly disturbed many bishops for pastoral reasons. Such overt political activity was seen as exceeding the proper bounds of the pastoral role. After the overthrow of Allende, the counterrevolutionary military regime tended to view the church with great suspicion because of its earlier association with the left. The bishops saw these consequences as a threat to the institutional stability of the church.

11. See "Mensaje pastoral del episcopado Nicaraguense," 17 November 1979, reprinted in *Nicarauac* 2 (April–June 1981): 70–82.

12. Thomas C. Bruneau, "The Catholic Church and Development in Latin America: The Role of the Christian Base Communities," *World Development* 8 (1980): 538.

13. For a recent profile of Archbishop Obando y Bravo see Stephen Kinzer, "Nicaragua's Combative Arch-Bishop," *New York Times Magazine*, 18 November 1984, pp. 75–96.

14. Phillip Berryman, "Latin America: La iglesia que nace del pueblo," *Christianity and Crisis* 41 (21 September 1981): 239–40.

15. Quoted in "Religious News in Nicaragua," *Envío*, no. 5, Central American Historical Institute, 15 October 1981, p. 2.

16. Ibid., p. 3.

17. Ibid.

18. Interview with Pablo Schmidt, Managua, 26 November 1981.

19. Cited in "Reflexión cristiana y revolución sandinista," *Cuadernos de Estudio* no. 15, *CELADEC*, December 1979, pp. 18–19.

20. Ibid., pp. 41–42.

21. Ibid., p. 20.

22. Interview with Alvaro Arguello, S.J., Managua, 7 August 1980. Father Arguello lost a brother in the insurrection. He is a strong supporter of the revolution.

23. "Comunicado oficial de la Dirección Nacional del FSLN sobre la religión," *Barricada*, 7 October 1980, p. 3.

24. Ibid.

25. "La iglesia en Nicaragua," *CELAM* 19 (January 1981): 11–21.

26. For a detailed discussion of the role of the church in the Salvadoran struggle see Tommie Sue Montgomery, *Revolution in El Salvador* (Boulder, Colo.: Westview Press, 1982), chap. 4.

27. Alexander Wilde, "Ten Years of Change in the Church: Puebla and the Future," in Levine, ed., *Church and Politics*, p. 269.

28. I do not wish to say that the bishops are entirely of one mind on this matter. There is diversity of opinion and tolerance of experimentation with regard to the revolution, but the stress on church unity has forced some public closing of ranks on these broad themes, resulting in a surface appearance of unity.

29. Daniel H. Levine, "Colombia: The Institutional Church and the Popular," Chapter 9 in this volume.

30. "Events Preceding the Declaration of the Bishops of Nicaragua on June 1, 1981, Concerning the Participation of Priests in Government Functions," *Envío*, no. 2, Central American Historical Institute, 15 June 1981, pp. 1–2.

31. "Comunicado pastoral de la conferencia episcopal de Nicaragua," in *Iglesia de Nicaragua: Tiempo de discernimiento y de gracia*, MIEC-JECI no. 25, July 1981, pp. 13, 15.

32. See "Primera respuesta de sacerdotes," ibid., pp. 19–20.

33. See "Comunidad de cristianos en la revolución se refieren al reciente comunicado pastoral de la conferencia episcopal," ibid., pp. 23–24.

34. "A Look at a Popular Nicaraguan Barrio," *Envío*, no. 4, Central American Historical Institute, 15 September 1981, p. 7.

6

Brazil: The Catholic Church
and Basic Christian Communities

Thomas C. Bruneau

The Catholic church in Brazil is widely acknowledged to be among the most progressive theologically and socially in Latin America and indeed the world. Since the late 1960s the church has increasingly defined itself on the side of the poor in Brazil, a commitment that has been manifested not only verbally but also in the formation and support of groups and programs relating to human rights, political amnesty, labor organizations, land rights, and particularly the brutal exploitation of the Indians. The implementation of this commitment has frequently brought the institutional church into conflict with sectors of the authoritarian regime that ruled Brazil after 1964, and the church has been recognized as the most important critic of the regime and its approach to modernization.[1] Even after the governments of Presidents Ernesto Geisel and João Figuereido initiated the process of "opening" in the mid-1970s, the church maintained its outspoken position and the government continued to harass and imprison laymen and clergy.

Despite general agreement on the church's role, there is some question about the extent to which it exerts influence on the Brazilian population in general even though more than 90 percent claim Catholicism when responding to the census. It is relatively easy to posit the formal and active position of the church in relation to the elites and the state, which have traditionally perceived it as an important institution, but it is another matter to ascertain the degree of influence it exercises among the general population. Because of the particular history of the church in Brazil, the size of the country and population in relation to the number of clergy, the traditional form of religiosity implemented there, and the vitality of Afro-Brazilian cults, there is broad agreement that the church is not particularly influential. This agreement is shared by anthropologists and sociologists who have studied local communities and conducted sample surveys as well as by the elites in the church itself.[2]

In my own work in the mid-1970s I concluded on the basis of a sample survey of two thousand questionnaires that the church did not exert influence among the population in general. Indeed, I argued that one of the main reasons for the innovation in the church, which led to its progressive orientation, was precisely its own awareness of its lack of influence. Thorough anthropological studies demonstrate the complexity of popular religious beliefs and practices and reinforce my conclusions about both the church's use of new strategies for penetrating the general milieu and the difficulty of doing so.[3]

The Basic Christian Communities

Probably the most important single theological and social innovation of the church in Brazil has been the formation of the basic Christian communities, or CEBs. Although there are no official or very reliable data on their numbers, a highly respected Brazilian scholar estimates that seventy thousand of these CEBs exist, involving some 4 million people.[4] The formation of the CEBs implies substantial change for the church itself as the laity assumes broader roles and responsibility, in many cases coming to define the church in a decentralized and participatory format that bears little resemblance to the hierarchical and highly structured institution it is commonly considered to be. Furthermore, the phenomenon of the CEBs holds important sociopolitical implications in Brazil, where there is little tradition of group formation, a long history of centralized and authoritarian decision making, and the military ruled in a bureaucratic and technocratic style from 1964 to 1985. Where the political parties have been "domesticated," unions and student associations either outlawed or controlled, and popular initiatives generally suppressed, the formation of the CEBs has created some group discussion and participation in a weakly defined civil society becoming restructured. Further, the content is important as at least some of the members of these groups demonstrate a high degree of awareness and go on to form other groups and organizations. This content is particularly significant now that the regime is opening; the CEBs provide a force to encourage the continuation of an opening and give it direction.

At the minimum, the formation of the CEBs represents a strategy by the church to regain influence in society. They may be and often are far more, and they can invert the general definition of the church, but nevertheless they remain a strategy. Those involved in the CEBs as leaders and apologists have emphasized that they have the support of the church and remain linked to it. Thus they may operate as sects, but not in the sense of an opposition of church-sect. Indeed, it seems clear that the CEBs emerge only when church personnel promote their formation. Therefore, although these units exist in a fantastic variety that makes it difficult to generalize about them, they represent a strategy by the church that has made resources available and promoted their growth and development.

This church support is not limited to a few isolated dioceses under progressive bishops without national repercussions. Rather, the phenomenon is national, involving the clear commitment by the National Conference of Brazilian Bishops (Conferência Nacional dos Bispos do Brasil, CNBB) as demonstrated in the defined priorities of pastoral planning, the publication of books and documents, and the promotion and support of five national meetings (1975, 1976, 1978, 1981, and 1983).[5] The theme of the CEB emerges clearly from the CNBB documentation, and it is obvious that many other aspects of pastoral planning (such as movements for rural and urban workers) are premised on their formation. Thus, rather than being an isolated and restricted phenomenon, the CEBs are the theme or topic defining the Catholic church in Brazil today. This does not mean that all bishops in all dioceses have encouraged their formation, but the majority have, and the movement is effectively national although concentrated in certain areas such as the North and Northeast and São Paulo, with fewer in the South. The formation and support of the CEBs suggest both a previous change in the church and an increasing momentum as they come to constitute a potential base of the national church.

There are several reasons or bases for the commitment of the Brazilian church to the growth of the CEBs. One of the initial bases is the continuing crisis in religious vocations. The priest-to-population ratio in Brazil has always been low and in recent times has decreased even further. In 1970 the ratio was 1 priest to 7,081 Catholics (approximately 90 percent of the people define themselves as Catholics) and by 1975 it was 8,528. There is an absolute drop in the number of secular priests on the average of .20 percent per year and of religious priests of some .60 percent. Thus some solution had to be found for parishes lacking priests, and though in some cases nuns have assumed important roles their numbers are also decreasing by approximately

1 percent per year. It became obvious to all observers that some way had to be found to supplement the dwindling clergy.

The second basis concerns the traditional structures for relating the institution to the people. The system of parishes has been studied and is generally considered to be inappropriate in many regions and social sectors of Brazil. They are too large, cumbersome, and generally encompass very disparate sections of society. Within parishes the traditional pietistic groups are archaic and involve but a very small proportion of the population in any parish. The more modern groups such as the Christian Family Movement and the *cursilhos*, with some exceptions, appeal to the middle and upper classes. The most active and important movement before 1964 for relating the church to sectors of the laity was Catholic Action. The movement became unpopular with the more important bishops by 1964 and most of its groups were abolished. The church, then, lacked effective intermediary structures for relating to society.

The third basis deals with the changing orientation of the church. A lack of priests and very weak and inappropriate intermediary structures made it difficult for the church to relate to society. It was even more difficult to relate to those strata of the population that came to be defined as the preferential option: the rural and urban poor, those marginalized in the modernizing society who failed to benefit from the "Brazilian economic miracle" of the early 1970s. These people had never been closely involved with the church, which had traditionally looked mainly to the urban middle and lower middle classes. Thus if the church were to approach the lower classes it would require new instruments or means specifically suited for that purpose. And as the new orientation of the Brazilian church was supported and legitimated by the Vatican and general assemblies of CELAM, so, too, the CEBs are legitimated. Pope Paul VI spoke of them in 1972 as did the Roman Synod in the same year; both Medellín and Puebla supported them; and Pope John Paul II encouraged their formation and met with some of their members during his visit to Brazil in 1980. The CEBs, then, fit within the general new and progressive orientation of the Brazilian church and are promoted for practical reasons.

If my earlier observations on change in the church are linked to the more specific reasons for the adoption of the CEBs as a program, a certain overlap is obvious. The church is aware of its loss of influence and is seeking to develop new means to relate to the lower classes, which had been traditionally neglected in the pastoral strategies. In a very simplified formulation, then, the church seeks to gain influence among the lower classes and requires new instruments and methods for achieving that end. My approach to analysis has been and continues to be to analyze the church as a large, complex institution that innovates in a changing environment to attain its goal of influencing individuals and thus society. I agree that any analysis of the church and its relationship to state and society must consider the role of different social classes and even class conflict. But I am not persuaded that those attempting to use the Gramscian approach to the analysis of church and society in Brazil are correct in downplaying the role of the church as an institution with a high degree of autonomy.[6]

It is very well to discuss the "people [*povo*] entering the church" and "the church making its option for the people in the class struggle," but that approach neglects the question why and how the church chooses an option that is not in line with its historical role in Brazilian society. In short, my response to critics of the institutional approach is that it at least provides some defined parameters for analysis and does not so easily allow one to get lost in a discussion of the definition of classes, their articulation, and so forth, while neglecting the dynamics of the institution vis-à-vis these very classes. Maybe the church in Brazil has developed "an irreversible historical consciousness," but this does not mean that its plans and programs will be continuous or even consistent. There have been rapid tactical changes in the past and may well be again.[7] In any case, the task is to see how church structures and popular needs or demands converge and then to analyze the particular solutions that are formulated.

It is common to discuss the CEBs by elaborating on each letter, or word, in the title.[8] Community means primary groups associated because of class and territorial proximity. In these groups the people meet, exchange ideas, and support one another. The groups offer their members the possibility to interact, discuss, and in fact become communities. The members speak in their own words, using their own terms, to express their own ideas and interests. By so doing, they eliminate the need for spokesmen with different class and educational backgrounds who have traditionally represented the people. Following from this, and because of the focus by the members on their own interests expressed in their own words, the possibility for critical reflection on their environment is encouraged, which in turn may lead to an understanding of the deeper causes of poverty and inequality. In short, community means interaction, equality and opportunity within the group, and the possibility to grow in a collective consciousness that has previously been missing in church and society in Brazil.

Ecclesial refers to the relationship with the church and religion. It cannot be emphasized enough that the groups have been formed through the initiative of elements in the church and are linked to the institution. The link is also maintained by the instrument for reflection, which is the Bible. The word of God is tied to the concrete concerns of the people, and one reflects the other. The normal methodology is drawn from the earlier Catholic Action experience and consists of "see, judge, act," which encourages the taking of consciousness or the development of awareness.[9] The strong religious symbolism of the people is drawn upon both to maintain some link with the past and to facilitate the interpretation of the present. The popular religiosity is given value, built upon, and facilitated by the reinterpretation. The Bible has been popularized and made readily available, so that it may be used in the reflection of concrete reality. Bringing the Bible into the hands of the people is important because they can then grasp the meaning of religion, as stated in the Bible, and not have to rely on spokesmen. There is a certain fusing of the clergy and the people and thus a democratic or participatory push for the community as a whole. The groups, then, are linked to the church but imply a redefinition of that church.

Base means both the basis of the church and that the basis is found in the people of the lower classes. Most of the documents note that the vast majority of the people involved in the groups are from the lower classes. They are found in the rural areas and the peripheries of the large cities and are generally marginalized from the benefits of society.

The materials so far available on the CEBs are limited and of dubious analytical value. Most of the literature is of a theological nature and is intended to encourage the formation of CEBs at both the elite (bishops and clergy) and the base levels by giving them a serious theological ground and linking them to some themes of popular religiosity. Other documents deal with the experiences of certain, possibly atypical, examples of the CEBs, and though fascinating and encouraging, they are difficult to interpret. Additionally, two studies exist that seek to give general statements of the CEB phenomenon. One, by Pedro Demo, was based on responses to a mail questionnaire by communities and though very perceptive has serious problems of accuracy.[10] The other study is mine and was also carried out as a sample survey but by means of an applied questionnaire. It, too, is not methodologically perfect for all CEBs. In my study the goal was to sample all groups, including the CEBs, and thus it is difficult to ascertain their exact extent, particularly because the definition of a CEB and even the names varied from one area or diocese to another. My tentative findings were that the church did in fact influence members of the CEBs, but I also indicated the general problems of methodology in studying these groups.[11]

Research in the Amazon

To study the phenomenon of the CEBs, as well as other topics, I became part of an interdisciplinary group of researchers looking at the general theme of the social impact of development in the middle Amazon.[12] This study grew out of my earlier research on the church in Brazil, which brought me to a number of areas in the Amazon. It seemed possible that studies in these areas could highlight certain phenomena found throughout Brazil but very difficult to define, isolate, and fully grasp in the more complex urban and even rural areas. In the Amazon, with its large size and scattered population (Amazonas, the largest state in the nation, had a population in 1980 of 1.5 million, of which Manaus alone had 643,000), which is only now being "developed" and integrated into the larger system, it seemed possible to conduct research on general topics with a greater degree of certainty as to results. As the Amazon is increasingly integrated we can study the dynamics of population movement, the establishment and reaction of institutions, and the formation of new groups and associations. By selecting a containable, if vast, area we can, it seems, have a fairly complete and accurate idea of the societal dynamics in the country in general. That is, though not seeking to generalize from one somewhat isolated site to the entire country, we could at least understand the dynamics that should be in line with other areas of Brazil into which the Amazon is being integrated.

Although the Amazon has long been a distant and neglected part of Brazil, during the 1970s its integration into the larger system was a priority of the military-directed government. The priority shifted from the original purpose of "opening up" the area and bringing in "people without land to land without people," as stated by President Emilio Garrastazu Médici in 1971, to that of extensive cattle ranching and mining to generate foreign exchange, but the overall thrust was to extend the political and economic system throughout the region. This goal in large measure has been accomplished with the extension of roads, development of settler colonies and farming areas, construction of dams and industries, and extension of the state and fiscal apparatus. The process has been anything but peaceful, and the overall impact continues as a matter of concern domestically and internationally.[13]

The area we selected is not what is termed a frontier region but rather one of long-settled population with well-established agriculture and commerce. It is, however, increasingly well integrated into the national system through roads, telephone, infrastructure, credit, and government agencies. The particular municipality where we conducted research had a population of fifty-three thousand in 1980 with twenty-seven thousand located in the city and the remainder in the rural area split between the margins of the Amazon River and along a road to Manaus, the state capital.[14] In this area the church is still defined as a prelacy because the population is small and widely dispersed. This prelacy includes five *municipios* with a total land area of 70,623 square kilometers and approximately eighty-five thousand people. Like other prelacies, this one is staffed by foreign clergy, nuns, and laity, although it is reasonably well integrated with the national church in Brazil through the CNBB and other organizations as well as an exchange agreement with one of the major archdioceses in Sao Paulo. The church in this area also follows the progressive orientation promoted by the national church, and its themes and dynamic are identified with those of the larger church, although most of the personnel and resources come from North America.

It was particularly important for this study that although this area had been settled for a very long period and was thus characterized by scattered developments along the river and its tributaries, it lacked a tradition of community or group formation. Such organization, however, is a priority for the church in the area and, as we shall see, groups have been formed, thereby allowing for a reasonable sample to be taken for analysis here.

The methodology used in the study included a review of census and other government data, other documents such as government agency assessments of the area, participant observation, focused interviews with selected religious and civil personnel, and a representative sample survey of 575 questionnaires administered by interviewers we trained. The sample covers one *municipio* and was drawn in a representative manner, using the then just available 1980 census data. The sample was stratified according to city, road, and river with the latter two weighted to achieve a good sample from each of the three ecological areas. The questionnaire included sixty-eight questions pertaining to migration history, work, agricultural production, commerce and credit, group membership, political and social attitudes, health, religious beliefs and practices, as well as standard controls for class, education, and the like. The application of the questionnaire was supervised by two members of the research team, verified at the time of application, coded in Brazil, and processed and analyzed in Canada. In my view it is the most reliable study yet done in Brazil that includes questions both on religious institutions and on beliefs and practices.

The Church in the Prelacy

Foreign missionaries were given responsibility for the prelacy in 1962, and the first bishop took office in 1965. Initially the church set up institutions such as schools and a hospital. For a time it became involved in development activities such as a producers' cooperative, a sawmill, and social centers. By the late 1960s, however, when the national church was adopting an increasingly critical and progressive role that was supported and indeed manifested by the CELAM meetings in Medellín in 1968 and Puebla in 1979, the prelacy also adopted this line. Its support was particularly obvious in the early 1970s, when a group of young and progressive priests helped elaborate the prelacy's local and international self-definition. In 1974 an exchange was worked out with one of the most progressive and important archdioceses in Sao Paulo to bring the prelacy even more in tune with the national church. The prelacy has never been heavily staffed, and today with six priests, seven or eight nuns, and approximately eight lay volunteers a great deal of movement (mainly by boat) is necessary to maintain contact with the people of the prelacy, which extends over five *municipios* and 70,623 square kilometers.[15]

As the orientation of the national church changed and became explicitly progressive as manifested in the CNBB, CIMI (Conselho Indigenista Missionário, Indigenous Missionary Council), CPT (Comisão Pastoral de Terra, Pastoral Land Commission), and CEBs, the prelacy followed suit. The bishop is extremely active in the CNBB and the CIMI, and CPT commissions have been founded in the prelacy with legal assistance provided through the church. As CEBs were encouraged elsewhere, so were they stimulated in the prelacy, which encouraged the formation of communities just at the time the national church began to define it as a priority. To reach the scattered population spread out along the rivers and lakes and the road, the prelacy encouraged the people to form community centers and chapels so they could gather for mass and other religious and social activities. The activities evolved to include courses dealing with health, cooperativism, and a variety of religious courses for groups of different ages. There was no tradition of community formation in this area, and the prelacy's strategy initiated these groups. As the national church evolved in its progressive orientation, so did the prelacy, with more emphasis on training and ultimately encouraging awareness or consciousness.

Probably the main manifestation of this emphasis was the establishment of a training center in the city of the prelacy in 1968. Following a similar dynamic in other parts of Brazil, the prelacy conducted various studies, reflections, and self-questioning sessions using local information and national and regional documents, and by 1977 the commitment for the formation of communities and development of awareness was key. The defined general objective from that time is "to promote liberating evangelization, that is, to collaborate with the Amazon people so that they can progress in an integral manner, having conditions to become liberated from ignorance, from disease, from oppression, from the stagnation, abandonment, and isolation in which they live."[16] The four lines of action receiving priority by 1980 were formation of the CEBs, training their leaders, promotion of a pastoral for the family and youth, and promotion and defense of human rights.

The priority is clearly and emphatically on the formation of CEBs, and the activities, publications, and commitment of time are certainly in line with this priority. Today there are approximately 164 CEBs in the five *municipios* of the prelacy (versus 68 in 1972) with some 91 located in the *municipio* where our survey was conducted. The training center gives courses for different pastoral agents, including a strong dose of socioeconomic content to encourage awareness and action. By 1980 one thousand community leaders had received one or more training sessions at the center, and contact was maintained by follow-up courses, visits to the communities, interchange between communities, and various written materials.

The experience of the prelacy in the formation of CEBs is similar to that in other areas in Brazil but more intense because of the ecology of the area. The number of personnel is not low in comparison to the population but is low when one considers the difficulty of transportation and the isolation. Thus a means had to be discovered to contact the population, and the community was the form chosen. The traditional links included infrequent and rapid visits by the clergy and nuns, and the traditional feasts and processions often had little to do with the institutional church. Thus as the orientation of the prelacy changed deliberately to seek increased influence, some new form of link had to be found: the community. The prelacy is probably a precursor in promoting communities, and it is more clearly the priority there than in all but one other diocese that I am familiar with in Brazil.

The prelacy has emphasized not only the CEBs but also the programs and movements promoted by the national church. It initially encouraged the formation of a cooperative and more recently has been involved in the formation and encouragement of the Sindicato dos Trabalhadores Rurais or Rural Workers Union. Growing in part out of the CEB experience in Sao Paulo was the formation of a militant union opposition, which took on a political form with the party reform of 1979. The party is the PT (Workers' Party), which has been encouraged by the church in some areas and certainly in the prelacy, which has published brochures pointing to the PT as the only authentic party. Individuals involved in the Sindicato, as well as the PT, have been linked to the training center and have both taken and taught courses there.

In sum, the prelacy, though originally a foreign church and staffed by North Americans, has become inextricably identified with the main themes and programs of the larger national church. In particular, it has promoted the CEBs and has worked through them to promote both the Sindicato and the PT. The education given to the leaders of the communities is of a very critical nature, and there is a constant process of review and evaluation. The prelacy, like the progressive church elsewhere in Brazil, has been attacked by state and municipal elites involving campaigns in the media, imprisonment, some repression, and generally tense relations. The prelacy has increasingly identified itself with the population in contrast to the elites and government. The organizational basis for the link is the CEB.

The church remains strongly visible in the area. It is no longer administering the schools and hospital but is very active through the communities. In the city, with its many government services and four church buildings, there is less emphasis on the CEBs (here called *grupos de quarteirao*, or neighborhood groups), and thus there are only nine for the city's population of twenty-seven thousand. For the other twenty-six thousand along the river and road, there are sixty-four for the former area and eighteen for the latter. The prelacy clearly has emphasized the formation of communities in the rural areas and particularly the riverine area.

The prelacy's presence in the area is confirmed in other data. While we were carrying out our fieldwork, the Office of Technical Assistance and Rural Extension of the State of Amazonas (EMATER) was also conducting a survey of some twenty-two communities in the *municipio*. That office provided us with the results of its study, and the presence of the prelacy is clear. For example, the study showed that the prelacy was active in nineteen of the communities (versus sixteen for local government). In sixteen communities the prelacy was conducting training courses and in twelve it was giving Bible courses. In short, what was most obvious from this study done by a government extension agency was the presence of the prelacy in greater degree than any other single organization or association except possibly EMATER itself, and its finding in this regard is open to question.

Thus if there is an area in Brazil where the church has been active in progressive ways, forming and training through the communities, and is present, it is in this *municipio*. It provides, I would argue, an excellent location to test the impact of the Brazilian church in stimulating CEBs and evaluating their impact on the behavior and attitudes of the population.

Results from the Survey

Our sample of 575 adult heads of households (88 percent men, or 505) was, as would be anticipated, largely Catholic, although 14 percent, or 81 individuals, belonged to other religions including the Baptists, Jehovah's Witnesses, and Seventh Day Adventists. Only 1 percent, or 7 people, indicated that they belonged to no church. Interestingly enough, only .30 percent, or 2 individuals, reported that they were Spiritists. This finding seemed reasonable for the area, where there is little traditional influence of the Afro-Brazilian cults and the dynamic of Umbanda in urban centers such as Rio de Janeiro and Manaus has yet to penetrate. The Protestant groups are far more active than the Spiritists. There is clearly an infusion of traditional religiosity in the area, and 44 percent, or 252, of the Catholics make promises and 10 percent, or 47, use *pajelança* in times of illness. The purpose here, however, is not to describe the variety of religious beliefs and practices but rather to analyze the degree to which the CEBs have expanded and their impact.[17]

We asked questions on membership in ten different types of groups as well as an open question. The groups listed ranged from dance or sports clubs to professional associations to cooperatives and unions to CEBs. These were termed *grupos de base* in the rural areas and *grupos de quarteirao* in the city. The questions were specific and indicate the importance we assigned to determining group membership. We found that most people do belong to groups. Table 6.1 shows that many belong to more than one group. Membership varied with 9 percent, for example, belonging to recreational groups; less than 1 percent belonging to the Masons, professional associations, and Lions, Rotary, and the like; 5 percent belonging to a cooperative; and, 31 percent belonging to the Rural Workers' Union. Most important for our

Table 6.1. Group Membership (percent)

Respondent belongs to	
No group	38
One group	37
Two groups	19
Three groups	6
Four groups	1

N = 575.

purposes here is the substantial number that belong to the CEBs. Of the 485 Catholic heads of household, 44 percent, or 212, reported that they belong either to the *grupos de base* or *grupos de quarteirao*. The priority given by the prelacy and its success is indicated by this one figure alone. I must emphasize that this survey was not specifically carried out to include members of such groups, and it was representative. Thus the data indicate simply that the church has been successful in recruiting members of its CEBs.

I noted above that the prelacy formed more groups in the rural areas than in the city and more in the riverine area than along the road (nine in the city, sixty-four along the river, and eighteen in the road area). The results from the survey indicate that membership does indeed vary and is fully in line with the number of groups reported by the prelacy. Thus in the city only 19 percent, or 32 people, belonged to the CEBs. In the rural areas we drew 65 percent of our sample, and 57 percent, or 180, belonged to the groups. Division by the three areas gives the results shown in Table 6.2. The results of the priority given to rural areas with particular emphasis on the riverine sections of the prelacy are clear. Within the eight sections of the riverine area of the *municipio* the distribution of membership in the CEBs is roughly the same, and all of this area is of the traditional settlement. In the road area, however, there are variations according to whether the settlement in the section is new or old. In the old settlement section, which is nearer to the city, the figure is 57 percent, whereas in the new sections it is only 32 percent (an average of 46 percent). The rate of membership in the CEBs is much higher in the more traditional areas of the river and road than in the city and the newer road sections.

There is no relationship between migration (number of moves) and membership in the CEBs. Nor is there a relationship between membership and such controls as education and income. There is a relationship, however, between membership and ownership of land, with 76 percent of the members

Table 6.2. Membership in CEBs (percent)

By area	
City	19
Road	46
Riverine	69
Average	44

N = 485 (Catholics).

owning land in comparison to 43 percent of nonmembers. This relationship obviously has much to do with the low membership in the city, where a minority own land, but roughly the same proportions of members in the road and riverine area—84 percent—own land. In sum, evidence from our survey shows that there is little difference between members and nonmembers, which included most controls as well as type of work and ownership of land. What varies is the areas where the respondents were located, which seems to indicate the priority the prelacy has given to forming communities in one area over another and possibly difficulties in penetrating the road area of recent settlements.

A strong relationship exists between membership in a CEB and frequency of attendance at mass. This finding can mean either that those joining were already the more frequent mass attenders (which seems most likely), or that on joining they began to attend more frequently. In any case, the relationship is strong, as can be seen in Table 6.3. The members of the CEBs, then, are linked to the church not only through these groups but also through closer involvement in the sacraments. It does seem possible, then, that the church can exert influence on these individuals in line with its progressive orientation as described earlier. The data, as we shall see, support this view.

In the late 1960s and early 1970s the prelacy encouraged the formation of a producers' cooperative. This cooperative came to include all levels of producers, large as well as small, and it now operates primarily as a commercial enterprise providing few benefits for the small producers with whom the prelacy is most involved today. The church no longer encourages people to join, nor does it encourage them to drop out. We found in our sample that only 5 percent, or 24 individuals, belong to the coop, although the membership varies from 9 percent for CEB members to only 2 percent for nonmembers. This finding seems to suggest that there was at least an initial tendency to join these cooperatives but that stagnation occurred with less active encouragement.

Table 6.3. Attendance at Sunday Mass (percent)

	Always	Frequently	Sometimes	Never
CEB member	66	21	13	0.5
Nonmember	30	27	38	5

N = 474 (Catholics).

The earlier encouragement for joining the coop has been replaced since the early to mid-1970s with a frank encouragement by the prelacy for the Rural Workers' Union, which is reflected in the data on membership from the survey. Some 32 percent, or 154 people, of the Catholic sample (which holds for other religions with the exception of Jehovah's Witnesses) belong to the union. Most important, for members of the CEBs the figure rises to 51 percent and for nonmembers it drops to 17 percent. The association is particularly impressive and holds regardless of such controls as socioeconomic status and ecological areas. The finding is unambiguous that the prelacy, through the CEBs, which predate the union, is successful in encouraging membership in the union as well.

The same can be said for stated political party preference. The prelacy has been relatively explicit in its support for the PT. We asked a question on party preference and found that 50 percent of our sample preferred none of them, although the figure was lower for CEB members than nonmembers (44 percent versus 52 percent). Most important, although the PT was third in preference out of five parties for the nonmembers, it was the first preference for the members of the CEBs (18 percent versus 14 percent for the next most popular party, the Social Democratic party [Partido Democrata Social, PDS]). Or, whereas 18 percent of the CEB members preferred the PT, only 6 percent of the nonmembers opted for it. Again, the influence through the CEBs is clear.

One of the goals of the CEBs is to work together—to cooperate—to resolve problems and achieve concrete goals. We asked a question on working together (*mutirão*) and found that some 41 percent of the Catholic sample, or 200 people, had worked in *mutirão*. The relationship varies in that 51 percent of CEB members work in *mutirão* in comparison to 34 percent who are nonmembers.

Most important, and following from working in *mutirão*, is a series of questions dealing with problems and who should resolve them. All but 10 percent of the sample indicated a variety of problems in response to an open-ended question and another 36 percent indicated a second problem. We then

Table 6.4. Who Should Resolve This Problem? (percent)

	CEB member	Nonmember
Person himself	11	15
Community	26	12
Patron and government	39	31
Church, coop, union	2	2
Only God	15	26
No problem/No solution	7	15

N = 479 (Catholics).

asked who should resolve the problem (the first one indicated), and the results are shown in Table 6.4. A number of observations should be made regarding this table. Despite the closer link between CEB members and the church, they do not expect it to resolve the problem. More important, they do not expect that only God can resolve it, which, combined with no solution/no problem is but 22 percent for CEB members in comparison to 41 percent for those who are not members (7 percent of members versus 15 percent of nonmembers did not note problems). In short, the CEB members are much more likely to think that there are solutions to the problem indicated, but they are less likely to feel that the individual himself should resolve it (11 percent versus 15 percent). Rather, more than a quarter of the CEB members indicated that the community should resolve the problem. CEB members also seem realistic in that 65 percent of them indicated that either the community or the government should resolve the problem in comparison to 43 percent of nonmembers.

These data clearly support the conclusion that the prelacy has been effective in implementing a strategy based on the CEB in that a great many members of CEBs appeared in a representative sample survey, and indeed a greater percentage of the sample belonged to these CEBs than to other groups or organizations. The distribution between the city and the rural area also holds, which is again in line with the strategy of the prelacy and is consistent with the situation in other parts of Brazil. More important, the CEBs seem to have the desired behavioral results such as membership in the union and attendance at mass and in attitudes, with particular importance for the voting preference and who should resolve problems. The strategy seems to be effective in that the CEBs give rise to the formation of other groups, and their members generally hold reasonably progressive sociopolitical opinions.

Thus in this admittedly somewhat exaggerated case of intense action and commitment to a strategy of change in the church through the CEB, the data support the importance of this entity. The CEB emerged in the context of a need for a new structure in a difficult geographical area and, with the general change in the Brazilian church, was formulated by the prelacy to promote religious involvement and sociopolitical awareness. Within the terms of the church and the prelacy it has been effective although a number of problems remain in this area as well as in other parts of Brazil. Urban centers are the most important areas, and here the CEBs and their members are few (19 percent). Clearly, it is much more difficult for the church to have an impact in the urban areas, but given their increasing importance in Brazil, they must also become a priority. For instance, the PT did not do well in the prelacy or in Brazil in general in the November 1982 elections, and this has much to do with its concentration in certain areas and relative absence elsewhere.

The groups, once formed, become available for other purposes. So far it seems that their orientation is much in line with the orientation the prelacy is seeking to give. Experience in the field shows, however, that the government is attempting to use or even take over these CEBs, and because it has resources, it may well be effective. Its success depends, however, on the extent of awareness; so far from my observations there and reinforced by the data, there is a good deal of awareness on the part of the members.

Notes

1. See my *The Political Transformation of the Brazilian Catholic Church* (New York: Cambridge University Press, 1974); Penny Lernoux, *Cry of the People* (New York: Penguin, 1980); and Helena Salem et al., *A Igreja dos Oprimidos* (São Paulo: Brasil Debates, 1981).

2. See Pedro Ribeiro de Oliveira, "Catolicismo popular no Brasil—Bibliografia," *Revista Eclesiastica Brasileira* 36 (March 1976): 272–80, for a bibliography on these topics as well as his research report on a survey, "Catolicismo popular no Brasil," no. 9, CERIS, Rio de Janeiro, 1970. For the bishops' statement see, for example, Documentos da CNBB, *Diretrizes Gerais da Ação Pastoral da Igreja no Brasil, 1975/1978* (São Paulo: Edições Paulinas, 1975), pp. 9–10.

3. See my *The Church in Brazil: The Politics of Religion* (Austin: University of Texas Press, 1982); and Carlos Rodrigues Brandao, *Os Deuses do Povo* (São Paulo: Editora Brasiliense, 1980).

4. Leonardo Boff, *Igreja: Carisma e Poder* (Petrópolis: Vozes, 1981), p. 197.

5. See, for example, Estudos da CNBB, *Comunidades eclesiais de base no Brasil* (São Paulo: Edições Paulinas, 1979); and Documentos da CNBB, *Diretrizes Gerais da Ação Pastoral da Igreja no Brasil, 1979/1982* (São Paulo: Edições Paulinas, 1980), which features the CEBs in several different sections.

6. For example, Luiz Alberto G. de Souza, "Igreja e sociedade: Elementos para un Marco Teorico," *Sintese* 5 (April–June 1979).

7. The rapid, if inconsistent, change at the time of the 1964 coup is a case in point. The title is from Carlos Palacio, "Uma Consciencia Historica Irreversivel (1960–1979): Duas Decadas de Historia da Igreja no Brasil," *Sintese* 6 (September–December 1979). I have formulated a response to the critics of an institutional approach and developed an elaboration of my own approach in "Church and Politics in Brazil: The Genesis of Change," *Journal of Latin American Studies* (November 1985).

8. See Frei Betto, *O que é comunidade eclesial de base* (São Paulo: Editora Brasiliense, 1981); and Clodovis Boff, *Comunidade eclesial: Comunidade politica* (Petrópolis: Vozes, 1978).

9. For a discussion of this methodology see Betto, *O que é comunidade eclesial de base*, pp. 29–32.

10. Pedro Demo, *Comunidade: Igreja na Base* (São Paulo: Ediçoes Paulinas, 1974).

11. More recent studies include Scott Mainwaring's, some of which is included in his chapter in this volume; Rowan Ireland's "Catholic Base Communities, Spiritist Groups, and the Deepening of Democracy in Brazil" (working paper 131, Latin American Program, Wilson Center, Washington, D.C., 1983), based on in-depth study in a community in the Northeast; and the forthcoming Ph.D. thesis by W. E. Hewitt for the Department of Sociology, McMaster University, on the CEBs in Sao Paulo. As indicated by the chapters by Berryman, Dodson, and Smith in this volume, as well as by Levine's 1981 book on Colombia and Venezuela, there are variations in the Latin American experience with the growth and roles of the CEBs.

12. The study is interdisciplinary with my participation as a political scientist, Chester Gabriel of McGill University, an anthropologist, and Rolf Wesche of Ottawa University, a geographer. The research was conducted in the area in mid-1981 and was supported by a research grant from the Social Sciences and Humanities Research Council of Canada.

13. For the overall system see, for example, Thomas C. Bruneau and Philipe Faucher, eds., *Authoritarian Capitalism: Brazil's Contemporary Economic and Political Development* (Boulder, Colo.: Westview Press, 1981); Luiz Bresser Pereira, *Development and Crisis in Brazil, 1930–1983* (Boulder, Colo.: Westview Press, 1984); and on some of the conflicts see CNBB, *Pastoral da terra: Posse e conflitos* (São Paulo: Ediçoes Paulinas, 1977).

14. Data from the Fundacão Instituto Brasileiro de Geografia e Estatistica, preliminary from the 1980 census.

15. In addition to interviews with the bishop, clergy, sisters, and lay volunteers for information on the church and its activities, I have found particularly useful a document prepared by Sra. Lucia Leite for an IBRADES (Rio de Janeiro) course in 1981, which focuses on the prelacy.

16. Untitled self-evaluation by prelacy reflection group.

17. For a good collection of articles on religion in the Amazon, see the special number of *Religião e Sociedade* 10 (November 1983).

7

Brazil: The Catholic Church and the Popular Movement in Nova Iguaçu, 1974–1985

Scott Mainwaring

This chapter examines the relationship between the Catholic church and the neighborhood movement of Nova Iguaçu, a large (more than 1 million inhabitants) working-class city thirty kilometers to the north of Rio de Janeiro. This case is interesting because of the importance and dynamic growth of the movement and its strong ties to the church. After 1974, the limited and dispersed efforts of the local population to obtain better urban services were gradually transformed into one of the best-known and organized movements in the state of Rio de Janeiro, and the Catholic church played an important role in the movement. The case is also highly suggestive about the way the church's role has changed during the process of political liberalization, which began around 1974—the same year the work that led to Nova Iguaçu's neighborhood movement began—and about the way the church contributed to the democratization process. Finally, the example of Nova Iguaçu illustrates some dilemmas confronting both the popular church and the popular movements and the alliances and tensions that exist between the church and these movements.

During the past decade, as the Latin American church has become a more vital force within the international church and within the political debates in many countries, the number of studies on the church has proliferated.[1] Until recently, however, the great majority of studies have focused almost exclusively on the hierarchy and on church-state relationships. This essay breaks from this perspective and insists upon the need to pay more attention to grass-roots organizations and to church–civil society relationships. The church's political significance in Nova Iguaçu—and more generally, through-out Latin America—cannot be comprehended through an exclusive focus on the hierarchy and on church-state relations. In Nova Iguaçu, although the bishop's support for progressive grass-roots experiences has been critical, it is the grass-roots organizations rather than the bishop that have been most important in supporting the popular movements. Furthermore, it has been the church's role in empowering civil society (especially the popular move-ments) rather than its negotiations with the local political elite that has been most significant.

The Church,
Ecclesial Base Communities, and Politics

During the early part of the twentieth century, after undergoing a lengthy period of institutional decline, the Brazilian Catholic church began to express concern about its weak linkages to the popular masses. In a famous pastoral letter written in 1916, Dom Sebastião Leme, the outstanding leader of the Brazilian church until his death in 1942, called attention to the weakness of the institutional church, the deficiencies of popular religious practices, the shortage of priests, the poor religious education, and the church's limited presence among the masses. Leme argued that the church needed to develop a stronger presence in the society and encourage more orthodox and acceptable popular religious practices.[2]

Despite marked institutional renovation in other areas, for several decades the church was only moderately successful in developing stronger linkages with the popular sectors. The real breakthrough did not occur until the emergence of the ecclesial base communities.[3] The CEBs seem to have originated in Brazil, where the first ones were created around 1962 or 1963. In some rural areas, progressive priests who were unable to say mass in a given area every Sunday because of the vast territories they had to cover decided to encourage the local people to meet for a Sunday service. This was not only a way of answering Dom Leme's old appeal for developing a deeper understanding of principles of Catholic faith and strengthening the church's ties to the popular classes, it also coincided with the trend to encourage greater lay participation and responsibility.[4] The base communities were originally intended as a means of strengthening the church, not, as they would become, a new form of the church.

The 1964 coup marked a watershed, both in Brazilian politics and for the Catholic church. Responding to fears of social chaos and economic crisis, the military overthrew the progressive populist government of João Goulart, beginning a period of twenty-one years of uninterrupted military rule. The military government repressed popular movements and initiated ambitious growth projects. Especially during the presidency of General Emilio Garrastazu Médici (1969–74), it silenced the most significant opposition forces. Partially in response to the repression, the Catholic church changed in a more progressive direction. Progressive grass-roots innovations such as the CEBs became a more central part of pastoral initiatives.[5]

A major turning point in the discussion about and role of CEBs came at the Medellín meeting of the Latin American Bishops' Conference in 1968, which encouraged the creation of base communities, now recognized as structures that could have some political significance.[6] By the early 1970s the number of CEBs started to grow rapidly. In their short history, the base communities have become a defining feature of the Latin American church; Brazil's most renowned theologian speaks of them as "reinventing the church."[7] New approaches to liturgy, catechism, community building, and theology have emerged within the communities.[8] The CEBs are known for encouraging both participation in religious life and a context that allows the members (mostly poor people) to take active responsibility for running group life: setting the agenda, making key decisions, and organizing for a variety of religious, social, and political activities. These innovations have profoundly affected the church in many Latin American countries; in this sense, the Brazilian church has exported aspects of its transformation to other Latin American nations. At the Puebla gathering of the Latin American Bishops' Conference in 1979, the bishops recognized that the base communities "create better interpersonal relationships, acceptance of God's Word, reflection about life and reality in light of the Bible; in the communities, the commitment to family, work, the neighborhood, and the local community are strengthened."[9] From modest beginnings, the CEBs in Brazil have grown to embrace an estimated eighty thousand groups with 2 million participants.

The proper role of the CEBs has become one of the major debates in the Latin American church. Conservative church leaders claim that the base communities are excessively involved in politics and threaten the church's specifically religious identity. They see the base communities as a threat to traditional hierarchical lines of ecclesiastical authority. Conservative hierarchies, such as the Colombian, have essentially renamed extant groups and called them base communities and have exerted strong pressures against the more popular and politically involved CEBs. While co-opting the name, they have fought for tighter clerical control over grass-roots ecclesial groups.[10]

The impact of the CEBs and the debate about them does not derive exclusively from their religious role. Based on their reading of the Bible, many CEB participants have become involved in popular movements, though their political activity has been characterized by a remarkable and generally understated heterogeneity. The case of Nova Iguaçu suggests that although Brazilian CEBs are not particularly politically sophisticated or even active, they can help strengthen popular movements that are working toward progressive social change. Furthermore, despite their political limitations, Brazilian CEBs have been significant in providing a basically democratic, participatory space in a generally elitist society.[11] The CEBs' political significance has been particularly great in Brazil, Chile, and Central America, where many CEB members have participated in revolutionary struggles.[12] Thus these grass-roots organizations have become an essential element of the religious and political future of several Latin American nations. It is within this general context that the significance of the case of Nova Iguaçu must be analyzed.

The Socioeconomic, Political, and Ecclesial Context in Nova Iguaçu

Located in the Baixada Fluminense, a large lowlands which has a hot climate, Nova Iguaçu became one of the most important orange-producing regions in the country around the turn of the century. Orange production entered a decline in 1926, when diseases started to kill the trees in some parts of the Baixada. The municipality's population grew from 33,396 in 1920 to 105,809 in 1940,[13] but the area was still predominantly rural. By the end of World War II, orange production had dropped off dramatically.[14]

After 1945, Nova Iguaçu began a new phase characterized by being a distant periphery of Greater Rio. As Greater Rio grew and as real estate prices pushed the popular classes into the favelas or the periphery, the city itself grew rapidly.[15] From 145,649 inhabitants in 1950, the population increased to 359,364 in 1960 and 727,140 in 1970, making Nova Iguaçu the fastest-growing major city in the country. In 1950, 46.60 percent of the municipality's population still resided in rural areas, but by 1970 this figure had dropped to 0.39 percent. This growth slowed during the 1970s, but the population still increased to 1,094,805. It is predominantly a working-class (generally unskilled labor) city with a high percentage of migrants. In 1980, 55.59 percent of the total population were migrants. Of 374,000 people in the work force, 76,000 were involved in industry, 155,000 in services, 54,000 in construction, 48,000 in commerce, and 19,000 in public sector jobs (see Table 7.1).[16]

The expansion of social services lagged far behind the city's growth. In 1980, only 37.7 percent of the municipality's population had running water. Only 30.3 percent had sewers; sewage is disposed through open canals and rivers, which is severely damaging to the local ecology and helps account for the bad health conditions. The city had only 265 doctors, 27 dentists, and 961 hospital beds, in all cases approximately one-eighth Rio's per capita level.[17] Between 1968 and 1972, the mortality rate for children in their first four years of life was 39 percent.[18] Partially because of a shortage of schools, in 1978, according to the mayor's estimate, 150,000 school-aged children were not enrolled, and most schools were in poor condition and seriously deficient in supplies. The illiteracy rate for people over ten years old was 17 percent in 1980, and only 39 percent of the population had completed high school. As of 1978, only about 15 percent of the municipality's garbage was collected, leaving some five hundred tons of garbage per day in open sewers and unoccupied land. Inadequate police facilities have led to one of the highest crime rates in the country. Less than 10 percent of the municipality's roads are paved, and the dirt roads create major transportation problems in rainy weather. A 1980 estimate showed that if the city administration continued to pave roads at the same pace as in the preceding decade, it would take 250 years to pave the streets that already existed.[19] The intermunicipality buses are in poor condition, overcrowded, and insufficient in number, and buses to Rio are very expensive relative to local income. The train takes two hours to cover thirty kilometers, is badly overcrowded, and has a high accident rate because of poor track conditions.[20]

The population of Nova Iguaçu has some tradition of battling to obtain better social services.[21] At least as early as 1945, there were isolated attempts to organize the population for this purpose. In 1950, the first neighborhood associations were formed. As the national and local climate of the late populist years (1958–64) stimulated a rich political debate throughout the society, the neighborhood movement expanded rapidly. In 1960, leaders of the neighborhood movement organized the first Congress of the Commissions for Urban Improvements of the Neighborhoods of Nova Iguaçu, mobilizing many neighborhood associations and obtaining some concrete

Table 7.1. Population of the Municipality of Nova Iguaçu

Year	Population	Percent in rural areas
1920	33,396	
1940	105,809	
1950	145,649	46.60
1960	359,364	28.34
1970	727,140	0.39
1980	1,094,805	0.29

Source: Instituto Brasileiro de Geografia e Estatística, *Censo*, various years.

concessions from the city administration. The precoup years saw other experiences of popular mobilization in the Baixada Fluminense, including a significant labor movement and occasional movements among peasants and rural workers. After 1974 the movements would draw upon this history of popular mobilization, in which several leaders had actively participated.

The coup wiped out the most important popular movements. Key leaders of the neighborhood movement were imprisoned, and the repression prevented efforts to coordinate the movement between different neighborhoods, reducing it to isolated efforts. The associations that survived articulated their demands individually, and there was little public sensitivity to them. The high levels of repression against the popular sectors and the disarticulation of local opposition forces made any popular organizing outside the church almost impossible.

The years following the coup were difficult for much of the local population. The city continued to grow at a rapid pace, bringing new social tensions. Real wages declined for most workers until around 1976, and the city's urban services failed to keep pace with the population growth. In addition to the official repressive apparatus, the infamous Death Squad was very active in the Baixada. By 1979 the Death Squad had executed 2,000 people in Nova Iguaçu, and another paramilitary organization executed 764 in the first half of 1980 alone.[22] The progressive local opposition leaders were imprisoned, and by 1970 the opposition party, the Brazilian Democratic Movement (MDB) entered a deep crisis. Statewide, the MDB fell into the hands of a conservative group closely linked to the federal government and known for being corrupt.[23] The local government party, National Renovative Alliance (ARENA), was conservative even compared with its counterpart in other major cities. It was notorious for corruption and was largely uninterested in resolving the urban problems confronting the population. Despite the local MDB's problems, ARENA was defeated in 1974 and subsequent elections.[24]

Meanwhile, the church of Nova Iguaçu was undergoing the changes that would make it the bulwark of popular movements. The diocese of Nova Iguaçu was created in 1960, and until 1966 its orientation was relatively conservative. That year, Dom Adriano Hypólito was named bishop and began to encourage the changes that led the church to become closely identified with the popular sectors.[25] At the first Diocesan Assembly, held in 1968, the diocese voted to establish base communities as one of its principal priorities.[26] Coincident with the constriction of civil society after 1964, the church began to create community groups—Bible circles, mothers' clubs, youth groups, catechism clubs—which reflected on faith and social reality. During the most repressive years, the base communities, which started to flourish during the early 1970s, were virtually the only popular organizations to promote critical political perspectives. Although these communities were involved only in rudimentary political actions such as signing petitions for urban services, their existence would prove important for the development of the Baixada's popular movements. Between 1964 and 1974, the only attempt to organize the local population in a more continuous fashion between 1964 and 1974 was the Movement of Community Integration, created by the diocese in 1968. This movement hoped to organize Catholics to get better urban services, but in 1970 it was dissolved by the repressive apparatus.

This picture began to change around 1974, when the military regime began to promote a "slow and gradual" liberalization process within the context of increasing divisions in the armed forces, the annihilation of the left, increasing opposition in civil society, and the "economic miracle." The *abertura* ("opening") profoundly affected the political process, including the church's role and relationship to popular movements. The liberalization coexisted with attempts to continue many key elements in the system of domination, with limited popular participation, tight control over major economic decisions, a strong executive, and an unegalitarian economic model. In this sense, the *abertura* was initially more an elite attempt to secure a continuation of important features of the system than a fundamental alteration in the regime.[27] During the early phases of political liberalization (1974–78), the liberal sectors of society benefited the most, but by 1978 popular movements were in a period of growth. In 1978, the first major strike in a decade occurred among the auto workers in the greater São Paulo region, and the Cost of Living Movement grew to national proportions.[28]

Political liberalization followed the same general contours in Nova Iguaçu as nationally, with a gradual easing of repression, especially after 1978. But the process in Nova Iguaçu had some distinctive features. The city administration and local government party were particularly discredited, especially by the late 1970s, remaining unresponsive to popular demands even though the repression was easing. The MDB in the state of Rio de Janeiro also remained discredited because of its close linkages to the military government. The Nova Iguaçu MDB entered a deep crisis that began around 1970 and lasted through the 1982 elections. Consequently, in contrast to other cities, where some MDB politicians supported the popular movements, the neighborhood movement remained politically isolated, with the church as its most significant ally. Finally, although the official repression eased up, the paramilitary Right remained active. The systematic repression of the Médici years (1969–74) disappeared, but the far right continued terrorist practices, including many incidents of repression against the Nova Iguaçu church and members of the neighborhood movement. The most spectacular incidents involved the kidnapping and torturing of Dom Adriano Hypólito in 1976 and the bombing of the cathedral in 1979.[29] The specter of repression was therefore one of the factors that conditioned the development of the neighborhood movement after 1974.

The Emergence and Growth of MAB: The Neighborhood Movement, 1974–1985

In the second half of the 1970s, there was an unprecedented growth of and interest in popular neighborhood movements.[30] The seeds of the Nova Iguaçu movement go back to 1974, when two young doctors committed to working with the poor began to practice in one of Nova Iguaçu's outlying neighborhoods.[31] Initially, they attended the population almost gratuitously and offered courses on health, but they gradually became aware of the limitations of this work. Medical treatment had only palliative effects on a region with widespread malnutrition, open sewers, no garbage collection, and other health problems, so they began to think about organizing the population to help change those living conditions.[32]

In 1975, the diocese's branch of Cáritas, an international organ of the Catholic church for serving the poor, hired these doctors and two others to start a health program. These four doctors would be responsible for transforming the previously isolated neighborhood efforts into a coherent popular movement. Committed to working with and attempting to mobilize the poor, the doctors made it clear from the beginning that they were not Catholics and that their contributions would be medical and political, not religious. This frankness led to good relations with Dom Adriano and the progressive clergy, including the Cáritas director, but the conservative clergy had reservations about their work.

In November 1975, the diocese began to hold health discussions led by the four doctors. Beginning the second meeting, in March 1976, Cáritas issued a report as a means of publicizing the meetings and disseminating ideas. At the second meeting the group's fundamental orientation was articulated: "The solution of health problems depends more on the population's unity and action than on the presence of a doctor. Having a health post is important, but it does not resolve health problems. Therefore, all the forms the population has of uniting to reflect on its problems and develop its consciousness and unity are important. Actions which are purely palliative, which are not concerned with the population's conscientization, discourage true learning and do not resolve health problems."[33]

In this early phase, the majority of people attending the courses worked at health posts. The doctors were satisfied with these courses, but they also wanted to reach a different public, the poor themselves. In 1976, they held health courses in six different neighborhoods throughout the municipality, usually visiting already established groups, most of which were connected to the diocese: Bible groups, mothers' clubs, baptism clubs, youth groups. These visits often strengthened the extant organizations or led to new embryonic organizations. The doctors emphasized awareness about the causes of health problems rather than medical treatment and encouraged the population to organize to get better urban services as a way of dealing with the problems.

The immersion in the neighborhoods represented an important step in the young movement. The clientele began to change, with fewer people who worked in health care but more people from a working-class background participating. All problems faced by the population, not just health issues, began to be discussed. Simultaneously, the population began to organize neighborhood associations to address these needs. From the beginning, these efforts emphasized the concrete needs of the local population rather than the more theoretical discussions characteristic of the church's conscientization work.

In May 1977, the movement began to call itself Amigos do Bairro (Friends of the Neighborhood) and assumed responsibility for putting out the newspaper that disseminated information. At the eleventh health encounter, in November 1977, the movement's objectives were stated explicitly: "Friends of the Neighborhood is a movement concerned with the good of all people, with a better and more dignified existence." At this same meeting, the concern was expressed that "Friends of the Neighborhood cannot be closed, it must communicate with all people and encourage all to participate."[34] This was a call to expand beyond church horizons and become a mass movement. Around this time, the movement began to define one of its principal strategies, direct confrontation with the city administration in fighting for urban services.

The movement continued to expand, involving a growing number of neighborhoods. This expansion dictated the need for more formal leadership structures, and at the thirteenth meeting, in March 1978, the movement voted to create a coordinating commission whose functions would be to "orient the movement, attempting to encourage the groups, but without dominating them; encourage the exchange of experiences; visit the neighborhoods; do a summary of the meetings; encourage the formation of new neighborhood associations; represent the movement whenever necessary; publish a newspaper about the problems and struggles of the neighborhoods; organize a central archive which includes the experiences of all the groups, important addresses, and other information for whomever needs it; offer mini-courses."[35] This leadership structure was an important step in expanding beyond isolated material needs to developing a mass movement with broad political horizons. Other steps in this direction occurred around the same time, including turning the health newspaper into a newspaper for the movement. A period of consolidation and rapid expansion was under way.

By May 1978, the bimonthly meetings involved people from eighteen different neighborhoods of Nova Iguaçu. At that time, the movement adopted the name Movimento de Amigos de Bairro, MAB (Friends of the Neighborhood Movement). The local associations continued to be the primary instrument for organizing the neighborhoods, and MAB became the means of coordinating the efforts of different associations and turning them into a cohesive project, capable of pressuring the state into becoming more responsive to local needs.

Two issues that arose in May 1978 had a major impact on the movement's development. One of the most active associations took a petition with fifteen hundred signatures to the city administration, but the administration refused to receive it, stating that it would accept demands only from people who had paid their building tax. The residents wrote to several council members (*vereadores*) protesting this policy, and the movement brought the issue to the attention of the local press. These pressures from different segments of the society forced the mayor to modify his initial statement on 25 July. MAB had achieved its first major victory in pressuring the city administration to re-evaluate its policies toward the popular sectors and for the first time had received considerable press attention and won allies among local politicians.

Around the same time, another serious conflict between MAB and the city administration occurred. The mayor agreed to attend a meeting with residents from one neighborhood, but he sent a representative instead. The residents were angry about his failure to come or to notify them beforehand. In protest to the initial decision to refuse to receive petitions and to the mayor's failure to listen to the demands of the local population, MAB decided to hold an assembly to discuss the administration's irresponsibility and what the residents could do about it. The assembly was held on 14 October 1978, with seven hundred participants representing thirty-eight neighborhoods, of which thirty-four had signed a letter to the mayor protesting the administration's lack of responsiveness. The assembly began a new period in MAB's development, marked by stronger linkages to local politicians and the press and by more extensive participation. The development of local allies would give the movement greater impact than it previously had.[36]

Until late 1978 and early 1979, even though MAB was becoming a mass movement, it was still almost exclusively concerned with immediate material needs of the local population. This focus began to change in late 1978 and early 1979 as the leadership became more interested in local and national politics. MAB participated in the solidarity movement with the 1979 auto workers' strike and with a teachers' strike in Rio and sent representatives to local demonstrations. The leaders began to support issues related to the democratization of the society such as party reform, political amnesty, and reform of local government. Organizational and political changes accompanied the movement's expansion and the parallel changes in the national political situation. In January 1979, MAB elected its first formal Coordinating Council, which met every week rather than every two months. The movement divided into five regional groups to attempt to ensure better sensitivity to grass-roots needs.

MAB's dynamism created a new problem for the city administration, which was accustomed to ignoring popular demands. During MAB's early phases, 1975–78, the administration, headed by a notoriously conservative and corrupt branch of the government party, consistently showed disrespect for MAB leaders. MAB participants were frequently told to meet with a city representative at a given time and place, only to arrive and find that the official was engaged elsewhere. After agreeing to hold bimonthly hearings to listen to the population's demands, the administration attempted to renege on the commitment.

MAB used this unresponsiveness as a means of further delegitimizing the city government. The movement publicized the government's repeated failures to meet promises, the disrespect it had shown for MAB participants, the financial scandals that surrounded the administration, and its failures to attend to the needs of the local population. Largely in response to the administration's repeated failures to meet promises and provide urban services, MAB decided to hold a second major assembly on 15 July 1979, again leading to an increase in the number of participating neighborhoods. It had three thousand participants, representing sixty neighborhoods of Nova Iguaçu. The importance the movement had acquired was evident in the publicity the assembly received and in the presence of important political figures, including federal senator Roberto Saturnino. The meeting was also successful in forcing the administration to agree to meet weekly with representatives from different neighborhoods of Nova Iguaçu. MAB, by now the most important popular movement in Nova Iguaçu, was in a new, more mature phase.

The party reform initiated in January 1979 was one of the most important steps in the *abertura*. The government dissolved the biparty system it had created in 1965 and established regulations for the creation of new parties. The party reform has deeply affected the entire subsequent political struggle, including the evolution of popular movements and the church and in this specific case, MAB. Although party reform had been a fundamental demand of the opposition, the government skillfully managed the reform to maximize divisions within the opposition, which split into five parties.[37] MAB's leaders had always experienced some internal divisions, but the party reform accentuated these divisions. Some MAB leaders opted for the largest opposition party, the PMDB (Party of the Brazilian Democratic Movement); others joined the Workers party (PT) or the Democratic Labor party (PDT). These party divisions reflected differences in basic philosophy about what should be done at that political juncture and how popular movements should be led. Some MAB leaders (mostly PT) were most concerned about grass-roots discussions and about making sure the common people led the process, and others (mostly PMDB) emphasized the importance of creating a mass movement that would participate in the redemocratization process. Ironically, then, the *abertura*, which facilitated the growth of the movement, also created conditions for internal competition and division.

Despite tensions between PT, PDT, and PMDB leaders, until December 1981 the existence of competing conceptions about how to run the movement probably helped MAB to articulate a careful balance between grass-roots work and broader political issues that made it one of the more successful neighborhood movements in the country. By late 1981, almost one hundred neighborhood associations were participating. The demonstration at the Government Palace in Rio on 13 June 1980, with seven hundred participants, was the first time MAB had gone to the state government rather than to Nova Iguaçu's government to demand urban improvements. This approach to the state government marked an important step in MAB's visibility and capacity to negotiate with the state. It meant dealing with a higher level of government and initiated a strategy of forcing the government party, the Social Democratic party (PDS), and the now extinct Popular party (PP), which controlled the state government, to compete in providing services.

MAB's successes have not made its tasks any easier; indeed, they have become more complicated as the movement has gained maturity. Mobilizing the local population remains difficult because of the region's security problems, the poor and (relatively) expensive transportation, and the limited time so many people have. Financial problems continue to plague the movement. Until the November 1982 elections, the city administration remained fairly unresponsive to MAB and to popular demands; the normally cautious *Jornal do Brasil* reported that "nowhere in the state of Rio is the Government party so discredited as in Nova Iguaçu."[38]

In December 1981, a period of greater internal conflict at the leadership level and some demobilization of the grass roots began. The most important problem was the accentuation of internal tensions in the movement, principally stemming from partisan disputes. In December 1981, MAB held the second Congress of Neighborhood Associations of Nova Iguaçu (the first had been held in 1960), became a federation, and held elections for a new Coordinating Council. The elections for the Coordinating Council led to sharp and unforeseen disputes. Many of the original leaders, including the four doctors, were not elected. Twelve of the nineteen original members remained, but the overall composition of the council changed. There were tensions between the new leaders and some of those who left, and charges of manipulation were made on both sides. Never before had MAB experienced such deep internal disputes. These tensions played into the government's hands. The regime fared relatively well until 1982 at institutionalizing an elitist system within the bounds of electoral politics because the opposition was somewhat disarticulated. Popular movements no longer had the dynamic growth that had characterized the 1974–80 period.

The 1982 elections for governor, federal and state congress, and local government stimulated many debates and conflicts within the movement. Officially, MAB adopted a position of autonomy vis-à-vis political parties. This meant that as a movement, MAB did not opt for any particular party and that it was open to all individuals, regardless of party affiliation. At the same time, however, many MAB leaders recognized the importance of electing individuals more sympathetic to the movement, so approximately a dozen MAB leaders ran for office, all in the PMDB or the PT.

The election results proved a major disappointment to the movement's leaders, most of whom had worked for the PMDB and the PT. None of the popular candidates of Nova Iguaçu were elected. Leonel Brizola won by a large plurality in Nova Iguaçu, and the PDT easily won the municipal elections. In the dispute for mayor, the election yielded the following results:[39] PDT, 129,789; PDS, 67,484; PMDB, 66,252; PTB, 20,084; PT, 7,262.

In Nova Iguaçu, a relatively conservative faction of the PDT came to power. Although less repressive and more open than past local governments, it also faced problems of corruption and lack of responsiveness. Throughout the state, Brizola implemented populist practices aimed at developing popular support. Faced with the severe economic crisis, the federal government's strategy of reducing resources to opposition governors, and a PDT minority in the state parliament, Brizola had difficulties in effecting major changes. At both the municipal and state levels, the opposition's winning of free, competitive elections but inability to introduce substantial improvements in popular living conditions created new problems for MAB. As one movement leader stated, "When the PDS was in power, everyone knew that the government was against the people. With Brizola, with the PDT, it is harder. Brizola says he is your friend, but in practice he is not much better than the PDS. But most people don't see this."[40]

Despite these new challenges and a temporary demobilization of the grass roots, MAB continued to be one of the most important popular movements in the state. In December 1983, the movement held new elections for the Coordinating Council, and the different factions once again improved their relations, beginning another phase of growth. In early 1984, the movement participated extensively in the campaign for direct elections. In November

1984, it held its largest demonstration ever, attended by about four thousand people, around issues of public health. By January 1985, when Tancredo Neves was elected president, MAB represented 120 neighborhood associations in the Baixada Fluminense.

The Church and MAB

During MAB's early development, the movement was highly dependent on the church. As the regime began to permit a limited liberalization, the popular movements gained more autonomy from the church for two principal reasons. First, the dynamics of the social process pushed them into a more autonomous position. Whereas earlier the popular classes could not organize outside the church, as the regime opened up, they gained more space for mobilizing and had less need to organize within the church. The church's politically limited organizations became somewhat inadequate as the strategic, organizational, and financial demands on popular movements became more complex. Conflicting ideas emerged regarding how the movements should be led as political organizations became reactivated and started to challenge the church's hegemony of the popular movements. The church often lagged behind in its political formulations, strengthening the tendency for other groups to assume the leadership of the most important movements. This nonchurch leadership was materialized in Nova Iguaçu through the role played by the four medical doctors and a number of other individuals associated with the Left.

Second, Dom Adriano and most other church leaders made a conscious effort to encourage the autonomy of popular movements, which they perceived as a means of strengthening the movements and opening them to non-Catholics. The diocese recognized that it did not have any special competence in the political decisions facing popular movements. It also perceived this option as a means of reaffirming its identity as a religious institution. Thus, in Dom Adriano's words, "It is advantageous for pastoral work that the movement be autonomous. That way, pastoral work can concentrate on the religious sphere, on the Bible Circles, religious ceremonies, base communities. The communities can continue focusing on the Bible and the social concerns which emerge from their faith."[41]

More Catholic activists assumed leadership positions, but the dependence on the church diminished as MAB focused more on popular mobilization and less on medical work. As the movement became better known, it relied less on support from local parishes. Even though it continued to encounter financial difficulties, it became more autonomous in this sphere, too. An important step in this regard was Cáritas's decision in 1978 that it would no longer finance the work of the four doctors on the grounds that in the new political climate it should use its limited financial resources to support work with the Catholic population. At the same time, the base gradually became less Catholic. As MAB became a mass movement and did less medical work, many CEB participants stopped attending the health seminars. People from other religious groups or who did not actively participate in any church joined the movement. Individuals with a history of leadership in the region's popular struggles started to participate, further diversifying the movement.

Nevertheless, the autonomy of the popular movements with respect to the church should not be overstated. In Nova Iguaçu, as in many parts of the country, a strong connection between the popular movements and the church continues to exist. It would be more accurate to say that the church and the movement have sought a relationship of autonomy than to assert that this autonomy exists in an absolute form.[42] The institutional church has continued to play an important role in MAB's development through several means:

1. Until November 1982, it helped protect the movement from the repressive apparatus. At critical periods, the diocese still can speak out against authoritarianism. When the church was attacked in the late 1970s, it was Dom Adriano and the Justice and Peace Commission that responded. When some urban squatters were involved in a difficult struggle for land in 1981 and 1982, it was the church that defended them. MAB lacked the resources to handle such a difficult case.

2. Many neighborhood associations hold their meetings in churches, which not only resolves the space problem but also serves as a visible sign of ecclesial support. The diocese provides space for MAB's office at the Formation Center, where the Coordinating Council meets weekly. Because one of MAB's major problems has been lack of financial resources, it has been important that the movement does not have to rent an office. The use of a diocesan building is also a source of legitimation, both in the population's eyes and in avoiding repression.

3. The diocese provides limited financial support, usually indirectly, as through helping to finance the health program. The diocese has loaned MAB a mimeograph machine, does not charge the movement for the use of electricity or water, and occasionally gives MAB small financial donations for its work toward social justice.

4. The diocese provides a moral legitimacy that encourages grass-roots

Catholics to participate. The church enjoys greater legitimacy than other institutions in Nova Iguaçu. Much of the population views the church as the one institution it can count on and as the only institution that will not act in pursuit of its own self-interests. The clergy are usually the only educated people who have ongoing contact with the population, so their credibility is unparalleled. Consequently, the support of most clergy has been very helpful to the movement.

The outstanding key to the close connection between MAB and the diocese has been Dom Adriano, who gave his full support to MAB from the beginning. In an interview, he stated, "We have an evangelical commitment to make a preferential option for the poor. So how are we going to realize this option? It's not enough just to talk and pray. As a Christian and as a pastor, I feel I have the duty to support the movements which work for the good of the people."[43]

The diocese's most important organizations have also supported MAB. Cáritas, for example, made possible the health work that led to MAB's creation, provides space for MAB's office, lets MAB use a mimeograph machine, and has hired two MAB leaders. The Justice and Peace Commission and the Pastoral Workers Commission (CPO) have generally backed MAB, although there have been some tensions between the CPO and MAB.

Most of the clergy have supported MAB, principally through developing a vision of faith that emphasizes social justice and political participation. Some priests have encouraged people to participate in MAB or to form neighborhood associations, and many let the associations use the churches for meetings. Characteristic of the support from progressive clergy for the popular movement was one foreign priest who arrived in a neighborhood of Nova Iguaçu in 1978. From the beginning his attitude was that the church should back the popular movements while respecting their autonomy: "The church has the grass roots, but it doesn't have many people who know what to do politically. It doesn't have people who can lead the grass roots. Therefore we must support the people who can. Also, it is not the church's role to lead the movement. What projects should be undertaken? How should the struggle be concretized? These questions go beyond the church's domain."[44]

When the priest arrived in 1978, he began to encourage the creation of more base communities and to promote a vision of faith linked to social justice. A few months later, several lay people and he prepared and distributed a questionnaire on the neighborhood's major problems. They invited all the residents—not just Catholics—to participate in the survey. At this point, a man who had participated actively in the region's popular struggles until the early 1970s and who had been jailed thirty-two times for political reasons under the military regime became involved. He had long ceased being active in the church, but the priest's orientation and willingness to work with non-Catholics encouraged him to attend the meetings. He spoke of how the church's transformation affected him: "For many years, even though I am a Catholic, I didn't have much to do with the church. The church felt it didn't need the poor. The priests didn't baptize our children, they didn't say funeral masses for peasants, they didn't give us any support. This bothered me. . . . The Church was against the common people and for the wealthy. . . . In '78, seeing that the church was helping the people, I began to participate again. It wasn't that I stayed away from the church for all those years, but rather the church that was removed from the people."[45]

After organizing the assembly and helping initiate a neighborhood association, the church changed its role. The population assumed control of the association, and the old activist became the outstanding leader. This association quickly became one of the best organized in all of Nova Iguaçu. Even though the movement had become autonomous, the church's support did not cease. The priest continued to encourage CEB participants to act in the association by stressing the value of political participation, and the meetings are still held in the church.

In addition to the support the bishop, many priests, and diocesan organizations have provided, grass-roots church movements have contributed to MAB's growth even though the base communities in Nova Iguaçu are primarily dedicated to religious reflection and are not politically sophisticated.[46] MAB and other movements do the political organizing, and the diocese focuses on evangelization, which includes encouraging people to live the social and political dimensions of faith. Yet by encouraging a large number of people to think more critically about politics, CEBs have helped create a willingness to participate in politics. The existence of CEBs meant that there was a large number of people with some prior experience of organization and participation, disposed to fight for urban improvements. Significantly, the neighborhood associations are generally strongest in areas where the church has encouraged the creation of CEBs. A MAB leader who was a longtime activist in the area's popular struggles reflected on how the grass-roots church work has strengthened the popular struggles:

> The people who participated before '64 were directed from above, by the parties and politicians of the period. The movement grew a lot but didn't have much substance. It made a lot of noise but

lacked continuity. Before elections, it grew rapidly, but after the elections, it gradually faded. Today's movements are different. Today, the work is more politically conscious. The participants know why they are there, they discuss more, participate more actively. Today they aren't just dragged along. That's what the difference is, that today the movement has a firm base. This difference is largely because of the church's work.[47]

In addition to helping create a grass-roots constituency that has bolstered the base of the popular movements, the diocese has encouraged the formation of popular leaders. Eight of the nineteen members of the initial Coordinating Council acquired their political education principally through the church, and six more had strong ties to the church. Nine members of the second Coordinating Committee had developed their political consciousness through the church, and at the neighborhood level, the predominance of Catholic activists is greater. A woman who first participated in the local CEB, later in the Pastoral Workers Commission and her local neighborhood association, and was eventually part of MAB's first Coordinating Council explained her own political evolution: "My political consciousness grew through the church. I was always a very religious person and was active in the church. But before coming to Nova Iguaçu, I had experienced only the closed church of Rio. It didn't get involved in politics, or if it did, it was on the government's side. Seven years ago, we moved to Nova Iguaçu. That's when I started to develop a political consciousness. I participated in the base community and learned a different understanding of the Bible, committed to the poor and to social justice."[48]

MAB, the Left, and the Church: Alliances and Tensions

Between the early 1970s and about 1978, there was a historically unprecedented alliance between the popular church and the left, which had traditionally seen the church as one of its principal enemies. After the total defeat suffered between 1968 and 1974, significant sectors of the left rejected vanguard approaches and became more concerned about basic human rights, more willing to work with democratic opposition forces, and more interested in doing grass-roots work with the popular classes. And even though they diverged with many political conceptions of the left, some popular dioceses opened a space for people committed to social transformation to work with the popular classes. In Nova Iguaçu, the diocese created the space that enabled the politically committed doctors to begin their work. Without the diocese's financial support, legitimation, and help in creating contacts with the already organized Catholic groups, it would have been almost impossible to do anything more than palliative medical work.

This alliance between the left and the church was important in the development of the neighborhood movement in Nova Iguaçu. Even though the population of Nova Iguaçu has a history of different forms of popular resistance and organization, it was not until a stable, politically aware leadership emerged that these efforts transcended immediate material perspectives. Before 1975, Catholics were organized in local ecclesial communities concerned with social reality, but there were no efforts to articulate a broad social movement that could change the way local government was run. It would take the active involvement of the four doctors committed to working with the popular classes to transform the isolated petitions into a significant popular movement. The presence of the doctors played a significant role in helping the local population to organize. One person who became a leader in the movement stated,

> The population was still completely passive, and there was almost no organization. Then the doctor arrived and everyone woke up. It encourages the people to have a doctor who shows some interest in their problems. He encouraged the people to reflect about the causes of the problems in the neighborhood. He asked, why do these problems exist? Then the people started to say that it was because of the miserable wage levels, because the city administration never does anything it promises, and so forth. Some people started to see that things weren't going the way they should, that it is better for us to demand our rights than to pay for medications.[49]

The four doctors and other individuals from the left helped raise broader political issues and actively worked to coordinate efforts between neighborhoods. The step from a movement concerned solely with the population's immediate needs to one whose leaders attempted to relate these needs to broader political issues was important. Popular movements can create pressures that cause authoritarian regimes to open up, but to do so, they must work beyond immediate material benefits toward issues related to democratization. Excessive focus on the broader issues easily leads to gaps between the leaders, who in a movement like MAB are politically sophisticated, and the rank and file, who generally are not very aware of the linkages between broader political issues and their immediate material needs. Yet exclusive concern with immediate material needs prevents a movement from contributing to broader social change and makes the movement susceptible to internal crisis once it has obtained the benefits it initially sought or, conversely, once it becomes frustrated from repeated failure.

The efforts to coordinate work between neighborhoods also gave a new character to the movement. From a relatively early time, the movement was concerned about articulation between the participating neighborhoods. This attitude was in marked contrast to previous neighborhood movements in Nova Iguaçu because only during the brief period before and after the 1960 congress had there been serious efforts to coordinate work between neighborhoods. It is also one of the characteristics that made MAB an unusually well-articulated movement. Coordinating work between neighborhoods created the possibility of a mass movement, with greater chances of pressuring the state. The new movement consequently provided different political experiences, which more local movements do not afford. Visitation between neighborhoods proved to be a source of encouraging other neighborhoods, expanding the movement, and exchanging ideas about how to work.

The role the doctors played in helping organize the local population is common to most popular movements in Brazil. The popular sectors have always expressed some resistance to domination, but without the input of leadership generally drawn from outside circles, these expressions have not led to political movements that could change the society. Even the post-1974 movements, which have been more autonomous with respect to political parties and intellectuals, have generally relied on outside support, especially in the early phases.[50]

Despite the strong presence of the Catholic left in the movement and despite the predominance of Catholics participating at the neighborhood level, the four medical doctors who began the movement retained the hegemonic orientation until December 1981. This phenomenon of a predominantly Catholic base and hegemonic non-Catholic leadership is common, but it has generated some tensions. Earlier I noted that Dom Adriano has fully supported MAB and its autonomy, but this perspective is not uniformly shared in the diocese. In contrast to some popular dioceses, where overwhelming numbers of the clergy are committed to the popular cause, the Nova Iguaçu diocese is somewhat divided, with a number of moderates and even some traditional conservative priests, some of whom openly and sharply disagree with Dom Adriano. Within the diocese there are many competing conceptions of the church's role, its relationship to politics, and consequently its relationship to popular movements. Although the predominant tendency has been to support MAB, some clergy have opposed the movement, and even some progressive Catholics have viewed it ambivalently.

Among progressive Catholics, the criticisms derive from the feeling of many priests that the left has done little grass-roots organizing and therefore should not lead the movement. They feel that MAB is controlled by intellectuals and that popular movements must be led by people from the popular classes. They argue that MAB's leadership is an elite with limited understanding of popular needs and values and that the movement has worked toward broader political issues at the expense of grass-roots work. Even though most of the diocese's priests and religious verbally eschew organizing the population for political purposes, some clergy delegitimize the efforts of "outsiders" in doing so. Finally, others criticize MAB for not developing more effective participation.

In MAB's case it is not clear that these criticisms are justified. More than half of the members of both of the Coordinating Councils have been workers, and the others live in simple conditions in Nova Iguaçu and have shown a long-term commitment to working with the popular classes. Furthermore, the movement's success in mobilizing the local population, contributing toward obtaining material improvements, and fighting for a more responsive local government suggests that it has captured popular needs and channeled them in an effective way. These positive attributes, however, do not eliminate tensions between some church people and MAB.

More important than the occasional tensions between progressive Catholics and MAB have been the conflicts between conservative clergy and the movement. One example of how the conservative clergy view MAB and especially the four doctors and other leftists in the movement will suffice to indicate the criticism they voice. One priest who has a moderate discourse but authoritarian practices and paternalistic attitudes openly discouraged people in his parish and in the mothers' clubs from participating in MAB:

> MAB was started by outsiders. It started here, in my parish, but escaped from my hands. They were doctors from Rio who wanted to do something about the misery of the Baixada. We didn't support them because they were outsiders. I didn't know why they were here. They were taking advantage of the grass-roots work I had done. . . . I feel suspicious about MAB. I see in it an ideology which I don't completely share, and the workers don't have a

means of defending themselves against this ideology. MAB takes
church people and makes them think things they might not want
to. . . . It is impossible to defend the workers against this
ideology.[51]

These criticisms reflect the tensions and debates found in the Brazilian
and Latin American church in general. The priest's views about avoiding
church participation in politics and encouraging clerical control of the popular sectors are common among conservatives. His discourse indicates a
competition for popular sympathies and control that is also common. His
opposition to MAB shows that even in progressive dioceses, the church often
has a contradictory political impact. Equally striking is the priest's attitude
that MAB could make people believe things that "they might not want to."
His attitude that the popular classes can easily be manipulated into participating in movements whose objectives they do not understand is question-
able. The popular classes may not understand the political debates that take
place at the leadership level of popular movements, and they can undoubtedly be manipulated in some ways, as the lengthy history of authoritarian
populism suggests, but far from being easily manipulated into participating,
they are usually suspicious of external agents who try to organize the population. There has been a generalized experience of needing to offer concrete
benefits to be successful in political work with the popular classes; they
participate only if they gain some benefit.[52]

The left is also sometimes critical of the church. Although the doctors who
helped start MAB appreciate the support they have received from Dom
Adriano, Cáritas, and other progressive clergy, their vision of how to lead the
popular movement differs from that of most progressive Catholics. One of
them said, "The church has the idiosyncracy, the internal contradiction, of
not admitting how it works. It leads the popular process, but then it claims
that this process is spontaneous, that it is the popular classes who are
directing their own process. It delegitimizes the kind of leadership, of
vanguard, needed to develop effective popular movements. For us, the
leaders must elaborate a project that indicates their ability to understand
popular demands. The challenge is in being able to capture and channel
those demands. The church delegitimizes that step."[53]

Notwithstanding the tensions between some MAB leaders and the diocese, one of the reasons MAB has been such a dynamic movement is the
combination of the leadership of the left and the strength of the popular

church. Whether MAB's relationship with the diocese will remain harmonious will be a key factor in the movement's future.

At the beginning of this article I noted the importance of paying more attention to grass-roots Catholic organizations, especially the ecclesial base communities. The analysis should make clear that these communities are a significant force, both in the Catholic church and in Brazilian politics. Although Brazilian CEBs are distinctive for their number, age, and close linkages to the hierarchy, base communities have also become an important source of change within the church in many Latin American countries. Not without reason have all sides of the ecclesiastical spectrum shown a keen interest in or concern about the CEBs.

In their political consciousness, action, and impact Brazilian CEBs are remarkably heterogeneous. As we have seen, the linkages between CEBs, popular movements, and political parties are very complex, far more so than most analyses have suggested. CEBs of the major industrialized areas such as São Paulo and Nova Iguaçu have the most sophisticated political consciousness, yet even in these cases this consciousness is rudimentary among the majority of participants. Furthermore, despite the presence of some leaders who are on the left and despite being one of the most successful neighborhood movements in the country, MAB's objectives and capacity to effect political change are relatively limited in the short run. In fact, by 1982 MAB faced serious difficulties, showing that even well-organized movements can be fragile and cyclical.[54] On the other hand, CEBs have helped introduce new social practices with an emphasis on participation and democratic methods and have strengthened popular movements throughout many parts of the country. Although the charge of the conservatives that the CEBs are deeply political has little to do with the reality of the vast majority of base communities in Brazil, their perception that CEBs affect political life is clearly correct. As Berryman and Dodson show elsewhere in this volume, this impact is even greater in Central America, where many CEB members have actively participated in the revolutionary process.

The chapter calls attention to the importance of not restricting analysis of the church's political impact to church-state relations. Political life includes a vast network of nonstate activities that can bolster different sectors of civil society. Despite infrequent interactions with or criticisms of the political elite, the Nova Iguaçu church has been one of the most important political forces in the region and has helped empower local popular movements. The analysis has also called attention to the limits to the church's involvement in popular movements; the competition among the church, political parties, and popular movements that frequently exists at the grass-roots level; the tensions and debates within the church concerning its proper linkages to politics; and the dilemmas the popular movements have faced. It is also important to emphasize that the relationship between the church and popular movements varies markedly from region to region and diocese to diocese.[55]

Finally, the chapter provides many suggestions about the way the church's political role has changed during the process of political liberalization. Even progressive church leaders feel that the church's work must change as civil society develops the capacity to articulate its own political mechanisms. One of the outstanding intellectuals of the popular church, Frei Betto, captured this new relationship between politics and religion in an important essay:

> The church cannot attempt to substitute political parties, unions, neighborhood associations, the mechanisms specific to the political struggle. . . . Asking the base communities to also become the union movement, a grass-roots organization, or a social center is a mistake. . . . The specificity of the base communities lies in their religious character. The people who participate in these communities are not motivated by professional, educational, or political interests. They are there because of their faith. This faith in Jesus Christ, lived and made explicit in communion with the church, impels the simple people to participate in the base communities.[56]

During the period under consideration, the Nova Iguaçu church changed from being the only institution capable of defending human rights to one among many forces interested in promoting social change. But though no longer alone, the church retains an important political function through developing a vision of faith that encourages people to participate politically.

Curiously, in the Brazilian case it has been precisely during this period of decreasing church involvement in the political sphere that the conservatives have most attacked the progressives for being too deeply involved in politics.[57] The explanation is not hard to find. On the one hand, the liberalization process has enabled the conservative sectors to claim that there is no longer any need for the church to intervene in politics and that the church should be apolitical.[58] Ultimately, of course, all conceptions of faith have political consequences; the question is really the nature of those consequences. On the other hand, the turn toward the right of the international church has strengthened the conservative sectors, even in Brazil, which probably has the most progressive Catholic church in the world. Thus the struggle for hegemony in the church goes on, and the grass-roots organizations and political involvement that have been at the center of this chapter remain central issues in the debates.

Notes

This material is adapted from a chapter in my book *The Catholic Church and Politics in Brazil, 1916–1985*, and it appears here with the permission of the publishers, Stanford University Press. Copyright © 1986 by the Board of Trustees of the Leland Stanford Junior University. I am grateful to Renato Paul Boschi, Richard Fagen, Daniel Levine, Guillermo O'Donnell, Robert Packenham, Donald Share, and Eduardo Viola for their suggestions on this chapter.

1. Among the best studies are Brian H. Smith, *The Church and Politics in Chile: Challenges to Modern Catholicism* (Princeton: Princeton University Press, 1982); Daniel H. Levine, *Religion and Politics in Latin America: The Catholic Church in Venezuela and Colombia* (Princeton: Princeton University Press, 1981); Thomas C. Bruneau, *The Political Transformation of the Brazilian Catholic Church* (New York: Cambridge University Press, 1974); and Bruneau, *The Church in Brazil: The Politics of Religion* (Austin: University of Texas Press, 1982).

2. D. Sebastião Leme, *Carta Pastoral a Olinda* (Petrópolis: Vozes, 1916).

3. Among other discussions on the CEBs, see Thomas C. Bruneau, "Basic Christian Communities in Latin America: Their Nature and Significance (Especially in Brazil)," in Daniel H. Levine, ed., *Churches and Politics in Latin America* (Beverly Hills: Sage, 1980), pp. 111–34; Frei Betto, *O que é comunidade eclesial de base* (São Paulo: Brasiliense, 1981); Clodovis Boff, *Comunidade eclesial, comunidade política* (Petrópolis: Vozes, 1979); Cândido Procópio Ferreira de Camargo et al., "Comunidades eclesiais de base," in Paul Singer and Vinicius Caldeira Brant, eds., *São Paulo: O povo em movimento* (Petrópolis: Vozes/CEBRAP, 1980); Affonso Felippe Gregory and Maria Ghisleni, *Chances e desafios das comunidades eclesiais de base* (Petrópolis: Vozes, 1979); Sergio Torres and John Eagleson, eds., *The Challenge of Basic Christian Communities* (Maryknoll: Orbis Books, 1981); Faustino Luiz Coutro Teixeira, "Comunidade eclesial de base: Elementos explicativos de sua gênese" (M.A. thesis, Pontifícia Universidade Católica of Rio de Janeiro, 1982). Despite the importance of the base communities, reflections on their significance by social scientists have been limited.

4. Among the earliest discussions of base communities are Bernardo Leers, "A Estrutura do Culto Dominical na Zona Rural," *Revista da Conferência dos Religiosos do Brasil* 99 (September 1963): 521–34; Antônio Rolim, "O Culto Dominical e os Religiosos," *Revista da Conferência dos Religiosos do Brasil* 100 (October 1963): 631–36; Raimundo Caramuru de Barros, *Comunidade eclesial de base: Uma Opção pastoral decisiva* (Petrópolis: Vozes, 1968); José Marins, *A comunidade eclesial de base* (São Paulo:

N.p., n.d., ca. 1968); José Comblin, "Comunidades eclesiais e pastoral urbana," *Revista Eclesiástica Brasileira* 30 (December 1970): 783–828.

5. I discuss the church's transformation at length in *The Catholic Church and Politics in Brazil, 1916–1985* (Stanford: Stanford University Press, 1985).

6. Conselho Episcopal Latinoamericano, *A Igreja na atual transformação da América Latina* (Petrópolis: Vozes, 1969), C. 15, para. 10–12.

7. Leonardo Boff, *Eclesiogênese: As comunidades eclesiais de base reinventam a igreja* (Petrópolis: Vozes, 1977).

8. On the theology and religious practices emerging from the CEBs, see Leonardo Boff, "As eclesiologias presentes nas comunidades eclesiais de base," in *Uma Igreja que Nasce do Povo* (Petrópolis: Vozes, 1977), pp. 201–9; Carlos Mesters, "A Brisa Leve, uma nova leitura da Bíblia," *SEDOC* 11 (January–February 1979): 733–65; Leonardo Boff, *Igreja: Carisma e poder* (Petrópolis: Vozes, 1981), pp. 196–212; Carlos Mesters, "Interpretação da Bíblia em algumas comunidades eclesiais de base no Brasil," *Concilium* 158 (1980); Marie-Dominique Chenu, "A nova consciência do fundamento trinitário da igreja," *Concilium* 166 (1981): 21–31; Almir Ribeiro Guimarães, *Comunidades de base no Brasil* (Petrópolis: Vozes, 1978), pp. 34–39, 117–215.

9. Conselho Episcopal Latinoamericano, *Puebla: A Evangelicacão no presente e no futuro da America Latina* (Petrópolis: Vozes, 1980), para. 629.

10. On this point, see Daniel Levine's article on Colombia in this volume.

11. I discuss the contributions and limitations of Brazilian CEBs in creating a more democratic political order in "The Catholic Church, Popular Education, and Political Change in Brazil," *Journal of Inter-American Studies and World Affairs* 26 (February 1984): 97–124. See also the commentaries on this article by Daniel Levine, Phillip Berryman, and Michael Dodson.

12. On Chile, see the article by Brian Smith in this volume. On Central America, in addition to the articles in this volume by Michael Dodson and Phillip Berryman, see Jorge Cáceres et al., *Iglesia, política y profecía* (San José: Editorial Universitaria Centroamericana, 1983). On the role of the churches in the Nicaraguan revolution, see Michael Dodson and Tommie Sue Montgomery, "The Churches in the Nicara-guan Revolution," in Thomas W. Walker, ed., *Nicaragua in Revolution* (New York: Praeger, 1982), 161–80. On the church's role in El Salvador, see Tommie Sue Montgomery, *Revolution in El Salvador* (Boulder, Colo.: Westview Press, 1982), pp. 97–118; and Jorge Cáceres Prendes, "Radicalización política y pastoral popular en El Salvador, 1969–1979," *Revista ECSA* 33 (1983): 93–153.

13. Data are from the official census.

14. On the development of Nova Iguaçu, see Leda Lúcia Queiroz, "Movimentos sociais urbanos: O Movimento Amigos de Bairros de Nova Iguaçu" (M.A. thesis, COPPE, 1981), chap. 2.

15. The population of Rio grew from 1,157,873 in 1920 to 1,764,141 in 1940; 3,281,908 in 1960; 4,251,918 in 1970; and 5,183,992 in 1980. Real estate prices in Rio increased 3.76 times in real terms between 1957 and 1976 (Conferência Nacional dos Bispos do Brasil, "Solo Urbano e Ação Pastoral," *Documentos da CNBB* 23 [São Paulo: Paulinas, 1982], p. 8). The expansion of the favela population outstripped the overall population growth, increasing, according to one estimate, from 57,889 in 1933 to 965,000 in 1961 (Fundação Leão XIII, *Favelas: Um Compromisso que Vamos Resgatar*

[Rio de Janeiro: Estado da Guanabara, 1962]). Today there are about 1.8 million favela dwellers according to estimates of the archdiocese of Rio. The figures can be debated, but the trend they suggest is clear.

16. Instituto Brasileiro de Geografia e Estatística, *Censo 1970*. For a socioeconomic profile of the Baixada Fluminense's population, see Cristina Saliby et al., "A política de habitação popular: Suas consequências sobre a população proletária do Grande Rio" (manuscript, Rio de Janeiro, 1977). The urban problems of Nova Iguaçu are not totally unlike those of the peripheral areas of greater São Paulo. For a discussion of São Paulo's recent development and urban problems, see Cândido Procópio Ferreira de Camargo et al., *São Paulo 1975: Crescimento e pobreza* (São Paulo: Loyola, 1976); Lúcio Kowarick, *A Espoliação urbana* (Rio de Janeiro: Paz e Terra, 1980); and Manoel Tosta Berlinck, *Marginalidade social e relações de classe em São Paulo* (Petrópolis: Vozes, 1975).

17. Movimento Amigos do Bairro, "Primeiro ciclo de debates populares do MAB" (mimeo, November 1980); 1980 census.

18. Quieroz, "Movimentos sociais urbanos," p. 79.

19. Movimento de Amigos de Bairro, "Primeiro ciclo de debates populares" (mimeo, 1980).

20. On the transportation situation, see Pastoral Operária de Nova Iguaçu, "A Condução do Trabalhador," in Carlos Rodrigues Brandão, ed., *A Pesquisa Participante* (São Paulo: Brasiliense, 1982), pp. 63–85. In the late 1970s, workers destroyed several trains in their rage over the constant delays and the maimings and deaths resulting from accidents. See José Alvaro Moisés and Verena Martinez Alier, "A revolta dos suburbanos ou 'Patrão, O Trem Atrasou,'" in José Alvaro Moisés et al., *Contradições urbanas e movimentos sociais* (Rio de Janeiro: Paz e Terra/CEDEC, 1978), pp. 13–64.

21. See Queiroz, "Movimentos sociais urbanos," chap. 2, on the pre-1974 popular mobilizations.

22. Maria Helena Moreira Alves, "The Formation of the National Security State: The State and the Opposition in Military Brazil" (Ph.D. dissertation, Massachusetts Institute of Technology, 1982), p. 500.

23. On the MDB in Rio de Janeiro after 1964, see Eli Diniz, *Voto e máquina política: Patronagem e clientelismo no Rio de Janeiro* (Rio de Janeiro: Paz e Terra, 1982).

24. In 1974, the top MDB candidate for federal deputy had 47,929 votes compared to 22,862 for the top ARENA candidate; the top MDB candidate for state deputy had 19,917 votes, compared to 9,974 for the top ARENA candidate; and the MDB candidate for federal senator outpolled the ARENA candidate by 99,628 to 43,352. Election coverage and data are found in *Correio da Lavoura* no. 2299 (November 16–17, 1974). In 1978, the MDB won 118,774 votes for federal senator and ARENA got 72,942 (*Jornal do Brasil*, 16 May 1982).

25. See the "Entrevista com D. Adriano," *Revista de Cultura Vozes* 75 (January–February 1981), for an introduction to Dom Adriano's perception of the church and politics. See also the interview with Dom Adriano in *SEDOC* 11 (November 1978): 496–511.

26. Information on the diocese's development came from interviews and from diocesan publications such as the annual *Plano Pastoral da Diocese de Nova Iguaçu* and

O Povo de Deus Assume a Caminhada (Petrópolis: Vozes/IDAC, 1983). Interviews with Dom Adriano Hypólito, the director of Cáritas Diocesana, a member of the Peace and Justice Commission, one of founders of the Pastoral Workers Commission, and an adviser to the Pastoral Workers Commission, were especially helpful on this subject. Also see Ivo Lesbaupin, "Direitos humanos e classes populares" (M.A. thesis, IUPERJ, 1982), pp. 16–19, on the Nova Iguaçu church.

27. An abundant literature is emerging on the liberalization process. My own views of the *abertura* are developed in two articles, both of which make reference to most of the literature. See Eduardo Viola and Scott Mainwaring, "Transitions to Democracy: Brazil and Argentina in the 1980s," *Journal of International Affairs* 38 (Winter 1985): 193–219; and Donald Share and Scott Mainwaring, "Transitions through Transaction: Democratization in Brazil and Spain," in Wayne Selcher, ed., *Political Liberalization in Brazil: Dynamics, Dilemmas, and Prospects* (Boulder, Colo.: Westview Press, forthcoming).

28. On the Cost of Living Movement, see Tilman Evers, "Os movimentos sociais urbanos: O caso do 'Movimento Custo de Vida,'" in José Alvaro Moisés et al., *Alternativas populares da democracia* (Petrópolis: Vozes/CEDEC, 1982), pp. 73–98. On the new labor movement, see José Alvaro Moisés, "Qual é a estratégia do novo sindicalismo?" in ibid., pp. 11–40; José Alvaro Moisés, "Current Issues in the Labor Movement in Brazil," *Latin American Perspectives* 6 (Fall 1979): 71–89; John Humphrey, *Capitalist Control and Workers' Struggle in the Brazilian Auto Industry* (Princeton: Princeton University Press, 1982); Maria Hermínia Tavares de Almeida, "Tendências recentes de negociação coletiva no Brasil," *Dados* 24 (1981): 161–89; Ronaldo Munck, "The Labor Movement and the Crisis of the Dictatorship," in Thomas Bruneau and Philippe Faucher, eds., *Authoritarian Capitalism: Brazil's Contemporary Economic and Political Development* (Boulder, Colo.: Westview Press, 1981), pp. 219–38. A fine overview of a number of social movements in São Paulo is Singer and Brant, eds., *São Paulo*.

29. Some of these incidents are discussed in the introduction to the "Entrevista com D. Adriano," *Revista de Cultura Vozes* 75 (January–February 1981). See also *Revista Eclesiástica Brasileira* 40 (March 1980): 177–82.

30. I use the term "popular neighborhood movements" rather than the more common "urban social movements" because it is more specific. Urban social movements encompass a wide range of middle-class activities, such as ecological movements, efforts to obtain better facilities from the state, and attempts to develop community resources such as athletic facilities. Some intellectuals who have studied urban social movements (Manuel Castells, Jordi Borja) have emphasized the transformative potential of all these movements. Although there is some possibility that the demands of the middle and popular sectors will lead them to join together to confront the state, in the Third World context it is equally likely that the middle strata and popular classes will desire different urban services.

In the past few years urban social movements have received significant attention. The works of Europeans Manuel Castells, Jean Lojkine, and Jordi Borja were seminal in reassessing these movements. By Castells, see *Movimientos sociales urbanos* (Mexico City: Siglo XXI, 1974) and *Cidade, democracia e socialismo* (Rio de Janeiro: Paz e Terra, 1980). Borja's most influential work is *Movimientos sociales urbanos* (Buenos Aires:

Siap, 1975). By Lojkine, see *Le Marxisme, l'etat et la question urbaine* (Paris: Presses Universitaires de France, 1977) and *La politique urbaine dans la region parisienne, 1945–1971* (Paris: Mouton, 1972). A fine critique of Castells's work is Paul Singer, "Urbanizacão, dependência e marginalização na América Latina," in Singer, *Economia política da urbanização* (São Paulo: Brasiliense, 1977). In this vein, see also Luiz Antônio Machado da Silva and Alícia Ziccardi, "Notas para uma discussão sobre movimentos sociais urbanos," *Cadernos do Centro de Estudos Rurais e Urbanos* 1st ser., 13 (1980): 79–95. Much of the Brazilian discussion has suffered from the same theoretical problems. Important critical contributions are Renato Boschi, "Movimentos sociais e a institucionalização de uma ordem" (Rio de Janeiro: IUPERJ, 1983); Renato Boschi, ed., *Movimentos coletivos no Brasil urbano* (Rio de Janeiro: Zahar, 1983); José Alvaro Moisés, "Classes populares e protesto urbano" (Ph.D. dissertation, Universidade de São Paulo, 1978); José Alvaro Moisés, "Experiências de mobilização popular em São Paulo," *Contraponto* 3, no. 3 (1978): 69–86; Paul Singer, "Movimentos de bairro," and "Movimentos sociais em São Paulo: Traços comuns e perspectivas," in Singer and Brant, eds., *São Paulo*, pp. 83–108 and 207–30; Anna Luiza Souto, "Movimentos populares urbanos e suas formas de organização ligadas à igreja" (paper, Rio de Janeiro, 1979); Ruth Cardoso, "Movimentos sociais urbanos: Balanco critico," in Sebastião Velasco e Cruz et al., *Sociedade e política no Brasil Pos-64* (São Paulo: Brasiliense, 1983), pp. 215–39.

31. The history of the neighborhood movement presented in this section draws extensively on Queiroz, "Movimentos sociais urbanos," even though my interpretation of the movement differs significantly from hers. Other information comes from extensive interviews with movement and church leaders; the movement's newspaper, *Encontro*; and the Nova Iguaçu newspaper, *O Correio da Lavoura*.

32. On the connection between this health work and the early development of the neighborhood movement, see Estrella Bohadana, "Experiências de participação popular em Ações de Saúde," in IBASE, *Saúde e Trabalho no Brasil* (Petrópolis: Vozes/IBASE, 1982), pp. 107–28.

33. *Encontro* 2 (March 1976).

34. *Encontro* 11 (November 1977).

35. *Encontro* 12 (January 1978).

36. On this phase of MAB's development, with more detailed information on the assembly, see *Encontro* 15 (July 1978) and 16 (October 1978).

37. On the party reform, see Thomas Sanders, "Brazil in 1980: The Emerging Political Model," in Bruneau and Faucher, eds., *Authoritarian Capitalism*, pp. 193–218; Robert Wesson and David Fleischer, *Brazil in Transition* (New York: Praeger, 1983), pp. 108–20. There is an extensive body of literature on parties and elections in the post-1974 period. See, among others, Bolivar Lamounier and Fernando Henrique Cardoso, eds., *Os partidos e as eleições no Brasil* (Rio de Janeiro: Paz e Terra, 1978); and Bolivar Lamounier, ed., *Voto de Desconfiança: Eleições e Mudança Política no Brasil, 1970–1979* (Petrópolis: Vozes/CEBRAP, 1980).

38. 27 September 1981.

39. *Correio da Lavoura*, 24 December 1982.

40. Interview, 21 January 1985.

41. Interview, 3 July 1981.

42. One of the strongest statements that the popular movements are still dependent on church support is Luiz Gonzaga Souza Lima, "Notas sobre as comunidades eclesiais de base e a organização política," in Moisés et al., *Alternativas populares da democracia*, pp. 41–73.

43. Interview, 3 July 1981.

44. Interview, 1 June 1981.

45. Interview, 2 June 1981. He refers to peasants because he lived in a rural part of the municipality until 1974.

46. On the political limitations and religious primacy of Brazilian CEBs, see J. B. Libânio, "Uma comunidade que se redefine," *SEDOC* 9 (October 1976): 295–326; Leonardo Boff, "Teologia à escuta do povo," *Revista Eclesiástica Brasileira* 41 (March 1981): 55–119; Frei Betto, *O que é comunidade eclesial de base*; J. B. Libânio, "Igreja—povo oprimido que se organiza para a libertação," *Revista Eclesiástica Brasileira* 41 (June 1981): 279–311; Paulo Cézar Loureiro Botas, "Aí! Que Saudades do Tempo em que o Terço Resolvia Tudo," *Tempo e Presença* 26 (March 1980): 3–10.

47. Interview, 26 June 1981.

48. Interview, 27 March 1981.

49. Interview, 18 May 1981.

50. The leadership of most popular movements has been closely linked to one political current or another, so the political conceptions of the parties, the left, and the ecclesial sectors involved in working with the popular classes have a major impact on the direction of these movements. It is impossible fully to understand the popular movements or the left without analyzing the linkages between them.

51. Interview, 12 September 1981.

52. On this point, see Antônio Ivo de Carvalho, "Saúde e Educação de Base: Algumas notas," *Proposta* 3 (December 1976): 19–33; Cristiano Camerman and Estrella Bohadana, "O Agente Externo na Favela" (paper, Rio de Janeiro, 1981); and Anthony and Elizabeth Leeds, *A Sociologia do Brasil Urbano* (Rio de Janeiro: Zahar, 1978), esp. pp. 26–52, 264–88. This observation is not unique to the popular classes in Brazil. A classic tenet of some strains of liberal political theory is the difficulty of getting people to participate in collective movements. See Mancur Olson, *The Logic of Collective Action* (Cambridge, Mass.: Harvard University Press, 1965).

53. Interview, 19 September 1981. For written criticisms of the church by different sectors of the left, see Queiroz, "Movimentos sociais urbanos"; Roberto Romano, *Brasil: Igreja contra Estado (Crítica ao Populismo Católico)* (São Paulo: Kairos, 1979); Ricardo Abramovay, "Marxistas e Cristãos: Pontos para um Diálogo," *Proposta* 16 (March 1981): 11–20; Vanilda Paiva, "Anotações para um Estudo sobre Populismo Católico e Educação Popular," in Vanilda Paiva, ed., *Perspectivas y dilemas da educação popular* (Rio de Janeiro: Graal, 1984), pp. 227–66; Octávio Guilherme Velho, "A Propósito de Terra e Igreja," *Encontros com a Civilização Brasileira* 22 (April 1980): 157–68.

54. Much of the literature on the urban social movements has been excessively optimistic about their capacity to promote social change. Recently a more critical literature has emphasized the limited nature and cyclical character of these movements. See Boschi, "Movimentos sociais e a institucionalização de uma Ordem"; Cardoso, "Movimentos sociais urbanos"; Renato Raul Boschi and Lícia do Prado

Valladares, "Movimentos Associativos de Camadas Populares Urbanas: Análise comparativa de seis casos," in Boschi, ed., *Movimentos coletivos no Brasil urbano,* pp. 103–43; Singer, "Movimentos de bairros" and "Movimentos sociais em São Paulo"; Fernando Henrique Cardoso, "Regime político e mudança social," *Revista de Cultura e Politica* 3 (November 1980–January 1981): 7–25. On a more theoretical level, see Albert Hirschman, *Shifting Involvements: Private Interest and Public Action* (Princeton: Princeton University Press, 1982); and Frances Fox Piven and Richard Cloward, *Poor People's Movements: Why They Succeed, How They Fail* (New York: Pantheon, 1977).

55. Some of this diversity in the relationship between the church and popular movements is apparent in the different studies in Boschi, ed., *Movimentos coletivos no Brasil urbano.*

56. Frei Betto, "Da prática da pastoral popular," *Encontros com a Civilização Brasileira* 2 (1978): 104, 95. On this point, see also Frei Betto, "Prática pastoral e prática política," *Tempo e Presença* 26 (March 1980): 11–29; Clodovis Boff, *Teologia e prática* (Petrópolis: Vozes, 1978).

57. See Herbert Lepargneur, *Teologia da libertação: Uma Avaliação* (São Paulo: Convívio, 1979); Boaventura Kloppenburg, *A igreja popular* (Rio de Janeiro: Agir, 1983); D. Eugênio Sales, "Comunidades eclesiais de base," *Boletim da Revista do Clero* 19 (September 1982): 20–33; D. Karl Josef Romer, "Por que o Livro de L. Boff, *Igreja: Carisma e Poder,* não é Aceitável," *Boletim da Revista do Clero* 19 (April 1982): 30–36.

58. This situation was anticipated in the prescient article by Ralph Della Cava, "Política a Curto Prazo e Religião a Longo Prazo," *Encontros com a Civilização Brasileira* 1 (July 1978): 242–58.

8

Chile: Deepening the Allegiance of Working-Class Sectors to the Church in the 1970s

Brian H. Smith

Since the Second Vatican Council (1962–65), at the official level Catholicism has emphasized renewing the internal spiritual life of the church by bringing it closer to the people and expanding its role of service to the secular world. The first goal has entailed a greater focus on the communitarian as opposed to juridical aspects of the church, more attention to biblical themes in catechesis and liturgical prayer, celebration of sacramental rites in the vernacular, and a call to lay persons and religious to play a greater role in the process of evangelization. The second has involved increased engagement by the church, especially through its lower clergy, religious, and lay leaders, in contemporary social problems such as poverty, injustice, racism, war, and violations of human rights.

As mentioned in the introduction to this volume, the bishops of Latin America in the post–Vatican II era have affirmed for the church in their region both of these dimensions of renewal—increased expression of vital faith among rank-and-file Catholics and more effective engagement by church members in public moral problems. In so doing, and because of the context of Latin America, these official commitments of the hierarchy at Medellín (1968) and Puebla (1979) moved the church closer to the popular classes—workers, peasants, urban slum dwellers, and indigenous peoples. These groups constitute the majority of Catholics and of the total population throughout Latin America (more than 65 percent), but historically, a lack of sufficient clergy and a close identification of the church with the middle and upper classes have kept them from being at the center of the church's pastoral attention. Moreover, these groups have borne the brunt of economic and political repression under military regimes that came to power throughout Central and South America in the late 1960s and early 1970s.

The clergy's attempt to be faithful to the spirit of Vatican II and thus make the church a more vital religious and social force in the lives of the majority of those under its pastoral care has led several national episcopal conferences in Latin America over the past fifteen years to adopt new pastoral strategies focused on the formation of small ecclesial base communities (*comunidades eclesiales de base*—CEBs) among the urban and rural poor. These groups (varying in membership from twenty to fifty persons) are predominantly led by nuns or by lay women or men (because of the continuing lack of clergy throughout the continent) and concentrate on deepening the understanding and the commitment of working-class Catholics with little formal contact with the church. Activities include reading and reflection on the Bible, shared prayer, preparation of adults and children for reception of the sacraments, in-depth group discussion on the relevance and application of biblical themes and symbols for contemporary social problems, and, flowing from this, some form of action to improve the socioeconomic situation of the local neighborhood or region. Hence the term "popular religion" in Latin America is taking on a new significance—it refers both to the traditional forms of personalistic and otherworldly oriented piety that continue to predominate and to a new spirituality that is biblical and communitarian, more closely linked with the structures and sacramental life of the church, and focused on the promotion of social justice. In fact, in some parts of Latin America (especially Central America) the term "popular church" now refers precisely to the new grass-roots communities among the poor that are growing in numbers and led predominantly by nonclerical personnel.

The new ecclesial base communities still affect only a small percentage of baptized Catholics in these popular classes in Latin America—certainly fewer than 20 percent. The vast majority of poor have not yet been exposed to the new pastoral strategies and continue to practice the traditional forms of popular religion, as is demonstrated in the chapter in this volume by Susan Rosales Nelson. The new CEBs, however, have been growing in countries where the political context has been characterized by insurrection, repression, or rapid social transformation—namely, Central America and the subcontinental region. In such contexts, their importance for both church and society goes far beyond their numbers because they frequently have been a critical focal point of social and political activity.

In Central America, for example, as both Berryman and Dodson illustrate, lay leaders trained in the CEBs have been an important source of recruits for revolutionary movements attempting to overthrow repressive governments (Nicaragua under Somoza, El Salvador, and Guatemala). As I have written elsewhere (and as Bruneau confirms for Brazil in his chapter), in several military regimes in the subcontinental region in the 1970s (Brazil, Chile, Bolivia, and Paraguay) new pastoral programs among the urban and rural poor rapidly expanded their social activities with the support of the national and international church in an effort to blunt the worst effects of economic and political repression. They established legal aid, health and nutrition services, and self-help employment projects when other private institutions (political parties, labor unions, neighborhood organizations) no longer were allowed to function, when abuses of human rights were at their height, and when government services were cut back.[1] In Allende's Chile and in post-revolutionary Nicaragua, CEBs, though few in number, provided some of the most important attempts to forge a practical synthesis between Christian faith and socialist political and economic commitments.[2]

Although such activities have made the church more credible and important in the eyes of many of the poor in these societies, they have also created some serious conflicts between the church and dominant economic and political elites. Military leaders have accused the church of allowing its new pastoral programs among the poor to be manipulated by leftist subversives, and persecution of CEBs has led to the disappearance and death of many recently trained lay leaders and the expulsion of many foreign clergy. Upper-income Catholics are scandalized by what they consider to be a distortion of religious faith in base communities and are withdrawing their support for, and participation in, the church.

Many Latin American bishops and the Vatican (as manifested in parts of the Puebla document, some statements by Pope John Paul II during his 1983 trip through Central America, and criticisms of Liberation Theology in 1984 by the Congregation for the Doctrine of the Faith) have become concerned because they feel the CEBs have become too intensely involved in social action. They are worried that the religious activities (prayer, Bible study, preparation for and participation in the sacraments) are being neglected or becoming too heavily politicized. Some groups in the new nonclerical popular church (especially in Central America) have openly criticized their bishops for not sufficiently disassociating the church from the old economic and political order and also for not allowing the emerging base communities greater voice in church decisions. The values prevalent in some of these base communities involve options for democracy and pluralism within the church, tendencies that are in conflict with patterns of vertical authority and formal unity at the core of church tradition.

Hence the new dimensions of popular religion in Latin America (although still involving only a minority) are creating serious problems for the church both in its external relations with secular powers and in its internal life among different sectors of its membership and across leadership echelons. These tensions are underlaid by differences of opinion both about the legitimacy and impact of the church's new public role on behalf of equity and human rights and about the meaning of religious symbols, authority, and practices in a period of rapid adaptation. The perennial mission of the church to preach and make the gospel credible and to offer the sacramental means of salvation to all regardless of nationality or class has not changed. Nor has its essentially hierarchical nature. What is changing (and has changed on occasion historically) are the means it chooses to achieve its religious and moral goals. When its strategies are shifting (as they are now in Latin America), the church's relations with different groups in society also often change—angering some and pleasing others, depending on whose self-interests are involved. Moreover, questions of legitimate adaptation of faith expression and pastoral responsibility arise within the institution among those concerned with preserving continuity with its tradition.

The rest of this chapter will examine both dimensions of change precipitated by the church's new pastoral activities among the popular classes—their impact on the church's relations with different political and economic forces in society and their consequences for the internal religious life of the church itself. The Chilean church during the 1970s will be the focus for analyzing these issues because it has undertaken major efforts to create ecclesial base communities among the poor in two very different social contexts—the democratic regime of Salvador Allende (1970–73), which attempted a constitutional transition to socialism, and the subsequent military regime (1973–), which is characterized by severe political and economic measures whose brunt has been borne most heavily by the working-class population.

Pastoral Strategies in the Late 1960s and Early 1970s

Although the Chilean church from the 1930s had one of the most well-developed Catholic Action programs in Latin America, the membership was predominantly middle class, and working-class culture was never adequately penetrated. The vast majority of Chileans (especially the poor), as in other parts of Latin America, continued to practice traditional forms of popular piety and had little contact with the institutional church. Even Catholic Action programs were declining in Chile in the late 1960s because they had become closely tied with the Christian Democratic party (PDC) during its rise to power, and many members had vacated Catholic Action to join the PDC or enter the government after the election of its candidate, Eduardo Frei, to the presidency in 1964. Moreover, although the PDC undertook reformist programs to promote more equitable distribution of resources in favor of working-class sectors, these did not fulfill the rising expectations of the poor. By the late 1960s, the left was arguing for a stronger national commitment to restructure economic and political institutions on behalf of the poor and on that basis gained ground in electoral politics, especially among low-income sectors.

For all of these reasons, by the end of the decade the bishops decided on a new strategy that was designed to evangelize more effectively vast numbers of nominal Catholics (particularly in the working classes), who previously had been on the margins of church life; develop among them a spirituality more in tune with the times that would include an ongoing commitment to work for social justice; recruit new cadres of leaders into positions of responsibility for the local churches, which were badly lacking in clerical leadership; and remain sufficiently independent of political parties to avoid the identification of church apostolates with the fate of any political movement.[3] In 1969 they authorized a program of decentralization of church structures into smaller units operating at the neighborhood level. These ecclesial base communities (CEBs) were to be small in membership (ranging from twenty to fifty), relatively homogeneous in social composition, and oriented toward biblical study, prayer, and sacramental worship, but were also to serve the social and economic needs of the secular community in which they were located.[4] They were to be guided and led by nuns and lay leaders because of the chronic shortage of clerics, which was exacerbated by a new exodus from the priesthood that began after Vatican II in 1965.

Significant as this new development in pastoral planning was, the lack of trained personnel, chronically weak allegiances to the institutional church by the majority of the poor, and long-ingrained patterns of popular piety made rapid creation of these base communities difficult. Moreover, the heightened politicization of Chilean society as the 1970 election approached and in the early 1970s when the Popular Unity (UP) government was in power further complicated the church's efforts to generate new forms of religious participation among the working classes.

After its election in September 1970, the Allende administration placed no official obstacles in the way of the church's evangelization efforts. There was, however, an intensification of mobilization efforts by all political parties between 1968 and 1973, and politics took on an all-pervading importance in the lives of Chileans. The parties of the left (Communist, Socialist, Movement of Popular Unitary Action, Christian Left) and Center (Christian Democratic, Radical) often held mass rallies and conducted neighborhood meetings on Sundays—the only nonworking day in the week for most Chileans (especially in the working classes)—or evenings. These were the precise times the new base communities inaugurated by the church were holding their sessions, which made it more difficult for the growing number of people with political commitments to participate in church activities as well.

Attendance at Sunday mass fell off dramatically during the Allende years, dropping from 32 percent attending once a month or more in Santiago in 1970 to 20 percent in 1973, and the new base communities that focused on Bible study, catechetics, small group prayer, and training of new lay leaders also attracted very few participants.[5] Moreover, because the Allende administration provided social services in health, nutrition, education, and employment for the working classes, there was no need for new church programs in these areas and the community-service dimension of base communities (as envisioned in the hierarchy's 1969 guidelines) remained underdeveloped during the Popular Unity years.

Many of the new base communities that did begin to function in the early 1970s, however, were quickly drawn into the vortex of partisan politics as they have been in postrevolutionary Nicaragua. The participants in small group discussion and Bible study programs often engaged in political debate among themselves and openly clashed with one another over the merits and problems of the UP government.[6] In some cases priests in working-class areas sympathetic to the objectives of the Allende administration—especially those involved in the Christians for Socialism (Cristianos por el Socialismo, CpS) movement[7]—made explicit efforts to raise the political awareness of participants in the base communities and demanded that the members make an active commitment to the transition to socialism and to parties of the left. Some of these clerics (and others in the group called "the 200") also publicly called for a new church, less controlled by the hierarchy (whom they criticized repeatedly for not backing the Allende government more fully), led by married priests and laity, centered on semi-independent base communities, and closely linked with secular organizations working for socialist objectives.[8]

Although few lay people were involved in these politically active base communities because small numbers in the working classes participated in any church programs during these years, these groups along with the CpS movement and "the 200" received much publicity during the early 1970s for their efforts to create a new church and to forge a synthesis of Christianity and Marxism. They were publicly praised by party leaders of the left (and by Allende himself) as an indication that religious believers and secular agnostics shared many humanistic values and could work together for common political and economic goals. Thus the social context gave an importance to such minority groups of Christians far beyond what their members would indicate.

These new pastoral strategies, especially the actions of CpS, eventually angered the majority of the hierarchy (as has happened in similar circumstances more recently in Nicaragua) because of what the bishops considered to be an explicitly sectarian (exclusive in membership) and partisan political emphasis. In April 1973 the bishops decided to prepare a statement criticizing the CpS movement. In a document outlining their misgivings (released in October 1973), the bishops explicitly condemned the practices of making base communities ideologically exclusive in membership and of linking them closely to politically partisan movements and programs and charged them with undermining episcopal authority. The main argument of the bishops was theological—namely, that the religious mission of the church was to all groups, and any effort to identify the church or its religious symbols with only one social or political line was a distortion of its universal mission and its transcendent spiritual message. They also argued that public and repeated criticism of the bishops from groups within the church threatened its unity and tradition and exceeded legitimate boundaries of pastoral adaptation at the local level.[9]

Thus throughout the late 1960s and early 1970s, despite new commitments by leaders of the institutional church to bring its programs and services closer to the daily lives of its nominal members in the working classes, base communities remained nascent. A combination of societal cross-pressures and a lack of felt need among the vast majority of the poor made it difficult for the church to create new religiously and socially vital evangelization programs in low-income areas. Many of the base communities that did begin to function rapidly moved in a direction frowned upon by the hierarchy, and some, along with several clerical leaders, were ultimately condemned by the hierarchy for not fulfilling the religious objectives of CEBs in continuity with church tradition.

New Church-Sponsored Social Programs at the National and Local Levels during the Military Regime

After the military coup in September 1973 churches were the only institutions allowed to function openly with any degree of relative freedom. Congress, the courts, political parties, labor unions, schools, universities, civic associations, and the media were either closed or placed under strict government surveillance. Moreover, during the first months after the coup the military carried out massive arbitrary arrests, conducted summary executions, and engaged in systematic torture of prisoners. Churches became the only places persons could go to seek protection or aid, and they almost immediately began a series of emergency humanitarian programs.[10]

As during the Allende years, new grass-roots church communities took on an importance far beyond their strictly religious significance. After 1973, however, with the aid of newly created church organizations at the national and regional levels, they became surrogates for other institutions and services no longer operational in secular society, thus attracting many more participants than during the previous regime. For these reasons, the church itself eventually came under heavy fire by supporters of the government.

Within a month of the coup a united ecumenical effort of Catholic, Lutheran, Methodist, Baptist, and Greek orthodox churches and Jewish synagogues was under way to coordinate relief services for the persecuted. In September leaders from these churches and synagogues established the National Committee to Aid Refugees (Comité Nacional para la Ayuda de los Refugiados, CONAR) with assistance from the United Nations High Commission on Refugees. By February 1974, CONAR had helped approximately five thousand foreigners (who had come to Chile during the Allende years as a haven of freedom from repressive regimes in other parts of Latin America) to leave Chile safely.

In early October, representatives from these various denominations inaugurated the Committee of Cooperation for Peace (Comité por la Paz Chilena, COPACHI) in Santiago under the copresidency of Lutheran bishop Helmut Frenz (a German citizen) and Catholic auxiliary bishop of Santiago Fernando Ariztía. COPACHI's purpose was to provide legal aid to prisoners and workers arbitrarily dismissed from their jobs and social and economic aid to families of both these groups of Chileans. Over the next several months, with monetary assistance from the World Council of Churches in Geneva arranged by Bishop Frenz, local offices or representatives of COPACHI were established in twenty-two of twenty-five provinces of the country to offer the same services in their regions as were provided by the headquarters in Santiago.

From October 1973 through December 1975 COPACHI initiated legal actions for more than seven thousand persons in Santiago alone who were detained, tried, or had disappeared. Its members also defended more than six thousand workers dismissed from their jobs for political reasons. It was successful in gaining reduced sentences for many who were actually brought to trial (a small minority of those in prison or who had disappeared), as well as compensation for countless numbers peremptorily fired.[11] It also collected information through interviews and visits to jails on the extent and nature of human rights violations and prepared detailed reports for major religious leaders on these abuses. Such reports also reached the outside world and helped substantiate denunciations of the Chilean government by international political organizations and the foreign media for very serious violations of human rights.

During 1974 the political repression became institutionalized with the establishment of a secret police organization (DINA), which administered torture houses. In addition, the model of economic recovery continued to exact a high price from the poor.[12] In this context of growing political and economic repression, COPACHI expanded its services. It provided technical and financial assistance to 126 small self-help enterprises and 10 rural cooperatives. In Santiago it supported a series of social services closely linked with, or operated by, the church's network of base communities—health clinics, soup kitchens for children, cottage industries, youth clubs, and rehabilitation and counseling centers for alcoholics (whose numbers rapidly increased as unemployment soared to 18.7 percent in Santiago by 1975).[13]

Thus in addition to new social programs coordinated or assisted by central church agencies, a series of new projects sprang up at the neighborhood level organized mainly by nuns and lay men and women active in CEBs and often supported with resources from COPACHI. These grass-roots projects attracted increasing numbers of persons to the CEBs (mostly from the working classes) who had nowhere else to go to discuss their problems frankly or to seek coordinated assistance.

Rectories, parsonages, and convents also became places of refuge for those seeking to escape arrest and torture, especially former leaders of labor union organizations and leftist parties. With the assistance of those working in COPACHI, people who were also active in CEBs enabled many hunted persons to gain political asylum in foreign embassies and leave the country unharmed.

COPACHI was closed in December 1975 under mounting government criticism that it was aiding primarily those opposed to government policies. Within days of the termination of COPACHI, in January 1976 the Catholic church set up a new organization in Santiago under its own control to carry out much the same activities as its ecumenical predecessor. It quickly established regional offices or affiliations with diocesan programs in twenty of twenty-five provinces. Over the next five years it provided services to about 900,000 Chileans (180,000 per year). On the average, 1 of every 60 persons in the country was assisted by the Vicariate of Solidarity each year from 1976 to 1980.

In light of continuing high social and economic costs imposed on workers by government-imposed recovery strategies,[14] the Vicariate of Solidarity expanded the support begun by COPACHI for local CEB-operated service programs for the poor. By 1980 in the capital city of Santiago (where one-third of the national population resides) it was assisting CEB-sponsored activities in health, nutrition, self-employment, and housing. These various services helped approximately 154,000 people, or 1 of 23 residents in the capital that year.[15]

In rural areas, where 30 percent of the land formerly part of the agrarian reform sector was returned to large landholders and 40 percent of small farmers had to sell their own land because they were unable to meet bank loan payments for fertilizer, tools, and marketing services,[16] the vicariate provided legal services for compensation to farmhands (more than 14,000 in 1980) who had been arbitrarily dismissed without severance pay. It also offered a series of training programs for rural union leaders in methods of organization and in agricultural law. In 1979 and 1980 such courses included 1,943 participants.[17]

Finally, the vicariate inaugurated a series of publications that circulated in working-class areas through church CEBs. After the coup 85 percent of the communications media in the country was bought up by government supporters (with the assistance of the government). All four television channels, thirty-five of forty radio stations, and all but one of the major weekly magazines were included in these purchases. To help offset the one-sided picture of national life presented in most of the media, the vicariate began to publish a biweekly twenty-four-page bulletin (*Solidaridad*) focusing on problems affecting the working class. Twenty thousand copies of each issue were being printed by 1980 reaching an estimated 100,000 persons (1 of every 105 persons in the country). In addition, the vicariate printed and disseminated pamphlets on topics such as the status of government investigations regarding persons who had disappeared, opinions of labor leaders on the exploitation of workers, and recent international church statements on social justice and human rights.[18]

As with its predecessor, COPACHI, the vicariate's service functions were closely linked to and administered by the network of local base communities in the church. In fact, these programs largely originated at the local level. They emerged out of CEB-sponsored meetings in which citizens formed committees, elected leaders, and decided on the most effective tactics to alleviate the worst effects of malnutrition, sickness, unemployment, and scarce housing in their neighborhoods. Vicariate of Solidarity personnel provided encouragement and technical expertise for such associations but did not dictate agenda or control the leadership.

Local residents and CEB members held regular meetings to manage the groups, while also examining the deeper causes of social and economic problems affecting their areas and discussing methods to make their efforts in confronting these problems more effective. In such sessions the various publications of the vicariate also served to inform and focus the discussions. In this way a critical consciousness was kept alive among many people in the absence of traditional political activities. Total inaction resulting from fear and apathy was avoided, and local leaders were kept from being co-opted by the government.[19]

Pastoral Activities in Base Communities since 1973

These new social service programs in the Chilean church that emerged after 1973 at both the national and local levels clearly had a positive impact on revitalizing the religious mission of the institution. The new services (some centralized but many operated through CEBs) brought thousands of Chileans into some form of contact with the church. Although almost all were baptized Catholics, the vast majority had had almost no contact with the institution for years before the coup. A large percentage of those who first volunteered in late 1973 and 1974 to work in the new nationally sponsored human rights programs were members of the middle classes with leftist sympathies. Their reassociation with the institutional church did not necessarily entail a participation in the sacraments or other religious activities, but it did signal a renewal of respect for the church and in many instances a reawakening of personal religious faith. This was especially true for many middle-class activists in parties such as the Movement of Popular Unitary Action and the Christian Left Movement.[20]

Moreover, at the neighborhood level in working-class CEBs a large percentage of church-sponsored social service programs in health, nutrition, and housing were staffed by volunteers formerly active in the Socialist or Communist parties, as well as by those in the PDC. This not only gave the leftists a new, more positive image of the institution but also brought about greater dialogue and understanding between themselves and sympathizers of center parties. Such a process of practical cooperation in humanitarian service to their neighbors, based on need rather than political affiliation, created mutual respect across party lines among working-class leaders that was sadly lacking throughout much of the Allende years. Such a mission of dialogue carried on under church auspices at the grass-roots level was not only important for the future political climate of the country if and when democracy returns but was viewed by many in the church as an essential part of its larger pastoral mission of reconciliation.[21]

Participation in the religious activities of base communities also increased after 1973. By 1975 it was estimated that there were at least twenty thousand actively committed lay members in base communities throughout the country.[22] At the time these included about ten thousand catechists who had received a two-year intensive training program in doctrine and Bible study. These catechetical leaders (mostly mothers) were in turn helping to prepare more than one hundred thousand parents to teach religion in their own homes and by so doing reached approximately four hundred thousand persons. Substantial numbers of teenagers also participated in the various programs of base communities, and by 1978 the number was over ten thousand.[23] Mass attendance (often celebrated in neighborhood chapels or other buildings in which base communities met) also dramatically increased after the coup, from 20 percent in Santiago participating once a month or more in 1973 to 42.8 percent in 1979.[24]

Moreover, many of those participating in the religious programs of the CEBs also took an active part in the nutrition, health, housing, and other community service projects affiliated with these same base communities. A survey in Santiago in 1977, for example, of 319 women engaged in several of the more than three hundred church-related soup kitchens in shantytowns found that although only 4.7 percent of those helping to prepare the food also participated in some religious activities of the local CEBs, 55.8 percent of those with top administrative responsibilities in these *comedores* were active in some religious function of the base communities.[25] Although these statistics indicated a division between those involved in social action programs and those engaged in religious work, they also showed that there was a small but significant group (especially those with leadership skills) who were combining a commitment to justice with an active religious faith—the ideal form of popular piety outlined in the documents of Medellín (1968), Puebla (1979), and the pastoral guidelines of the Chilean bishops for CEBs in 1969.

An additional sign of vitality in these base communities was the large number of nonclerics who exercised effective leadership positions. The primary responsibility for both the social and the religious activities of the CEBs fell on laity (especially women) and nuns. Prayer groups, Bible study, catechetical training, preaching, distributing the Eucharist, and officiating at weddings (by nuns) were mostly conducted by women because of the scarcity of priests and the chronically low church participation by Chilean males. Almost one-half of the approximately 5,500 nuns in Chile in 1975 were engaged in direct pastoral work in base communities, particularly in working-class areas. Because of the scarcity of priests (2,100 in Chile in 1975, or 1 for every 4,300 baptized Catholics), these sisters were given administrative responsibilities not only for local CEBs but also over entire parish territories when no clergy were in residence. By 1976, 80 of the 750 parishes throughout the country (10.7 percent of the total) were under the exclusive control of nuns and, although not ordained, they were performing priestly functions (except granting absolution for sins and saying mass).[26]

In addition, 167 married men were functioning as deacons in Chile by 1979, acting as leaders of nonsacramental worship services, administering baptism, and officiating at weddings—most of which rites were performed at the local level in CEBs. Moreover, almost all of the church-sponsored social services linked to CEBs were carried out by lay persons and sisters.

Finally, the new social and religious programs of the church that began after 1973 showed the greatest vitality in working-class areas, especially in urban shantytowns.[27] It was in these neighborhoods where government-sponsored political and economic repression was the greatest, and the church provided a haven in which many workers found the inner spiritual strength and material aid necessary to survive. For the first time in its history, the institutional church began to be socially meaningful to many nominally

Catholic workers, and, in turn, its religious message was made credible to them through its official commitment to human rights and justice.

Challenges Facing the Church as a Result of New Pastoral Strategies among the Popular Classes

As important as all of the new activities of the church were after the coup, several problems remained unresolved. These involved cultural and geographical obstacles to effecting lasting changes in the patterns of traditional piety; differences of opinion across leadership levels of the church as to the style of its new ministries; growing alienation from the church by upper-income Catholics; and church-state tensions over the political impact of the church's new social and religious programs.

Lingering Obstacles to the Formation of Base Communities

Despite the increase of middle- and working-class participation in religious activities after the coup, the vast majority of Catholics in the country by 1980 still did not participate as regular members of base communities. The estimated twenty thousand actively committed laity in CEBs in 1975 constituted a very small percentage of the baptized. Even if this twenty thousand became one hundred thousand by 1980 (a very generous extrapolation) they constituted only 1 percent of the approximately 9 million Catholics in the country.[28] Moreover, there were long-standing cultural obstacles to rapidly increasing the rate of participation in CEBs. In urban areas women and teenagers constituted the vast majority of the churches' new cadres of activists because adult men participated in much smaller proportions in these new structures. This pattern reflects a chronic cultural view prevalent in Chile (and in other Latin American countries) that religious activities are only for women and children. The lay deaconate for men helped to alter this image somewhat and offers male leadership role models that are neither clerical nor celibate. This program, however, is merely in the beginning stages (167 ordained by 1979), and it will take some time and great efforts to attract more men into the church's formal ministerial life.

Furthermore, both geographical and cultural factors in rural areas continued to present serious difficulties to the establishment of small base communities and the generation of new attitudes and behavior. The five dioceses of the far north in the desert and mining regions, as well as the three southern-most dioceses in the island and polar regions, are still considered mission areas. Clerical and religious personnel have been even more scarce there than in other parts of the country, and the people live in isolated areas scattered over wide stretches of territory. The majority of baptized persons in both of these regions (who constituted 11 percent of all Catholics in the country in 1980) still practice the form of popular religion that is very traditionalistic, private, and associated only seasonally with the church on the occasion of religious processions or festivals in which cultic dances are performed. Peasants and small family farmers in the countryside in other parts of the country (who constitute at least an additional 15 percent of the Catholic population of Chile) continue to display similar patterns of piety.

Hence at least one-fourth of the church's membership, which is located in desert, mountainous, island, and rural areas and most of whom are poor, by 1980 had yet to be exposed in any systematic fashion to its new pastoral orientations encouraging small base communities. This phenomenon and the inclusion in urban CEBs of only a small percentage of Catholics as active members indicates that the Chilean church is only beginning to penetrate working-class culture with its new methods of evangelization. Although the progress in 1980 was greater than ten years before (and the church's reputa-tion much higher), base communities still remained in a nascent stage of development.

Differences of Opinion among Church Leaders on the Style of New Ministries in CEBs

Although new religious programs and ministries of the church were only in preliminary stages of growth in the years following the coup, significant differences of opinion began to emerge within the church on the critical pastoral, disciplinary, and even doctrinal issues precipitated by a decentralization of its structures. These pertained to approaches to popular piety, models of church development, Liberation Theology, decision making in the church, and ministerial eligibility.

During interviews I conducted in 1975 with 186 Chilean Catholic lead-ers,[29] all thirty of the bishops asserted that the correct theological posture regarding the vast majority of poor was to accept the traditional devotional practices as valid because they believed these were the only faith expression possible for most. Less than two-fifths of the priests, nuns, and lay leaders, however, were willing to accept these practices as theologically permissible, and many were critical of what they considered overindividualistic or superstitious aspects still prevalent in popular piety.

Eighty percent of all respondents (including bishops) agreed that some changes should be made in expressions of popular faith, linking them more closely to the new communal life of the church as expressed in CEBs. When asked, however, what pastoral strategy should be used to effect such a development, three-fourths of the bishops said they preferred to work with existing forms of piety—participating themselves in religious processions and celebrations honoring regionally popular saints and using these occasions to celebrate mass and hear confessions. Two-fifths or more of the priests, nuns, and lay leaders, however, took a more structural approach to the problem. They indicated that priority should not be given to encouraging the continuation of traditional forms of piety but to minimizing such practices through the creation of new organizations among the lower classes (CEBs) so as to stimulate a more biblical and critical social consciousness among the poor. The negative attitude toward popular piety as a superstitious distortion needing to be corrected, which Thomas A. Kselman describes as normally characteristic of institutionalized religion, clearly manifested itself in these opinions expressed by lower church leaders in Chile.

Six years after officially endorsing a new approach to popular religion in 1969, however, the bishops were not willing to reject the older forms of popular piety and place all of their emphasis on CEBs alone. Neither did they fall into the second category of critics of popular religion Kselman describes, who view it primarily in sociological terms as an expression of class. They saw in it some genuine religious meaning beyond cultural conditioning and were also concerned that an exclusive focus on CEBs would probably mean a loss of contact with the church for the vast majority of poor who still were not yet participating in these new base communities. Local church leaders, involved much more than the hierarchy with the creation of CEBs and not responsible for large territorial areas (dioceses) as are the bishops, were more concerned with generating a new form of spirituality albeit with smaller numbers of Catholics. Such differences are understandable given the different responsibilities and locations of higher and lower church leaders, but they also produced inconsistencies in pastoral emphases and meant that not all the energies of the church among popular classes were to be devoted to CEBs.

Higher and lower church leaders also differed significantly over preferred models of church membership and over the usefulness of Liberation Theology as a pastoral strategy. Only one-third of the bishops expressed preference for a church community that emphasized the necessity of a profound commitment by all even if this would result in a smaller but more vital institution. The overwhelming majority (70 percent) of local pastoral leaders interviewed, however, chose this model (which is close to a Protestant approach) over traditional Catholic emphases on universal membership and varying degrees of permissible commitment and participation. Moreover, three-fifths of the hierarchy also felt that there was no place in Chile for pastoral strategies based on Liberation theology methods (combining religious faith and training with discussion and direct action to change substantially economic and political structures, preferably in a socialist direction). A strong minority of priests, nuns, and lay leaders (40 percent) thought such an approach desirable and feasible, and many told me they were regularly emphasizing this method in their local base communities.

In addition, 70 percent of the bishops felt that important church decisions should be made by the hierarchy alone (perhaps with some prior consultation with local church leaders). More than one-half of the nuns and close to two-thirds of the lay leaders, however, believed that church decisions should be reached either by a dialogue toward consensus across all levels of the institutions or be determined primarily by representatives of local CEBs.

Finally, critical differences of opinion between bishops and many local church leaders occurred over ministerial eligibility. Whereas 60 percent of the bishops did not think married laymen becoming priests was a possible, or even desirable, option for the church, 81 percent of local church leaders felt it either possible or necessary for the future of Chilean Catholicism. Moreover, although only two of the thirty bishops supported the ordination of women as priests, more than one-third of the leaders in base communities (including more than one-half of the nuns) viewed this option as desirable.

Some of these differences of attitude between higher and lower church leaders had been developing since at least Vatican II in the mid-1960s. The new role of the Chilean church after the coup in the promotion of human rights, social justice, and religious evangelization among the poor, carried out through an expanding network of base communities, necessitated the granting of more de facto power to many nonclerics who had never before exercised such responsibility. These rapid changes stimulated new values and judgments among local leaders that were at variance with those of the bishops, who, along with their announced approval of more vibrant local church communities, also remained committed to traditional Catholic disciplinary and doctrinal concepts such as the male celibate clergy, strict hierarchical authority, and a universal church as opposed to an exclusive or sectarian model of religious incorporation. Moreover, the bishops continued to fear a heavy politicization of church programs as had happened in the early 1970s, particularly in a new context when such involvement of CEBs in political issues led to serious church-state conflicts.

All of these differences may be understandable, but in the short run they limited the coherence of the church's pastoral efforts in the latter 1970s. They also manifested latent tensions across leadership ranks over issues on which there is no room for compromise at the official church level (universal lay membership, hierarchical authority, and a male celibate clergy). Were such tensions to become overt and exacerbated, they could lead to serious authority conflicts between the bishops and lower-level leaders similar to those that occurred in the early 1970s regarding Christians for Socialism and "the 200."

Alienation of Upper-Income Catholics

Many wealthier Catholic laity in Chile (who constitute between 5 and 10 percent of the baptized) distanced themselves from the church after the coup. Most were strong supporters of the military government throughout the 1970s and thought the church's new commitments to the poor identified the institution too closely with opponents of the regime. Many also believed that the church was betraying its traditional religious mission by placing so much emphasis on temporal activities as opposed to strictly spiritual functions that characterized much of its thrust before the 1960s.[30]

Several of the bishops and priests whom I interviewed in 1975 in different parts of the country remarked that they were concerned about the growing alienation from the church among wealthy Catholics. Many in this group were reluctant to volunteer for new forms of lay ministry in base communities—deacons, catechists, and Bible study and prayer group leaders. These activities require a sense of communal solidarity and willingness to share one's faith in public with others, but upper-income Catholics still preferred more private forms of piety and a sacramental participation that involves no verbal witnessing or personal sharing. They also shied away from involvement in social and economic programs sponsored by the church as part of their religious commitment. Indeed, some found such new emphases threatening to their class interests.[31]

Such upper-class alienation worried the hierarchy. For pastoral reasons, the bishops want the church to be open to all regardless of class or political affiliation. For financial reasons, the bishops need help and support from this group to maintain programs. Just when the hierarchy was undertaking a wide range of new social commitments, support from the very Catholics with the resources to shoulder responsibility for them was being lost. Although contributions to the church increased after the coup, they still constituted only a minuscule percentage of the cost of running human rights and service projects for the poor. Financial self-sufficiency by the Chilean church, a goal articulated by the hierarchy in 1964, was even more unrealistic in 1980 than when it was first stated in the mid-1960s. Over 95 percent of the financial resources to support new social projects by the church still came from abroad at the end of the 1970s.[32]

Moreover, some wealthy Chileans engaged in active public campaigns to discredit the church. They used their social and political influence under the new regime (in government, business, the media, and education) to slander many clergy as Marxists and to mount periodic propaganda campaigns in the press and on television charging that church-sponsored programs were dangerous to public order. Others actively promoted challenges to episcopal authority from within the church. From time to time after the coup, the religiously reactionary Society for the Defense of Tradition, Family, and Property (TFP) used its ready access to the media to question the orthodoxy of the hierarchy and most of the clergy. In 1979, for example, TFP published an open manifesto calling upon Catholics not to obey bishops, most of whom it claimed were in heresy because of their social stands.[33]

Although few Catholics were active in these antichurch campaigns, their resources and access to power gave them considerable influence beyond their numbers in the new regime. Their alienation was not only pastoral but a political loss because they included several key policy makers in the private and public sectors who no longer took the church's social message seriously. Their presence clearly limited the church's possibility of influencing decision making in the early years of the present government.

Church-State Conflicts

Closely related to upper-class alienation from the church were chronic tensions between church and state that sometimes erupted into public conflict. The military, although acquiescent to the inauguration of church-sponsored human rights and social service programs in the aftermath of the coup, soon became very critical of such projects. The military considered most of those aided by the Committee of Cooperation for Peace between 1973 and 1975 to be enemies of the regime—workers, students, intellectuals, and leftist and centrist party leaders. Government leaders thought such an organization was simply a haven for dissidents, and by mid-1974 they began to pressure the heads of the various churches to close it down. Several of its members were arrested, and articles appeared in the media discrediting its work as Marxist-inspired. At the same time, local base communities in working-class areas came under close surveillance by 1975, with the secret police (DINA) paying unemployed workers, who were desperate for resources to feed their families, to spy on CEBs and pass on information of their activities to the government. Lay leaders in these programs were arrested and tortured, and many foreign priests were forced to leave Chile.[34]

As we have seen, this pressure led to COPACHI's dissolution in December 1975. Although its successor, the Vicariate of Solidarity, was designed to eliminate the partisan image attached to the church's social programs, it did not succeed for the fundamental reason that the political and economic context for the poor did not change substantially in the late 1970s. Conditions remained bleak, and no major social institutions (labor unions, political parties, community organizations) were able to gain sufficient freedom to meet basic needs or effectively articulate popular demands. As a result, many of those in political or economic trouble continued to come to the church for assistance.

Popular needs thus helped push the church into continual opposition, and by late 1977 spokespersons for the government and those in the progovernment media began to discredit the vicariate just as they had COPACHI. Charges were made that the vicariate was harboring Marxists and taking money from abroad to support political dissidents in Chile. Diocesan affiliates of the vicariate in various parts of the country were raided and personnel harassed. Such attacks were renewed periodically as part of the junta's efforts to maintain a climate of fear throughout the country. Rectories, convents, and base communities experienced similar raids and surveillance, and in 1980 harassment tactics against neighborhood church projects linked with CEBs increased for a time once again.

How can we assess the impact of these activities? Clearly, even though the bishops spoke out firmly after 1976, no significant reduction either of repression in the country or of vilification of the church in the media ensued.[35] Indeed, such public criticisms by Catholic bishops only confirmed the judgments of high military leaders and their civilian supporters that the church was attempting to undermine the legitimacy of the regime and compete with it for political power. Neither the "quiet diplomacy" of bishops in the first two years of the regime nor their more prophetic public denunci-ations thereafter convinced the military that the fundamental public objec-tives of the church were humanitarian service and moral clarification, not struggle for political power.

Developments in the Early 1980s and
Prospects for the Future

Although my analysis has concentrated on the consequences of the church's new pastoral activities among the popular classes in the 1970s, both for its external relations with society and its internal religious life, the same trends have continued in the early 1980s. In fact, the challenges in both realms have become more sharply delineated with no resolution of tension likely in the near future.

In the aftermath of a carefully controlled national plebiscite in September 1980 granting the military at least nine more years of rule, Cardinal Raúl Silva Henríquez of Santiago, president of the Vicariate of Solidarity, an-nounced a cutback in its staff and a decentralization of several of its functions to local dioceses and zones within dioceses. Local church personnel were also urged to concentrate more on strictly religious activities. Later, in a July 1981 press conference, Father Juan de Castro, then executive director of the vicariate, stated that the institution for too long had been a "foreign body within the church." He argued that the time had come for the church to return to its "proper mission" of preaching the gospel and helping individuals arrive at personal religious conversion.[36]

Some interpreted these words and actions as an attempt by the hierarchy to diminish the debilitating political attacks on the church by a regime that seemed in 1981 to be well established in power for the next decade. One-third of the hierarchy (including the cardinal himself) were close to manda-tory ecclesiastical retirement age and wanted to leave church-state relations in an atmosphere of relative peace for the next generation of episcopal leaders. Such tactics may have also been meant to mollify upper-income and conservative Catholics, whose alienation and withering attacks on the clergy were thought by some bishops seriously to damage church unity.[37]

But other interpretations were less sanguine. Some argued that such announcements undermined the church's credibility among its new adher-ents in the working classes, who had come to depend on the church for many basic needs. Local CEBs would not have the resources or trained staff to carry out programs effectively on their own. Moreover, if religious conversion was to proceed among those groups, such critics argued, and if base communities were to continue to grow, effective social services would have to continue both in the vicariate and at the diocesan level so as to act as a support for CEBs, thus enabling them to remain as the church's concrete sign of commitment to the poor. A dichotomy between spiritual conversion and concern for justice could no longer be upheld by serious church spokespersons, they said, after so many official church statements to the contrary at Vatican II, Medellín, Puebla, and in several documents of the Chilean bishops throughout the 1970s.[38]

This debate within the church has not yet been resolved because the political and economic crisis has worsened since 1981, forcing the church to maintain its policies of the 1970s. A severe depression began in 1982, which has continued to the present and has resulted in soaring unemployment (officially over 20 percent in 1984 but unofficially much higher) and further cutbacks in government spending. In the midst of dramatic failure of the regime's economic policies, political opposition significantly increased in 1983 and 1984 with monthly street demonstrations and work stoppages demanding a return to democracy, mounting terrorist activities against government property, and repeated calls by opposition parties (albeit still divided among themselves) for the resignation of General Augusto Pinochet. The reaction of the government has been to refuse any change in policy direction and to repress severely public manifestations of dissent. It reimposed a state of siege in November 1984, conducted massive arrests in urban shantytowns, and increased internal banishment and the use of torture against opposition leaders, especially those in the working classes.

In face of these tactics, the vicariate has continued its human rights services to those suffering the brunt of the new wave of political repression. It has also continued to raise and channel international financial support for the church's various local service programs closely linked with CEBs. Together with leaders and members of the CEBs it has helped to plan and carry out a number of public events (such as Masses for Peace and demonstrations on behalf of life) aimed at maintaining calm but also clearly demanding greater public participation in decisions about the country's future. Such actions have precipitated renewed attacks on the church by the government and its supporters. These have included the reappearance of charges of subversion against church groups in the carefully controlled media, more expulsions of foreign clergy, and a return to police harassment and arrest of vicariate and CEB leaders.

In such a tense context the hierarchy has not taken a definitive stand over the church's future pastoral strategies among the popular classes. The appointment of several new bishops since 1983 by the Vatican—including a successor to Cardinal Silva of Santiago, Archbishop Juan Francisco Fresno —has strengthened the number of those in the episcopal conference who favor a more spiritual focus in the CEBs and nonconflictual relations between church and government. The hierarchy, however, has not been blind to the brutal consequences of the regime's economic and political policies since 1983. The bishops have continued their support for the vicariate's human rights work as central to the church's apostolate and have endorsed the social service dimension of CEBs during the economic crisis. They have also continued to speak out in opposition to government policies that violate human rights, increase economic hardship for the poor, refuse serious political dialogue with the opposition, and harass or vilify pastoral leaders at the local church level.[39]

Although the economic and political context of the mid-1980s has put off the resolution of the internal church debate that emerged early in the decade over the proper focus of popular pastoral strategies, the disagreements are still there even if dormant for the moment. The majority of bishops (now strengthened by similar positions outlined by the Pope and Vatican in the early 1980s and by recent additions to their own ranks) are concerned that the social and political dimensions of CEB spirituality not overwhelm the religious aspects (prayer, Bible study, sacramental preparation and participation). They clearly see this religious activity not only as primary but as separate from social commitment. Although not nearly as fearful of the implications of decentralization, pluralism, and lay initiative as Levine describes the Colombian hierarchy to be, or as Dodson explains is the case for the bishops in Nicaragua, the Chilean hierarchy clearly want to exert more control of CEBs than in the past and move them away from intense social and political involvements as soon as possible. Their memory of the Allende years and the CpS movement is still vivid.

Many in the CEBs, however, believe both religious and social aspects are part of one commitment to God and humankind and that religious faith is nourished in and through the work for justice. They see the social services of the vicariate and the CEBs as the most credible sign the church can give to its transcendent values and beliefs. To them, these symbols shine through and become real to the world at large in the lives of Christians committed to alleviating suffering. This itself, they claim, is a form of prayer and an act of belief in God and nothing to be feared from a religious point of view.

The debate is unlikely to be resolved in the immediate future. Indeed, such debates have a long history in Christian and other religious traditions. But the differences outlined here do have immediate practical consequences for the church in Chile. Should a more exclusively religious emphasis be given to the CEBs in the future and social services be dramatically curtailed, many of the new adherents may leave the base communities. If this were to happen, their contact with, and participation in, the church would be lost. Moreover, if there is a change in regime in the near future and a new government were to cease political repression, alter the economic model so that its costs would not be as severe on the poor, and increase public welfare programs and services, many of the humanitarian projects of the church would become less necessary and people would look elsewhere for the effective delivery of social services. Those primarily interested in this dimension of the CEBs could better achieve their objectives in other places, as did many Chilean Catholics in the early 1960s, when they ceased participating in Catholic Action programs and went to work full time for the PDC and the Frei government.

If there is a large group of new adherents to the CEBs who are there primarily for the social service dimension—and hence belong in the category of spirituality described above—the CEBs will dramatically shrink in numbers of participants either if the hierarchy insists on a more strictly religious focus in CEBs or if the political and economic climate of the country improves significantly.

If, on the other hand, social service activities continue to characterize a good part of the life of the CEBs for some time to come, the numbers of new adherents will probably continue to grow. This is a more likely scenario because the economy is in very bad straits. If there is a change of policies, or even a new government, economic recovery will be a long, hard process and public social services and employment opportunities will not dramatically increase for some time. The church's humanitarian efforts among the poor will, therefore, most likely continue.

This latter scenario would give the church more time to deepen the allegiances of its new adherents, while moving more Chileans whose primary concern is service to participate in the CEBs' religious functions as well. A synthesis of both emphases of prayer and social action in the individual lives of CEB members—the ideal articulated by Medellín, Puebla, and the Chilean bishops themselves in 1969—would, under such circumstances, have a better opportunity to develop. If such a synthesis does occur among the church's new adherents, when the political and economic context improves they might still continue to participate in the religious activities of the CEBs while pursuing their social objectives elsewhere. Mainwaring's findings in the CEBs of Nova Iguaçu in Brazil during the period of redemocratization confirm such possibilities.

Although such a scenario would enhance the church's prospects for furthering this new form of popular religion among the working classes without losing its religious focus, such an outcome is not free of problems. As indicated earlier, those at the local level working to create and sustain CEBs in Chile have a very different vision of the future of Catholicism than do the bishops, and theirs is much closer to that of the CpS and "the 200" fifteen years ago. They prefer a church much closer to some Protestant models than to the Roman Catholic tradition—decentralized, democratic, with fewer but more committed members, and with equality in ministry for females, males, and married persons. These ideas are currently being nourished by the day-to-day practice of the CEBs. Even if church leaders solve other problems associated with the new popular piety (conflicts with the state, alienation of upper-income Catholics, insufficient male participation), the issue of conflicting ecclesiologies between higher and lower leaders will not be settled easily. It has much more serious, long-range implications for the church than the tensions between the two spiritualities described earlier because it affects the traditional nature of the institution.

This conflict is latent now because the serious economic and political problems of the society are taking so much time and energy of those working in the CEBs. If the context changes and some of the pressing demands for social services by the popular classes subside, the leaders and members of the CEBs are likely to begin pressuring the hierarchy on a new agenda for the inner life of the church. This agenda is the most critical long-term consequence of the newer forms of popular religion in Chile and for the universal church as well in the post–Vatican II era.

Notes

1. Brian H. Smith, "Churches and Human Rights in Latin America: Recent Trends on the Subcontinent," in Daniel H. Levine, ed., *Churches and Politics in Latin America* (Beverly Hills: Sage, 1980), pp. 155–93.

2. For Chile, see Brian H. Smith, *The Church and Politics in Chile: Challenges to Modern Catholicism* (Princeton: Princeton University Press, 1982). For Nicaragua, see the chapter by Michael Dodson in this volume.

3. During the late 1960s the Chilean hierarchy made efforts to put some distance

between the official church and the PDC not only because of the "drainage" of lay elites out of Catholic Action into the party but also because by 1968 it was becoming clear that the left might gain the presidency in 1970. Although the hierarchy in 1962 warned of "persecution, tears and bloodshed" for Christians should a Marxist win the presidency in 1964 (clearly placing the moral weight of the church behind Frei's candidacy), as the 1970 election approached such condemnations ceased and the bishops took an officially neutral position regarding parties (Smith, *Church and Politics in Chile*, pp. 111, 135).

4. Episcopal Conference of Chile, *Orientaciones pastorales II: Comunidades de base* (Santiago: Tipografía San Pablo, 1969), pp. 8–9. This emphasis on small base communities was also urged by the Medellín Conference of Latin American bishops in Colombia in 1968.

5. Statistics on Sunday mass attendance are from my own secondary analysis of random, stratified, door-to-door opinion survey data conducted in the capital in 1970 and 1973 by the Centro de Opinión Pública of Santiago. My interviews with bishops, priests, nuns, and lay leaders throughout Chile in 1975 (N = 186) are the basis for the judgment about a lack of vitality in the new base communities during the Allende period.

6. Even in working-class areas there was not unanimous support for the UP. The PDC, and to a much lesser extent the conservative National party (PN), had a significant base of support among various groups of workers. My secondary analysis of public opinion survey data collected by the Centro de Opinión Pública in Santiago in February 1973 (a month before the last parliamentary election) indicated that among blue-collar industrial workers, the UP's base of support was 52 percent, the PDC's 31.9 percent, the PN's 2.8 percent, with 13.3 percent undecided. Among the nonindustrial workers (artisans, independents, and those in domestic services), the left gained 22.4 percent, the PDC 37.4 percent, the PN 15.7 percent, with 24.5 percent undecided. Similar cleavages also characterized several occupational groups in the middle class (office workers, sales personnel, small business persons). Among these groups, the UP received 36.6 percent support, the PDC 30.1 percent, the PN 16.1 percent, with 17.2 percent undecided (Smith, *Church and Politics in Chile*, Table 7.8, p. 221).

Such cleavages carried over into the local church-sponsored programs that functioned with some regularity during the Allende years. My interviews in 1975 throughout Chile with local clergy, religious, and lay leaders responsible for these base communities confirmed that, especially during the latter part of the Popular Unity administration, the problem of serious polarization of religious meetings was fairly widespread and, in their perspective, quite disruptive to effective evangelization (Smith, *Church and Politics in Chile*, p. 262).

7. This movement, which began among eighty clerics active in working-class parishes in Santiago in April 1971, spread to other areas of the country and by mid-1973 included approximately three hundred members. The leadership was exclusively clerical, and the overwhelming majority of members were priests, nuns, and Protestant pastors. Their goal was to make local church structures more supportive of socialist objectives. For an extensive account of their aims and strategies, see Smith, *Church and Politics in Chile*, pp. 230–80.

8. For example, the declaration of principles for a base community inaugurated in a working-class neighborhood in Valparaiso in 1971, guided by a priest active in Christians for Socialism, required that all members be both Christian and revolutionary and that no one could participate without previous acceptance by the membership (Ignacio Pujadas, "Comunidades de cristianos revolucionarios: Declaración de principios," *Pastoral Popular* [Santiago] 22 [March–April 1972]: 48–50).

For other statements by Christians for Socialism espousing a new, more sectarian (exclusive in membership), and political model for the church, see Juan Menard, "La iglesia de hoy es para el mundo de ayer?" *Pastoral Popular* 22 (March–April 1972): 51–64; Secretariado Nacional de los Cristianos por el Socialismo, *El pueblo camina . . . y los cristianos?* (Santiago: Prensa Latino-americana, 1972); Gonzalo Arroyo, S. J., "Historia y significado de CpS" (mimeo, Padre Hurtado, Jornada Nacional, 1972); Diego Irarrazaval, "Que hacer? Cristianos en el proceso socialista" (mimeo, Padre Hurtado, Jornada Nacional, 1972; translated and reprinted in English by Church Research and Information Projects, New York, 1975).

9. Episcopal Conference of Chile, "Christian Faith and Political Activity," in John Eagleson, ed., *Christians and Socialism: Documentation of the Christians for Socialism Movement in Latin America* (Maryknoll: Orbis Books, 1975), pp. 179–228.

10. One reason why both Catholic and Protestant churches did not suffer the same immediate restrictions placed on other major social institutions was that the military had proclaimed the preservation of Christian moral and religious values as a reason for the coup. More important, major church leaders of all denominations were very cautious in their public statements about the coup, and none unequivocally denounced the new government's massive violations of human rights. The military wanted at least tacit legitimation for the new regime by the churches, and, in exchange, ecclesiastical leaders wanted to prevent restrictions on the religious activities of their churches and also to be allowed to undertake humanitarian aid to those suffering persecution. Both church and government leaders, therefore, had mutual interests in avoiding confrontation at the start.

11. El Comité de Cooperación para la Paz en Chile, "Crónica de sus dos años de labor solidaria" (mimeo, Santiago, 1975).

12. Soon after the coup, to curb soaring inflation rates (over 600 percent by September 1973), the military announced major cutbacks in public services, including health and nutrition programs in urban shantytowns that had been expanded by the Allende administration. Wage adjustments were also pegged at a lower rate than price rises and collective bargaining was outlawed. Land reform programs were suspended, and cooperatives and socialized farms, instituted by the Frei (1964–70) and Allende (1970–73) governments respectively, began to be returned to previous large landholders or parceled out in small plots to poor families who were given neither the tools nor credit to work the land productively for profit. The government also began to sell off to the private sector large state enterprises in industry and public utilities nationalized during the Frei and Allende years. Many workers lost their jobs in the process (Lester A. Sobel, ed., *Chile and Allende* [New York: Facts on File, 1974], pp. 153–62).

13. Local church-sponsored health clinics in Santiago offered treatment to seventy-five thousand patients during the first two years of military rule. By late 1975

approximately four hundred soup kitchens also linked with CEBs and, with financial support from COPACHI, were providing hot lunches to more than thirty thousand undernourished preschool age children daily. By late 1975 COPACHI employed more than three hundred full-time lawyers, social workers, and medical personnel throughout the country, who also offered advice and backup support to church personnel in CEBs carrying out these local service programs (U.S. Congress, House, Subcommittee on International Organizations of the Committee on International Relations, "Prepared Statement of José Zalaquett Daher, Chief Legal Counsel, Committee of Cooperation for Peace in Chile," in *Chile: The Status of Human Rights and Its Relationship to U.S. Economic Assistance Programs*, 94th Cong., 2d sess., 1976, pp. 57–65).

14. After 1975 there were some improvements in the economy. Inflation decreased dramatically (from 600 percent in 1973 to under 40 percent by 1979), loans from foreign private banks soared to nearly $3 billion in new credits in 1980, exports increased, and foreign reserves totaled more than $1 billion in 1980. But these gains did not help the majority who were poor because unemployment remained high (over 13 percent in 1980), wage increases continued to be pegged lower than price rises (diminishing purchasing power of the poor by almost one-half between 1973 and 1980), health and housing expenditures by government were cut back, and labor union activities remained severely restricted.

15. In 1980 in Santiago the Vicariate of Solidarity aided the following services operated through the church's CEB network: 74 community health clinics, assisting annually more than 22,000 patients; 160 feeding centers providing daily hot lunches for more than 13,000 children and adults; 105 cottage industry centers administered by unemployed men and women; 74 artisan and handicraft projects run by prisoners to gain income for their families; and 68 housing committees to pressure the government to provide needed services in shantytowns (water, sanitation, electricity) and protect slum dwellers from eviction by private land speculators (*Vicaría de la Solidaridad: Quinto año de labor, 1980* [Santiago: Arzobispado de Santiago, 1980], pp. 15, 67, 87, 111–13).

After COPACHI was disbanded in 1975, Chilean Protestant churches (which included 1 million members, or 10 percent of the population) set up separate development projects to assist peasants and workers. Lutherans, Methodists, and some evangelical churches formed three umbrella organizations—Service (DIAKONIA), the Social Action Federation of Christian Churches (Federacíon para la Accíon Social de las Iglesias Cristianas, FASIC), and Evangelical Christian Aid (Ayuda Cristiana Evangelica, ACE). The first concentrated on rural projects (agricultural cooperatives, credit and marketing assistance, health care), and the latter two supported urban service programs such as feeding centers, food purchasing cooperatives, health clinics, hygiene education, housing committees, literacy training, and cottage industries. Many of these programs were also administered through small church groups similar in style of operation to the Catholic CEBs. All of these Protestant and Catholic service programs were made financially possible by donations from international organizations (religious and secular) headquartered in the United States, Canada, and Western Europe. Between 1974 and 1979, this aid totaled $88.5 million (Smith, *Church and Politics in Chile*, Table 9.2, p. 326).

16. Thomas G. Sanders, "Counterreform in the Chilean Campo," *American Universities Field Staff Reports*, South America Series, 1980, no. 32, p. 9.

17. *Vicaría de la Solidaridad*, pp. 128, 133.

18. Ibid., pp. 146–68.

19. The military regime made some efforts in 1974 and 1975 to sponsor new social organizations (especially for women and youth) as a way to train new leaders imbued with the authoritarian ideology of the regime. Such efforts met with some success among the staunch supporters of the regime in the wealthier sectors of the population (upper 10 percent) but were much less successful among the middle class and not at all among workers. It was among this latter group (which constitutes almost 70 percent of the population) that CEB service organizations were most active.

20. Fontaine, "Algunos aspectos de la iglesia chilena de hoy," *Mensaje* 24 (June 1975): 246–51. This judgment was also confirmed by my own observations and conversations with several persons active in COPACHI in 1975.

21. These judgments are based on personal observations and experiences in the Santiago working-class parish I served in as a priest in 1975 and on conversations with priests, nuns, and lay leaders in other working-class parishes throughout the country. As is evident from the public reemergence of traditional left versus centrist political splits at party leadership levels in 1983 and 1984, any reconciliation thus far has taken place primarily at the rank-and-file levels.

22. This estimate was given to me by Bishop Carlos Camus, then secretary of the Episcopal Conference, in an interview in September 1975.

23. Enrique García Ahumada, F.S.C., "Nuestra catequesis actual," *Mensaje* 26 (November 1977): 657–61; Carlos Sánchez, "El difícil despertar de la juventud chilena," *Mensaje* 27 (January–February 1978): 17–20.

24. Statistics on Sunday mass attendance for 1979 are taken from a random stratified door-to-door survey (based on the same 1973 sample of the Centro de Opinión Pública) conducted by Centro Bellarmino (N = 963) (Renato Poblete, W. Carmen Galilea, and P. Patricia van Dorp, *Imagen de la iglesia de hoy y religiosidad popular de los Chilenos* (Santiago: Centro Bellarmino, 1980), p. 38.

25. Cristian Vives, "La solidaridad: Una forma de evangelizar y participar en la iglesia" (mimeo, Santiago: Centro Bellarmino, 1978), pp. 22–23.

26. Katherine Ann Gilfeather, M.M., "Women Religious, the Poor, and the Institutional Church in Chile," in Levine, ed., *Churches and Politics in Latin America*, pp. 188–224.

27. A study of thirty-six base communities in 1978 sponsored by the Episcopal Conference discovered that two-thirds were located in working-class areas, with a heavy proportion of members being housewives and students (Episcopal Conference of Chile, *La comunidad eclesial de base: Una experiencia pastoral chilena* [Santiago: Ediciones Paulinas, 1978]; see also Thomas G. Sanders, "Popular Religion, Pastoral Renewal, and National Reconciliation in Chilean Catholicism," *American Universities Field Staff Reports*, South America Series, no. 16, 1981, pp. 1–12).

28. A random stratified door-to-door survey of 963 Catholics in Santiago in 1979, for example, conducted by the Jesuit-sponsored research institute Centro Bellarmino discovered that 87.9 percent of the respondents did not belong to any religious

organization of the church, and 93.9 percent indicated that they did not work for any social action project. Moreover, 73.8 percent manifested no or only a low level of understanding of central doctrines of the church. More than one-half (53.1 percent), however, felt close to the church, more than three-fifths (63.5 percent) were in accord with the positions of bishops and priests, more than seven-tenths (71.8 percent) believed the church to be interested in their problems, and more than three-fourths (75.8 percent) favored the church's commitment to the defense of human rights. Although this response showed a substantial approval of and respect for the church by a majority of Chileans (many of whom were helped by its new services), it also indicated how few actually gave their time to work in any of its new social programs or participated in its new religious activities even during the immediate postcoup years of expanding local base communities (Poblete, Galilea, and van Dorp, *Imagen de la iglesia*, pp. 42, 47, 48–49, 61, 70–71).

29. I included in my nationwide interviews (N = 186) all thirty active bishops, forty-one priests working among different social strata in eighteen of twenty-three provinces, thirty-one priests in a random stratified sample in Santiago, thirty-three nuns acting as pastoral leaders in CEBs among different social classes in seven provinces, and fifty-one lay men and women leaders of CEBs in urban areas (mainly in Santiago).

30. Renato Poblete, "Los católicos de derecha," *Mensaje* 28 (May 1979): 251–52.

31. In the survey of Catholic attitudes conducted in Santiago in 1979 by Centro Bellarmino, it was found that wealthier Catholics as a whole went to mass more often and had a better knowledge of doctrine than did the poor, but they were also more critical of the clergy, felt more alienated from the church, and were less willing to accept a commitment to justice and to human development as integral parts of Christian life than were working-class Catholics (Poblete, Galilea, and van Dorp, *Imagen de la iglesia*, pp. 156–58).

32. Between 1974 and 1979, voluntary tithing contributions to the church rose from $155,106 to $1.4 million annually. The total amount of internally generated funds in five years from this program (called Contribución a la Iglesia) reached just over $4 million. Compared to the $88.5 million contributed from private and public agencies abroad in the same period, this figure is small (Smith, *Church and Politics in Chile*, Table 9.2, p. 326).

33. Sociedad Chilena de Defensa de la Tradición, Familia y Propiedad, *Iglesia del silencio* (Santiago: Edunsa, 1976), pp. 377–400. In 1980 strong criticism, including libel, against the present leadership of the Chilean church was again voiced in the secular media by some groups sympathetic to the TFP and its brand of Catholicism (Jaime Ruiz Tagle, "Iglesia, gobierno y pueblo," *Mensaje* 29 [July 1980]: 308–11). For further information on the strategies of Catholics on the right since the coup, see Smith, *Church and Politics in Chile*, pp. 336–40.

34. Between 1973 and 1975, 314 foreign priests (12 percent of the total number of clerics in the country) left Chile, many under government threats or pressures for purported political activities during the present or previous governments.

35. In April 1974, after the Catholic bishops issued their first systematic, but only mildly critical, analysis of the situation in the country since the coup, one of the four

members of the ruling military junta, Air Force General Gustavo Leigh, stated publicly that he had "great respect for the church, but like many men, without realizing it, they are vehicles for Marxism" (Sobel, ed., *Chile and Allende*, p. 171).

Between mid-1976 and mid-1980, the Episcopal Conference issued several much more sharply worded public statements criticizing continued torture and arbitrary detention, lack of adequate investigations into the cause of disappearances, failure on the part of the government to allow participation by the public in important national decisions, and the immorality of economic strategies exploitive of workers and peasants (Smith, *Church and Politics in Chile*, pp. 310–11).

36. Teófilo Rondón, "Chilean Hierarchy Ceding Ground under Pressure," *Latin American Press* (Lima) 13 (16 July 1981): 2.

37. These were the opinions expressed to me by Father Juan de Castro, at that time executive director of the vicariate, in an interview I conducted with him in Cambridge, Massachusetts, in November 1981. He also believed that the announced cutbacks in the vicariate's staff would not entail a diminished commitment to human rights and social services because all the activities of the CEBs would continue with greater decision making at the local level as the visibility of their national sponsor, the vicariate, decreased.

38. For a summary of such arguments see Cristian Vives, "Iglesia y pueblo," *Mensaje* 30 (June 1981): 100, 237–40.

39. Thomas G. Sanders, "Catholicism and Authoritarianism in Chile," *Thought* 69 (June 1984): 235.

9

Colombia: The Institutional Church and the Popular

Daniel H. Levine

"Popular" is an ambiguous and highly charged word in Latin America today. Much of the confusion and tension is rooted in a struggle to control the meaning and direction of "the popular" in culture, society, and politics, to structure "popular" organizations, and to shape their relation to central institutions.[1] Struggle over the popular is particularly visible in Catholicism, where the definition of "popular religion," its expression in base communities (*comunidades eclesiales de base*, or CEBs) and similar groups, and its proper link to central church institutions have lately become major foci of debate and conflict. The stakes are considerable: controlling the popular and shaping the structure, orientation, and agenda of popular religious groups and practices yield major influence over the future of Catholic ideology, as carried in a potentially massive net of grass-roots organizations and activists throughout the area.[2]

This essay explores these issues through analysis of the evolving position of the institutional Catholic church in Colombia as it considers and reconsiders popular religion and the popular in general, while developing strategies of incorporation and control. I argue that the way central church agencies conceive of the popular and the provisions they make to incorporate it into the institution's symbolic and organizational structures rest above all on the church's sense of itself and of its key interests. At the same time, ironies emerge, for as we shall see, the very foundation and initial sponsorship of participatory grass-roots organizations spur new awareness and touch off processes of group and personal change that may undercut the controls so carefully built in from above. Groups founded on one model may escape its limitations, as members come to use the church's structures and ideas to frame and legitimate alternative expressions of their interests. It is the *intersect* that counts, the ongoing linkage between the institutional and the popular that shapes belief, structure, and practice. Both the general issues and the specific case of Colombia are important. I begin with a brief statement of the issues.

General Issues

Despite a flood of recent research, publication, and polemic on the general topic of religion, society, and politics in Latin America, little systematic attention has gone to studying the ways in which institutional churches have reached out to contact and shape popular religion and popular organization; even less to understanding the impact of this process on the churches themselves.[3] But the institutional and the popular cannot be separated. Popular religion is not an autonomous, somehow "natural" product. Indeed, much of the stock of symbol and metaphor, as well as the organizational forms and practices often considered "popular" are historical products, born of the relation of subordinate social groups to dominant institutions, among them the churches. The link is constant, for the churches as institutions provide legitimacy, support, continuity, and a sense of meaning and moral authority to popular religious expression.

Neither institutional churches nor popular organizations and practices are static: each changes continuously. Within the churches, as conventionally accepted notions of authority, unity, and membership change, new patterns of legitimation, organization, and action emerge to reshape the way church leaders see the popular and build links to it. As these concepts filter to the base, they are taken up and used by popular groups as a foundation for their own organizational efforts and as a base for defining and legitimating new interests. Of course, the popular is not static either: the interests of popular groups evolve and change in accord with their situation and with the alternatives available at any given time in a specific society.

Full understanding of the relation between the churches and the popular requires careful attention to the meanings given to "church" and to the way different concepts of the church intersect with alternative definitions of the popular. In contemporary discussions, a broad distinction is often drawn between visions of the church stressing hierarchy, juridically defined roles, and the guiding force of authoritative doctrine (church as institution) as opposed to those seeing the church primarily as a historical community of believers and highlighting values of solidarity, shared experience, and multiple sources of power and authority (church as community, as People of God).[4] These models define very different projects for the church, particularly through the contrasting senses of unity and belonging on which they rest. The first builds unity around ecclesiastical structures, with average members in a distinct and subordinate relation to clergy. The pervasive stress on hierarchy, organizational unity, and clerical dominance converges in a style in which goals and orientations flow from the "church" to "the world." The very use of these terms stresses separation: society is to be suffused with Christian principles; the world is to be reconquered for the church. The second model builds religious unity on the solidarity of community and shared experience. Institutional unity thus rests on social unity, with the stress on homogenous, class-based groups. The emphasis on solidarity undercuts clerical dominance and reduces the centrality of ecclesiastical structures. The church is part of the world, and orientations are sought in daily experience. Action may thus stem from social analysis, without the mediation of authoritative doctrine. Society is remade, not rechristianized.

How do these models intersect with notions of the popular? Two concepts must be explored: "popular religion" and "base."[5] As to popular religion, three meanings are especially salient: (1) a pattern of inherited magic and superstition to be purified through reinforced ties to the church; (2) the spiritual tradition of the poor and humble in general, who are encouraged to express their faith in renewed structures of community and participation; and (3) the beliefs and practices of popular classes, rooted in their class situation and giving voice to its contradictions and dilemmas. All these usages rest on a sense of class, with "popular" tied in some way to being poor and subordinate, but this social identity is used very differently in each. The first two consider poverty in the abstract, removed from the structures of any specific society. Only in the last does class provide a potentially independent ground for reflection, organization, and action.[6] The idea of "base" meets a similar fate. As used in the definition of base communities (CEBs), base has at least two meanings: a subunit at the base of the hierarchical structures of the church; and a "basic" social group with base referring both to primary affiliation group and to the CEBs' subordinate class character, lying at the base of a social pyramid.

Beyond matters of definition, these usages all clearly embody distinct notions about the proper linkage of the popular to central cultural and political institutions. Abstracting popular ideas, groups, parties, and the like from social class and tying "base" to the hierarchical structures of the church binds any aspect of popular religion tightly to institutional membership and clerical control. With purification or enhanced participation of the poor and humble in general at issue, maintaining a link to religiously legitimate goals depends on the mediation of clergy and the sanction of authoritative doctrine (in this case, the social thought of the church). Membership is heterogeneous and ties to the hierarchy remain central.[7] Here, the church "goes to the poor," works with the poor, speaks for the poor—always in a guiding role. In contrast, when base and popular are grounded more explicitly in class, the poor become concrete and immediate. The general stress on solidarity and sharing experience with the poor is sharpened to embrace not "the poor" in general, but rather the poor produced by specific social structures. The church, in this case, does not "go to" the poor. Rather, it arises from the poor and accompanies them in the struggles of daily life. Membership is clearly homogeneous, and ties to the hierarchy are less central to the legitimate constitution of a group.[8]

Discussions of the institutional church and the popular today thus come together around issues of class, class division, politics, and the meaning of unity. Defining the base of the church in class and community terms calls conventional structures and roles into question. As religious unity is sought through sharing and solidarity on a class basis, the mediation of ecclesiastical agents and structures becomes less essential. These roles are not eliminated, but their unquestioned authority wanes as new sources of legitimate orientation and leadership emerge. Most important, the stress on class sketched out here opens new dimensions of "politics" for the churches. First, the link of church-related and sponsored activity to politics as conventionally defined (state, parties, movements, and the like) is accentuated as members and leaders alike are moved to express their faith in actions to promote justice. Second, and equally crucial, issues of power and equality move into the churches themselves, as the very nature and bases of unity are called into question. It is precisely the convergence of politics in these several senses that makes debates over the popular so salient in Latin American Catholicism today.[9]

I noted earlier that Colombia is a particularly instructive case. Several issues make it so. First, on the Latin American Catholic scene, Colombia can be taken as the conservative anchor of an ideological spectrum whose opposite pole is often seen in Brazil. In contrast to the Brazilian church, widely known for progressive theology and ample support of CEBs and popular organizations generally, the Colombian church is widely recognized for its conservative theology, with stress on traditional concepts of hierarchy, authority, and unity leading generally to clericalization and firm control of such groups. The church has long held a uniquely central role in Colombian life, and more than most churches in the region it has maintained a vital and powerful net of mass organizations. The organizational record is illuminating, for as Colombian society has changed, church leaders have experimented with different structures and styles of group formation as they seek to penetrate popular classes under changing circumstances.

It is also important to note the Colombian church's strong ties to international Catholicism. The evolving position of its leaders and central institutions closely reflects trends in the church as a whole. Colombia is home to the Latin American Bishops' Conference (CELAM), and Colombians dominate its leadership and permanent staff. For many years now, CELAM has been the focus of opposition to "progressive" currents in Latin American Catholicism, most recently centering its attack on the concept and practice of a "popular church." In this regard, both CELAM and the Colombian hierarchy and established authority in that hierarchy are very close to current papal policies.

Finally, the pervasive stress on hierarchy and established authority in the Colombian church is echoed and reinforced by the dominant mentality and structure of the political system. The Colombian state, the major political parties, and groups such as unions or associations are all generally inhospitable to independent grass-roots organizations. Operating on clientelistic lines, they tend to break up and isolate class-based and independent initiatives, encouraging instead the formation of dependent, vertical ties to existing elites and structures. Thus, even if popular groups were to seek them out, they are unlikely to find reliable and durable allies on the national or regional scenes. These structural constraints are amplified because there is no significant ideological or institutional challenge to the social or political status quo in Colombia, and none has been visible for some time.[10]

Attention to these structural traits should not obscure the realization that Colombia enjoys relatively open politics, with few formal limits on organization and action. As a result, one rarely finds activism driven into the churches and rooted in religiously inspired popular groups because of restrictions in society and politics at large. In this regard, Colombia is far removed from cases like Central America, Chile, or Brazil. In any case, Colombia's recent political history, and above all the still fresh memory of massive violence, continue to produce an almost automatic rejection of "politics" at the grass roots. The quickest way to turn off a discussion with Colombian peasants is to speak of "politics."[11]

For all these reasons, the explicitly political thrust of popular religious organizations and base communities has been limited in Colombia. The hierarchy resists it, the structural patterns inhibit it, and the potential clientele is often suspicious and wary. Nonetheless, conflict over the popular has been extensive and bitter in the Colombian church. Indeed, the Colombian hierarchy has repeatedly condemned the very notion of a popular church with a vehemence so disproportionate to reality that one suspects the bishops see in it a basic challenge to the church and to their authority. The two are hard to separate, for Colombia's bishops place the hierarchy and its agents at the very core of church life. From this perspective, the maintenance of unity around the bishops is of critical importance, as are the continued subordination of laity to clergy and the organization of tight linkages between any Catholic groups and the central structures controlled by the bishops. In sum, the institutional church in Colombia sees a threat in the popular because its leaders see the stress on class, solidarity, and shared authority as a challenge to the structure of power within the ecclesiastical institution and hence to the very survival of the church as they know it.[12]

The main body of this essay explores these issues in detail for Colombia. I begin with a brief sketch of models of the church predominant in recent years. This "sense of the church" is linked to changing organizational strategies pursued by the hierarchy. The Bishops' Conference also sponsors national training programs, three of which are considered in detail to get a sense of the bishops' view of the popular: the training of "pastoral agents," the development of base communities, and the stress on permanent deacons and lay ministers. These sections are followed by analysis of the emergence of distinct, competing lines and methodologies of "popular work" in the late 1970s. Several case studies of popular organizations and base communities are then considered, drawing on recent fieldwork among peasants and city slum dwellers. A concluding section places these data and issues in the context of the changing nature of debates within the church itself.

Models of the Church, Images of Authority

The models of the church held by Catholic leaders shape the way they see themselves, the institutions they lead, and their proper relation to

social and political issues. These visions of the church (ecclesiologies) provide an important mediation, through which religious ideas are crystallized in
structures of organizational life, patterns of authority, and legitimate goals,
commitments, and actions.

In general, ecclesiological debates in the Colombian church have followed
the lines traced in Latin America and in the church at large over the last
decade or so. But although the language of debate has shifted a great deal,
the Colombian case shows striking continuities with the past.[13] Of these,
three are especially noteworthy: a concept of authority that makes hierarchy
central to church life; a concern for unity seen as the joining of a heterogeneous base around hierarchy, clergy, and the structures they control; and a
related vision of the link between church and world rooted in notions of
Christendom, which hold that the church (properly constituted) brings values and guidelines to the world.

Let us consider authority first. All institutions embody some notion of
authority, shaping structure, group relations, and prevailing understandings
of legitimacy. But authority is not the same everywhere; not all authority is
authoritarian. In fact, intense debate over the nature and proper exercise of
authority has been central to Catholicism since the Second Vatican Council,
and these discussions have been aired with particular intensity in Latin
America.

In Colombia, the bishops have long claimed authority of broad scope,
basing their claims explicitly on the structure of roles and statuses the
ecclesiastical institution provides. This position remained substantially unchanged into the 1960s. A tentative step toward reconsideration came in
1969, with a document entitled *La iglesia ante el cambio* (The church facing
change).[14] Here the bishops note a "state of crisis" whose resolution required full-scale rethinking of the church, the world, and the relation between them. They draw an explicit link between social change, intrachurch
relations, and recognition of the changing nature of authority in the church.
Thus, "in the search for these new relations, the greatest difficulties arise on
issues of authority, the teaching office of the church, the sacramental ministry, and social change: four areas closely linked in the life of the church, and
of the church in the world."[15]

But this interest in innovation faded quickly; signs of caution, doubt, and
withdrawal appeared almost immediately. As it became clear that new authority models, innovations in the ministry, and greater openness to social
change had the practical effect of giving average believers, as well as lower
clergy and religious, the right to create autonomous programs with minimal

control, the hierarchy drew back sharply. In documents and actions, the bishops attacked the new ecclesiologies, condemned notions of a "popular church" that began to surface in the 1970s, and reaffirmed the central role of the hierarchy as a constitutive element of church life.[16]

They utterly reject the translation of traditional Catholic concepts into sociological categories: the gospel poor into the proletariat, sin into social injustice, and evangelization into social and political reflection and action. Such conceptual innovation is seen to attack the very bases of Catholicism, gutting its transcendental core and undermining the apostolic authority of the bishops. They counter by reaffirming the church's mysteries and the necessary role of clergy and bishops in their interpretation. Above all, they stress unity, unity of several kinds: the unity of laity, clergy, and bishops; the unity of all social classes in the church; and the unity of meaning and action in this world and the next. As I suggested earlier, the Colombian hierarchy's reaffirmation of these positions reflects a general trend in the Latin American church, reinforced in recent years by the policies of Popes Paul VI and John Paul II. Initial openness to institutional renewal and social action was soon followed in many cases by a concern for reestablishing hierarchy, authority, and unity, spurred by fear of the destructive consequences of an overly sociological view of the church's base, structure, and role.[17]

A great deal has been written about this process, and one document chosen from many may help clarify matters. As part of the preparations for the regional bishops' conference held in Puebla in 1979, the episcopal conference of each Latin American nation submitted a detailed report to CELAM summarizing its own situation and position.[18] The Colombian contribution is lengthy and pays special attention to matters of popular religion and popular religiosity, while taking pains to refute the concept of a "popular church" as a "church of the poor."[19]

The bishops work on the concept of the church, reaffirming their traditional stances. In their view, any religious organization, indeed all manifestations of religiosity, must be placed in a context in which the authority of the hierarchy and its officially designated agents occupies a central position. Links to bishops and clergy are thus the only core around which a coherent and legitimate religious life can be built. The loosening and constant questioning of these links is taken as a source of social and political troubles; their reaffirmation is seen as the only sure foundation for resolution of national problems. Of course, any definition of church unity rooted in sociological, and especially class, considerations is rejected. To the bishops, the very existence of the church is threatened by attempts "to question the age-old structures of the church, and to begin only from the people, from their values, struggles, and contradictions; to rethink faith only from the perspective of the commitment to liberation of the poor and oppressed; to revive prophetic charismas in the very heart of existing ecclesiastical institutions, in order then to condemn anything not in line with these premises."[20]

The explicit link between authority and unity has been the special public concern of Msgr. Alfonso López Trujillo. López Trujillo was for a long time secretary general and then president of CELAM; he is now archbishop of Medellín and was recently named a cardinal. López Trujillo is widely seen as a key spokesman for papal positions within Latin America. In a recent communication, he argued that the church is faced with a dangerous wave of "laicism," which if unchecked could overrun and eventually eliminate the hierarchy. He takes special pains to reject "horizontal" models of the church, which stress shared experience and the diffusion of power and legitimate authority. These are foreign to Catholic thinking:

> Working above all from a sociological perspective, the kind of structure of the church is thrown into question. *Horizontal* relations are to replace *vertical* ones. The fabric of communities [CEBs] must not be *vertical* (bishop-priest-layman) but rather *horizontal* (bishop-priest-layman on the same level). Why the recourse to such spatial images? If the goal is to avoid the extremes of "clericalism" or "authoritarianism" which would make the communities domains at the pleasure of the hierarchy, with no real space for lay action, then the intent is not censurable. But if such "horizontal" structuring produces a confusion of the missions [which] different statuses and vocations hold in the church, then the matter is one of grave concern.[21]

In sum, with the brief exception of *La iglesia ante el cambio*, Colombia's bishops have thus consistently upheld the centrality of hierarchy to church structures, practices, and the legitimacy of religious expression in general. Moreover, as I have shown elsewhere, the public record fits well with the bishops' private views.[22] Although they know of debates on authority in the church as a whole, they see the reformulation of authority as a secondary priority in their own church and society. Their church remains highly clerical and authoritarian; their society remains grounded in largely unquestioned structures of class and institutional patterns.

Hierarchy remains central to unity, and together these two notions undergird a mentality of Christendom.[23] Thus, though the bishops are largely content with the church's current structures and guiding principles of authority, they have staked out an increasingly critical social role. In public comments, the traditional mix of triumphalism, anticommunism, and moral lamentation has yielded to studied denunciations of poverty, inequality, and injustice. But such critiques are approached from the position of an institution giving guidance as part of a general rechristianization of the social order. To be valid, orientations must come from the church and, more specifically, from its official leaders. Borrowing from and cooperation with non-Catholic and secular elements is suspect. In this way, although church leaders may criticize injustice and promote reform, they do so within a tradition of clerical domination. Democratization or reform within the church is rejected: the bishops seek to modernize church structures and reach out to society. No basic reshaping of either is in the cards. Their church remains highly clerical and authoritarian; their society remains grounded in unquestioned relations of class and power. The next section shows how these perspectives shape church organizational strategies in Colombia, now as in the past.

Organizational Strategies

The Colombian church has long created mass organizations. This extended effort is best understood as an expression of the church's central role in national life. As a dominant institution, the church has looked to organization as a means to secure and maintain a mass base. Although the perceived threat has changed over time (secularization, liberalism, Marxism, the "popular church"), the hierarchy's response has been consistent: a search for reliable yet vigorous organizations as a bridge extending their resources and authority into society at large. To the bishops, doctrinal orthodoxy, structural subordination, and loyalty define the ideal Catholic group, now as in the past.[24]

The history of official Catholic organizations in Colombia falls easily into four broad periods: (1) decentralized social action and charity (to about 1930); (2) cultivation of Catholic Action movements, with a stress on workers and peasants (to the mid-1960s); (3) decay of Catholic Action and centralization of organization under direct episcopal control, with distinction of pastoral from political action (to the mid-1970s); and (4) the current stress on small groups tied closely to the hierarchy through the training of pastoral agents, the formation of lay ministries, and the promotion of base communities.[25]

The early history of lay Catholic organizations in Colombia contains a series of scattered initiatives. In 1913 the Bishops' Conference issued guidelines for such groups, stressing charity plus social action. The perceived threat of liberalism and secularizing influences among youth and labor led to sponsorship of such groups as the Young Catholic Workers (Juventud Obrera Católica, JOC), later a seedbed for Catholic unionism. The big push began in the late 1930s, when, inspired by European Catholic Action, the hierarchy sponsored the formation of a series of labor and peasant groups, entrusting their day-to-day management to the Jesuit-run National Coordination for Social Action. This Jesuit presence set a pattern ensuring orthodoxy, loyalty, and subordination by having priests serve as "moral advisers" at all levels.

Colombia's Catholic Action movements were strong for many years, but their relations with the church entered into crisis in the late 1960s. Ideological and generational changes in the Jesuit order made the bishops lose confidence in Jesuit programs for training lay leaders and guiding mass organizations. At the same time, established groups such as trade unions struck out for greater autonomy, resisting episcopal pressure for control and reliability. In reaction, the hierarchy took steps to centralize control, while clarifying the proper place of such groups in a Catholic scheme of things. The management of groups and training programs was taken away from the Jesuits and given to a new department of the Bishops' Conference. Various training institutes were purged; "unreliable" clerical advisers were replaced. Stress was now on developing leaders who would be loyal to the institutional church. Indeed, loyalty appears as a basic criterion in recent training materials for lay leaders. Thus, "Any ideological position which Christians assume must be taken in accord with the general doctrine of the church and with the teachings of the bishops in particular. It makes no sense to uphold as Christian an ideological position already condemned by the church. Unfortunately, this sort of thing makes for ambiguities. Christians must be radical in their loyalty to the church."[26]

Church structures are thus to be modernized and purified. Loyalty is underscored and central control reaffirmed at every turn. But ambiguities are at once apparent. The bishops want to promote social and pastoral action while avoiding dangerous political involvements and heading off challenges to their own authority. But any pastoral activity soon comes up against issues of action and power. Even a studied neutrality can be seen to take sides, if only by leaving established structures unchallenged. Moreover, in the long run group vitality rests on developing experienced leaders and serving the interests of members. These inevitably clash with demands for constant external control and supervision. The official solution to these dilemmas has been evasion: sensitive (that is, political) roles are reserved for laity "acting on their own" and prohibited to clergy or leaders of official Catholic groups.[27] In this way, the hierarchy can reach out to the poor but remain shielded from politics and class division. Lines of authority are kept clear, and the contamination of politics is avoided. Once again López Trujillo puts the issue sharply. He notes that in speaking of "the people,"

> Defending their rights is not the same as giving free rein to class struggle. Bear in mind that it is a law of language that some expressions are so ideologically contaminated that it is a difficult business to rescue their original content and tone. To organize for class struggle, even if we judge it compatible with our faith, has consequences of its own . . . a confused people sees a sterile division in the heart of the Church, robbing [it of] its true mission and mediating capacity.
>
> Language gains not the instrumental force of communication and dialogue, but of harangue alone: catechism sows slogans and nurtures reflexes of violence; homilies become fiery political speeches which may gain applause on the stage, but which elsewhere produce only the short circuit of bitterness.[28]

Three Official Programs

The ambiguities of the bishops' stance and the vehemence of their public positions are rooted in fear, above all fear of class division and of politics. These are feared for their potential impact on the church's place in society and for the potential challenge they embody to relations of power and authority within the church. Given this pervasive fear, it comes as no surprise that Catholic organizations should stress loyalty, control, and a restricted range of "safe" activities. The hierarchy's studied response to the challenge of the popular church is well exemplified in three programs mentioned earlier: training pastoral agents, developing base communities, and promoting permanent deacons and lay ministries generally. Let us consider these briefly.

The institutional church in Colombia jealously guards the identification, training, and legitimation of pastoral agents. The Bishops' Conference runs a number of national programs in this area and has developed several correspondence courses and pamphlets for training purposes. These materials ground all reflection and any consideration of action in authoritative and lengthy expositions of official Catholic social doctrine.[29] The bishops are given a key guiding role, the position of clerical advisers is reinforced, and great attention is devoted to defining the meaning of "laity" as a basis for membership in the church.

Strict distinctions are maintained between lay and clerical roles and activities, with the former clearly subordinate to the latter. Indeed, the most striking trait of all these materials is the dominant role given to clerical guidance. In this way, training programs are geared to produce reliable intermediaries, who will represent the institution's central interests in work with popular classes. This means binding such classes to bishops and clergy in ties of symbolic legitimation and controlled membership. Strong warnings are given of the danger posed by false prophets. They "pay little heed to announcing the true gospel message. The temptations of political acclaim seduce them [and] laden with revolutionary promises they divide the community. They do not give the word of God, but speak only the language of men."[30]

Reliability is enhanced by the ultimate goal of transforming laity into clergy or what might be called "miniclergy"—in any case, into official agents of the institutional church. The bishops' programs for base communities are a case in point. The first and most basic point to bear in mind is that the bishops do have a program. CEBs do not spring full blown "from the people": in Colombia as in every recorded instance, CEBs emerge from and maintain links to the institutional church. After all, these are "base ecclesial communities": base for basic; ecclesial for religious and church-linked; community for sharing and human solidarity. The continuing link of CEBs to larger church institutions is critical. After all, the church is nothing if not flexible. Over the years, Catholic leaders have shown a vast capacity to absorb all sorts of movements. They are domesticated if possible but cut adrift readily should they prove problematic or threatening. Moreover, old structures are often simply renamed to keep up with the trends of the moment. Such is often the case in Colombia. Officials of the Bishops' Conference point to large numbers of CEBs throughout the nation,[31] but a close look reveals that these are mostly older groups renamed. Only rarely have attempts been made to build genuinely new structures. A search through church documents and guidelines for CEB formation shows clearly that for the bishops, base means simply "lowest level" or "beginning," base as in basic. As a result, CEBs in Colombia are seen primarily as small-scale incarnations of the church, cellular units linked tightly to existing structures.[32]

For the bishops, the crucial dimension of the CEBs is the ecclesial. One official pamphlet lists eight constitutive traits, with most detailed attention going to the requirement that such communities be "hierarchically organized with a ministerial quality." This definition has a double meaning: close ties to existing ministries plus service as a source of new ministries and future clergy.[33] In the report to Puebla cited earlier, the Colombian stance is stated clearly:

> The best conditions for nurturing a vocation of service to the church are found in the heart of the Christian community. The Holy Spirit never stops enriching the church with varied gifts and charisms to be placed in service to the community. It is the hierarchy which is charged with discerning their proper content and exercise. Today, these different conditions converge principally in the CEBs as the beginning of an era of lay ministries in the church. The same holds for permanent deacons. CEBs are a fertile ground, as much to find and nurture vocations of deacons as to exercise their ministry as promoter, animator, and unifying link between the communities and their pastors (parish priests and bishops). Many CEBs already have lay ministers officially named by the hierarchy. They also have fine conditions for permanent deacons. Many have sent young people to seminaries and religious orders.[34]

These comments suggest that the production of clergy or miniclergy is a controlling goal in the bishops' views of CEBs in Colombia. The status of permanent deacons and lay ministers warrants a word of its own. These older, often ancient offices and functions have been revived throughout Latin America, partly in response to the scarcity of clergy and also as an expression of the desire to stimulate lay activity. In many instances, those filling these posts have had a significant impact: leading Bible study groups, encouraging openness and broader participation, and stimulating social and political awareness by linking religious reflection directly to the experiences of daily life.[35] The new lay ministers remain, in theory, rooted in their communities and social groups and therefore sensitive to local needs and desires. But in Colombia, the bishops' goals are manifestly more narrow. The overwhelming concern for security and reliability generates a push toward clericalism: continued control by clergy and the production of new (if lesser) clergy.

The three programs just considered are all designed with control in mind. The central thrust and limitations of these initiatives stand out sharply when set against available alternatives. The next two sections consider the alternatives in two ways. First, I will look at the net of groups and programs linked to CINEP (the Jesuit research and social action center) and to the radical Christian journal *Solidaridad*. Then I will consider in detail several cases in the development of base communities in peasant and urban settings. These are inspired, respectively, by official and alternative notions of what popular work and base communities are all about.

Popular Work: Alternative Views

In Colombia, the intense hostility to autonomous popular initiatives by both church and government makes it difficult to document the structure, methods, and activities of alternative lines of popular work. Groups are suspicious of outsiders and typically prefer to work without publicity. In this way, they avoid potentially devastating encounters with ecclesiastical or political authorities. As one activist notes, the groups are isolated: "This is not Brazil, where one has the bishops' support. Here in Colombia the hierarchy is opposed, and as we are few, it is easy to destroy us. So this is our plan: sow the seeds, let them grow, and later, when these seeds are trees, with strength of their own, *then* to be ready for the ecclesiastical and official onslaught. But should it come now, when the people are not mature, all this will collapse."[36]

Despite these limitations, there is enough evidence to build a portrait of the popular alternative promoted by CINEP and *Solidaridad*. They challenge the bishops on all fronts, giving particular weight to four elements: class unity as the basis of popular religious organization; the utility of Marxist analysis; the need for new structures of authority in church and society; and the primary role of political action in religious organization and commitment. All these issues are discussed at length in *Solidaridad*. For example, the June 1981 issue deals extensively with the meaning of a "popular Church." In particular, the anonymous writers in *Solidaridad*[37] confront the bishops' stress on lay ministries, arguing that this strategy amounts to evasion of the real problems the "base" confronts. From this perspective, the central issue is not reform of church structures but reworking of their social and political position in the context of needed revolutionary change.

For *Solidaridad*, the bishops' fear of losing ties to power and privilege heightens their drive for control and their insistence on loyalty. Control is stressed so heavily that innovation is choked off, and alternatives are driven out of the church:

This gives a special tone to the relations of Christians to popular struggle in Colombia. Or, to state it differently, to the birth of our own popular church. Our groups of Christians feel like spiritual orphans. Communion with the hierarchy is very hard, and this explains why in so many instances there has been such stress on *breaking*. A hierarchy which doggedly turns its back on the people, in the long run creates a people which turns its back on the hierarchy. This situation has forced many priests to work clandestinely, weakening the impact of their work with the masses. In our country, fidelity to the church is particularly conflictful.[38]

As these comments suggest, the immediate problem of those linked to the CINEP-*Solidaridad* line is survival, and survival within the church. A loosely linked net of popular groups does exist, and continuous efforts are made to retain some ties to central church institutions. Leaders and activists alike fear being forced out of the church and thereby losing the cover of its moral authority and the symbolic legitimation membership provides. As a result, in contrast to the experiences of the mid-1970s,[39] direct conflict with the bishops is avoided. As one CINEP organizer put it:

We have evaluated these experiences and discovered that the hierarchy does have power. Of course, we knew this, but we had not felt it in practice, not in the flesh. But then we found that they do have the power to destroy all this. So it is foolish to attack them so openly. At the same time, we drew another conclusion: the hierarchy has meaning to the people. Attacking the hierarchy means losing contact with the people. Attacking the hierarchy only sows suspicions toward us among the people. Another conclusion is that we gave all this an overly political cast. Christian commitment, yes, but very political. All in good faith, of course, but the result was documents which were too political. We were Christian groups, but we looked like political groups, with a commitment which was above all political.[40]

These comments suggest a search by radical groups for a new operative style that balances political goals with more explicitly religious activities and orientations. This new turn stems as much from a healthy respect (at last!) for the appeal of traditional religious categories and symbols as from the fears of repression just cited. The result is a set of groups that operate quietly, scattered in the interstices of church structures. Open conflict is avoided, and wherever possible some intrainstitutional shelter is sought: a sympathetic bishop here, a religious order there. In the process, groups form and dissolve as occasion arises, and the very notion of centralized, nationally structured organizations begins to fade. As one Jesuit notes, "Beyond the fact that groups form and dissolve, far more important is the dissolution of the very notion of Christendom. This is gone, and hence the groups built on that vision also fade away."[41]

As I have suggested, this view is optimistic, for Christendom is far from gone in Colombia. Indeed, its resurgent strength gives real foundation to the fears of radical organizers and the popular groups they inspire. Training institutes really are purged and difficult clergy transferred or suspended on short notice. Moreover, the bishops recently launched a major campaign within the international church, lobbying heavily in Rome in an effort to bring CINEP to heel. CINEP's leadership has been changed, and its efforts face growing restrictions. The campaign was kicked off by unprecedented public denunciation in 1981. The bishops' words bear repeating:

> With pastoral distress, and impelled by the requirements of truth
> and ecclesial unity, we must declare that our call to those priests
> who are a notable part of institutions of investigation or study cen-
> ters, and who share the theses of "Christians for Socialism" has
> proven fruitless. They persist in ideological goals which break the
> communion of the Lord's church. Hence, in the spirit of the Apos-
> tolic Call for Reconciliation, we declare that CINEP, its publica-
> tion "Controversy," the journal *Solidaridad*, as well as the popular
> ecclesial communities, are infused with ideologies and goals in
> grave conflict with the doctrine and discipline of the church.[42]

Popular Work: Case Studies

Debates over the popular often remain abstract and theoretical. Hence a look at experience is appropriate to grasp how and to what extent the conceptual differences outlined here make for really different sorts of praxis. As groups crystallize and routines are built into daily experience, many of the implications of these models come alive, and one can see clearly the limitations imposed by the clientelistic mentality and structural patterns that pervade Colombian society. I will consider two distinct CEB experiences: the first in a series of peasant parishes and hamlets in the diocese of Facatativá; the second in a poor invasion neighborhood on the outskirts of the city of Cali.[43] The program in Facatativá approaches the bishops' ideal with only minor local variations, whereas the Cali experience is tied closely to the radical alternative, both in style and content and through intense personal links to CINEP and *Solidaridad*. Limitations of space make complete analysis impossible, but even a brief look is instructive.

To begin, let me stress one common element. In each case, the impulse to form CEBs comes in some way from clergy and religious. Acting either through official diocesan programs (Facatativá) or on their own (Cali), these individuals bring people together, get the groups started, and keep them going through constant attention. They link scattered and often diverse groups together both through physical contact (meetings) and by providing common themes and orientations. In the course of my fieldwork I found no autonomous popular groups that predate this intervention. It is worth repeating that CEBs are a church-related and sponsored product, linked from the beginning (albeit in strikingly different ways) to the larger institution.

Now differences begin. Facatativá, located in a region of largely poor and isolated peasant communities, has a long-term commitment to rural promotion, with CEBs playing a central role. The diocese devotes many resources to promotion of CEBs, with effort concentrated in a group of pilot parishes. The program was begun with significant external funding from Catholic Relief Services of the United States. This money has paid for a small permanent staff and covers expenses of publication, transport, and the development of a center for regular meetings among clergy, religious, and community members. The full-time staff (a pastoral specialist, an educator, an agricultural extension agent, and a project evaluator) maintains links up and down the church's hierarchical chain: up to the national and regional training programs and down to a net of clergy, sisters, and lay activists who move the communities on a day-to-day basis. The diocese sees considerable success, pointing to the growth of lay interest and participation, the spread of new groups, and the development of numerous self-help projects arising from the solidarity CEB membership provides.

The urban example has seen little similar help. Cali is a major industrial city that has undergone phenomenal growth in the last thirty years. The archdiocese responded to this challenge with a series of innovative programs in the late 1960s but in recent years has drifted with little coherent focus. Laissez-faire reigns in Cali, and the result is a series of relatively autonomous initiatives, particularly in the invasion barrios constantly forming on the city's periphery. The archdiocese is always short of personnel and thus is disposed to accept initiatives if they respond in some way to the needs of pastoral attention. In many cases, then, small groups of clergy and/or sisters have gone to live in Cali's barrios, with the goal of sharing popular experience, gaining local confidence, and gradually building organizations. The task is harder than in Facatativá, for Cali has little of the pervasive religiosity and unquestioned respect for clergy and sisters that one finds in the Colombian countryside. Moreover, Cali's barrios are often heterogeneous, composed of migrants from many regions with few long-standing ties. As a result, CEBs must compete with other groups for a diverse and uncommitted clientele.

What are the communities like? Let us begin in the villages and hamlets of Facatativá. Consistent efforts are made here to promote the creation and regular operation of CEBs with strong links to a net of official ecclesiastical agents. Both church leaders and lay members value such links. Priests are constantly encouraged to pay close attention to the communities, and in two pilot parishes I visited (each embracing hundreds of isolated hamlets) a group of sisters was dedicated exclusively to this work. All these efforts are tied together at the center through the diocese's permanent staff, which keeps up a steady stream of directives, study groups, reminders, and the like. Average members value the link to the church as well, for it gives legitimacy and moral stature to group activities, while tying the groups into the net of contacts and resources the church can provide.

The results are mixed. Although CEBs are indeed promoted, the pervasive clerical domination and central control inhibits group autonomy and curbs internal democratization. Group meetings are often like charades: priests and sisters ask for suggestions, denounce paternalism and clericalism, and insist that "it is up to you." They then proceed immediately to lay out detailed programs, which are typically adopted in toto. Moreover, the extreme vertical structuring of the program impedes any experimentation with local coalition building—for example, a search for common ground and common effort with political or peasant groups around local problems. All significant action and interpretation are cleared with sisters and with the parish priests, and independent initiatives are discouraged. One program I looked at attempted to go in the direction of greater testimony and witness and met with trouble. Here, an independent priest worked as a laborer, sharing the lives of local families and gradually joining with them in a mix of religious reflection and social action. He was soon denounced to civil, military, and church authorities. The parish priest refused to defend the program, and it collapsed.

But the portrait is not monochromatic. One might argue that with time and experience such groups will eventually create structures and forms of expression with a dynamic of their own and thus gradually move beyond clerically defined limits. This may be so, and two examples illustrate the point. In one instance, a savings and loan cooperative has been formed, providing needed credit to peasants in the area. The original initiative came from the diocesan team, whose members worked for more than a year to start the cooperative, which rests above all on the base provided by CEB members. Despite these clerical origins, the cooperative quickly expanded to include both members and nonmembers of the CEBs and has now assumed a vigorous life of its own. As CEB members expand their horizons to found other groups, and as these gradually attain a measure of independence, conflicts arise. In this case, the parish priest has openly and repeatedly complained that the cooperative and similar groups are not sufficiently integrated into parish life. Group members feel the clergy does not grasp their needs and seeks only subordination. The following is one opinion, highlighting three areas: education (an adult literacy program), pastoral (the diocese's extension activities), and the cooperative:

> The priests say these are not integrated into the parish, but this is absurd. All our leaders are the same leaders promoted by education or pastoral who are now in the cooperative. They are members, activists, leaders. They are presidents of local civic action committees, presidents of the cooperative. They do catechism in the villages, preparing couples for marriages, parents for baptisms. They are active in every social and civic program. How can they say that they are not linked to the parish? I just can't see it. They say this is not integrated, but I believe that no matter how tied a leader may be to the parish, this does not mean he must depend on the parish for everything . . . this is what they want, but it is not possible. The cooperative needs independence, pastoral and education, too, because each has programs specific to it. What we need is coordination, not control.[44]

The problems in the parish are linked to the clergy's view of their role and of their proper link to politics. The speaker continues:

Things have been difficult lately, precisely because they have not made a real political commitment.

Who?

The priests, the new ones. And as long as there is no real commitment, things will not go well. People want more. They now look for hard facts, works you can touch and see. People don't believe any more in the Eucharist all by itself. I think Jesus came not only to save souls, but also to fill bodies.[45]

At the same time, in a number of CEBs one finds stirrings of a localized interpretation and reinterpretation of the programs provided from the top. One lay leader, a very poor and devout peasant, put it this way:

Yes, programs come from the diocese, but lately they are difficult and boring, too long and too complicated. So people get bored. And they have become more aware. They say, "Let's talk concretely about the problems we have in the group, the families in our hamlet, and see what solutions we can find." So we search in the gospels where Jesus tells his disciples to do this and that, and there we find ideas. Just as yesterday the Lord told this to his disciples, today he is speaking to us in the same way: do good for others, and there we end the meeting . . . so we get together to discover what is going on, to see if we can solve things. We don't worry that there is hunger in Africa; we are hungry here. Or that in Africa, Vietnam, Israel, Egypt, or Korea there is war. Here we are also at war. What happens is that in some places the fight is one way, and in others it is different. The whole thing doesn't bother me too much.[46]

A final aspect of the life of the CEBs which should be borne in mind is the impact of the plain fact of regular get-togethers and Bible study. Before the communities existed, local religious life consisted mostly of sporadic attendance at mass or participation in a massive devotion or procession on special holidays such as Christmas or Easter. A trip to the church was difficult for many peasants, and priests visited the hamlets only rarely. Pilgrimages to local shrines were undertaken, if possible, in cases of dire need. With the foundation of the CEBs, several new phenomena emerged. First, people gather regularly to read, listen to, and discuss the Bible and to worship, led by sisters and local lay ministers. Religious practice is thus more regular and is carried out in a familiar and comfortable ambience—most often in a member's home. Devotion is also more understandable, for both the Bible and the liturgy are in Spanish. All my interviews, with peasants and city dwellers alike, speak to the importance of these changes.

In addition, having regular meetings at fixed times and places clearly encourages responsibility and a sense of community, while breaking down the barriers of isolation and mutual suspicion so common in this region. One of the pilot parishes I visited has long been known as a guerrilla stronghold, a "red zone." The constant conflict here between guerrilla forces and the army creates high levels of tension, nervous illness, and a pervasive suspicion. But the meetings have changed things. As one woman from a particularly remote and conflict-ridden area put it,

> Another thing. People here lived in fear, fear of the army, of the guerrillas. This fear hasn't gone away, but it is better now. Now people talk among themselves with more confidence.
> *Why?*
> It must be the meetings, the church. Because as for the rest, what is there? What is there? We don't even have a schoolteacher. The only thing that functions is this. This is the only way people can meet others apart from those in their own hamlet.[47]

More radical and direct attempts at culture change through the CEBs meet a mixed fate in Colombia, and the barrios I visited in Cali illustrate the point well. Lay participation and more democratic internal governance are notable. They are attributable partly to the less clerical tone of local culture and partly to the sisters' genuine care in avoiding directive roles. Meetings are much less like charades and often take place with no clerical presence. A woman long active in one local CEB explains how the meetings are run:

> Well, it's like this, we develop it this way. We all work to understand better, even me, because you know there are so many things a person doesn't know. No? The Bible. We read the gospels and we study every little bit. And here we have people who have never known anything. They read it there [in church], the Father reads the gospel and that's it. Because he says a whole world of things people pay no attention to. But here we try to explain things ourselves. We don't have them explained to us, but ourselves we draw it out, we discover what we think.[48]

Internal openness and the characteristic orientation of the groups stem from their origins and development. CEBs in this barrio arose from initiatives by a small group of sisters who bought a house in the neighborhood. All work for a living, and in dress, speech, housing, and the like they identify closely with the community. Contacts with neighbors were gradually developed with formal programs begun only after considerable time had passed. CEB formation was in fact the last link in a chain, which began with the creation of a cultural center in the barrio. A lending library was set up. Study circles and short courses were offered on topics ranging from national history and unionism to theology, community affairs, and mundane, useful topics like nutrition and sewing. These activities attracted many residents and provided a base for subsequent group formation.

In the beginning the sisters were helped by a group of enthusiastic foreign priests staffing the local parish. They made church premises available, legitimated the programs, and collaborated in a general stress on cultural change and on the sociopolitical aspects of religious action. Attempts were begun to reorient religious ritual and devotion, for example, by changing the pattern of traditional Easter activities. Vigils, processions, decorations, and offerings were not eliminated, but their content and focus were reformulated in a more community-focused direction. The symbols of Christ's suffering, death, and resurrection were given a more direct social and political interpretation.

Class identity and political commitment in these groups were further promoted through participation in regional and national nets of similar groups. On several occasions the CEBs in this barrio have selected and financed delegations to national meetings—a major step for poor people. The general orientation is of a piece with the CINEP-*Solidaridad* line. Here is the opinion of another member:

> People come with such and such a problem and we start from there. This is where one can really feel the work of the group, because you know in the life of poor people there is so much pressure, so many economic problems . . . on the one hand, patience is needed to stay in the fight. On the other, well, you have to learn to stand up and ask for help. Not to remain closed off, but to communicate, tell your problems to your neighbors, to the group. This is the base of our activities—that all develop a critical awareness. Because in isolation nothing gets done, nothing can be accomplished. Not for oneself, not for others.[49]

Base communities in this barrio have generally thrived. Although some residents objected to their "red" tone and sought out other groups and parishes, overall response was good. These CEBs clearly found a bit of open space in the church's institutional structures and made the most of it. They benefited from the laissez-faire stance of Cali's bishops and from the active support of clergy and sisters in the barrio itself. But such groups are highly vulnerable. Apart from the political troubles their activities may bring, there is always the danger of a sudden loss of church toleration and support. The danger is immediate: in 1982 the contract of the foreign priests was terminated on short notice, and they were replaced by a series of local clergy who were notably ill at ease with the style and content of group activities.[50]

At the time fieldwork was carried out (1983) the situation was a standoff, and the groups persisted. But the long-range view is bleak, for even continued support from the sisters will not overcome the hurdles posed by a hostile priest. Loss of sympathetic clergy further involves a moral conflict because the link to the church's moral authority and to its central sacraments is thrown into question. Finally, we should never forget that barrio residents are, after all, very poor people. Despite their general rejection of paternalism and clerical control, they see clergy as a crucial resource with links to the institutions of the larger society.

In all these cases, in barrios and peasant villages alike, it is clear that CEBs arise and survive linked to the church as an institution, or at the very least to some part of it. Deliberate institutional choices underlie their creation, and long-term survival without some tie to the institution is difficult to conceive. Only the slow development of genuinely independent resources and leadership can ensure group survival. Indeed, in a curious way, it may be that the structural richness of the more controlled peasant environment, by spinning off cooperatives and other self-help projects, will lay the groundwork for greater independence than can be achieved by a verbally more radical but structurally weaker set of communities in the city.[51]

In this essay I have considered evidence on the ways in which key elements in the Colombian Catholic church understand the popular and organize groups and guiding ideas to deal with it. But beyond reviewing evidence in this way, it is important to ask why popular religion and "the popular" as an area of concern have taken center stage in the Colombian church, as they have in Latin America generally.

Clearly, current debates are only the most recent stage in a long process of change. In Colombia, the shift is visible in changing organizational strategies, which themselves respond to shifts in the prevailing focus of ideological concern. The early mass movements of Catholic Action fought against secularization, moral decay, liberalism, and leftist influence. As these fears faded amid rising concern over the implications of violence and politics for the churches, more controlled pastoral programs emerged, pulling back from direct political commitment and action. Now, churches in many countries (Colombia included) have taken a major role in defense of human rights. All these concerns make sense in a relatively clear sequence of threat and response. But why the popular?

I would argue that focus on the popular subsumes and unifies these earlier issues because of the way in which the popular as a concept and axis of debate joins the life of the institutional church with society and politics as a whole. Facing up to the meaning of the popular forces church leaders to grapple simultaneously with the internal political challenge posed by independent grass-roots organizations, with the ecclesiological significance of their class composition and political orientation, and finally with the practical problems posed by their politically charged activities. All sorts of thorny questions are raised. Do class-based groups have a legitimate place in the church? Is political commitment a necessary outgrowth of faith? Who speaks for the church anyway? What gives authority and why should it be obeyed?

Framing the question of the popular in this way helps make sense of the underlying thrust of official church programs. Authority is reinforced, unity is rebuilt around hierarchy and clergy, and the church's long-standing role as norm-giver to society at large is affirmed once again. In pursuit of these goals, bitter attacks are launched on the very idea of a popular church, and its adherents are put under heavy pressure. All in all, the thrust of this response is to pull the debates back to an earlier point when the church, identified with and united around its bishops, spoke with one voice to condemn Marxism, violence, and politics. Clerical control, lay subordination, and the assertion of narrow ideological parameters are all means to the recreation of this end.

These considerations suggest a number of specific consequences for the future of the institutional church in Colombia and for the quality of its links to the popular. First, it is hard to avoid the conclusion that in many instances the Colombian hierarchy has simply renamed existing groups. Even the most traditional organizations, wholly opposed to CEBs in structure and orientation, are held up as instances of CEBs in action. At the same time, those opposing the bishops are increasingly forced to work apart from the institutional church. Their ideological legitimacy is hard to maintain, and sheer survival is often at issue. Future relations of such groups to the institutional church are likely to remain strained and distant, as the hierarchy moves steadily and forcefully to check independent expressions of the popular.

A second consequence is that attempts to build new political commitments into the fabric of religious life will be excluded, rejected, delegitimized, and where possible destroyed by the bishops. In a number of Latin American cases, CEBs have recently served as substitutes or surrogates for political action, which is restricted or impossible in society at large. They provide an institutional shelter for activism and dissent, while nurturing the practice of democracy in the groups' daily experience. None of this is likely in Colombia. The bishops want no part of political commitment in any of these senses. They do not fear confrontation with the state, although they prefer to avoid it. What they fear above all is conflicts over power within the church and their implications for established patterns of authority and unity.

In the final analysis, the way we think about things organizes how we act, what we seek, and how we see and interpret events. Of course, this is not a matter of ideas and perceptions alone. The predominant ideas of a culture are closely linked to structures. They are carried by institutions and expressed in the daily routines and expectations of a variety of groups. The concepts and self-images that dominate the praxis of the Colombian Catholic church spring as much from inner sources (doctrine, theology, organizational routines, traditions) as from the bishops' great fear of the popular. Moreover, as I have suggested, these concerns and pervasive fears fit well with the clientelistic mentalities and structures of Colombian politics. In this way, the ideas and structural patterns central to both ecclesiastical and political life converge to inhibit and control the popular. Popular beliefs and practices are seen in ideologically narrow terms; popular organizations remain subordinate to hierarchical control.

But more is involved than mere control, for the inner continuities in the church's sense of itself suggest that even if the threat of the moment should change, any group the church promotes will have a characteristic structure and style of action. New organizations may indeed penetrate popular classes, but links of authority and institutional membership cut across lines of class to reaffirm hierarchy at every turn. The revival of notions of Christendom in Colombia, as in the church in general, suggests that no matter how "critical" or "progressive" officially sponsored groups may appear, they remain constrained in spirit and popular in name alone.

Notes

The field research on which this essay is based was made possible by grants from the Horace H. Rackham School of Graduate Studies of the University of Michigan and by the National Endowment for the Humanities Basic Research Grant RO-20271-82.

1. Of course, the issue is not new, nor is it peculiar to Latin America. Much recent fine historical work has been devoted to clarifying the relation of popular to institutional religion and, in particular, to rethinking the meaning of popular religion and popular culture generally. The following sources are particularly helpful: James Obelkevich, ed., *Religion and the People, 800–1700* (Chapel Hill: University of North Carolina Press, 1979); Natalie Zemon Davis, "Some Tasks and Some Themes in the Study of Popular Religion," in Charles Trinkaus and Heiko Obermann, eds., *The Pursuit of Holiness in Late Medieval and Renaissance Religion* (Leiden: E. J. Brill, 1974), pp. 307–36; and Carlo Ginzburg, *The Cheese and the Worms: The Cosmos of a Sixteenth Century Miller* (New York: Penguin, 1980). For more contemporary accounts see Thomas Kselman, *Miracles and Prophecies in Nineteenth-Century France* (New Brunswick: Rutgers University Press, 1983); Ralph Della Cava, *Miracle at Joaseiro* (New York: Columbia University Press, 1970); Douglas Brintnall, *Revolt against the Dead: The Modernization of a Mayan Community in the Highlands of Guatemala* (New York: Gordon and Breach, 1979); Kay Warren, *The Symbolism of Subordination: Indian Identity in a Guatemalan Town* (Austin: University of Texas Press, 1978); and Michael Taussig, *The Devil and Commodity Fetishism in South America* (Chapel Hill: University of North Carolina Press, 1980).

2. The literature on contemporary Latin America is vast and growing rapidly. On base communities see Thomas C. Bruneau, "Basic Christian Communities in Latin America: Their Nature and Significance (Especially in Brazil)," in Daniel H. Levine, ed., *Churches and Politics in Latin America* (Beverly Hills: Sage, 1980), pp. 225–37, and his *The Church in Brazil: The Politics of Religion* (Austin: University of Texas Press, 1982), which has an extensive bibliography. Sergio Torres and John Eagleson, eds., *The Challenge of Basic Christian Communities* (Maryknoll: Orbis Books, 1981), provides a range of recent statements. See also Brian H. Smith, *The Church and Politics in Chile: Challenges to Modern Catholicism* (Princeton: Princeton University Press, 1982); Michael Dodson and Tommie Sue Montgomery, "The Churches in the Nicaraguan Revolution," in Thomas W. Walker, ed., *Nicaragua in Revolution* (New York: Praeger, 1981); and Scott Mainwaring, *The Catholic Church and Politics in Brazil, 1916–1985* (Stanford: Stanford University Press, 1985), which gives special attention to the relation of the popular to the institutional church in Brazil. See also Penny Lernoux, *Cry of the People* (New York: Penguin, 1980). Much of the force of conflict and debate grows from the innovations of Liberation Theology. On this point see Daniel H. Levine, "Religion, Society, and Politics: States of the Art," *Latin American Research Review* 16 (Fall 1981): 185–209, and the studies reviewed there. A particularly instructive account of the link between theology, organization, and action is Brian H. Smith and T. H. Sanks, "Liberation Ecclesiology: Praxis, Theory, Praxis," *Theological Studies* 38 (March 1977): 3–38.

3. But see Smith, *Church and Politics*; Bruneau, *Church in Brazil*; and Mainwaring,

Catholic Church. A stimulating discussion of the church's attitude to society is Juan Luis Segundo, *The Hidden Motives of Pastoral Action: Latin American Reflections* (Maryknoll: Orbis Books, 1978).

4. I discuss these alternatives in "Authority in Church and Society: Latin American Models," *Comparative Studies in Society and History* 20 (October 1978): 517–44. For greater detail see my *Religion and Politics in Latin America: The Catholic Church in Venezuela and Colombia* (Princeton: Princeton University Press, 1981). A particularly useful account remains Avery Dulles, *Models of the Church* (New York: Doubleday, 1974).

5. See Segundo Galilea, *¿Los pobres nos evangelizan?* (Bogotá: CELAM, 1977); and Enrique Dussel, "La 'base' en la teologia de la liberación: Perspectiva Latinoamericana," *Concilium*, April 1975. This entire issue of *Concilium* is devoted to debates over base communities. See also Pablo Richard, "El neo-conservadurismo progresista latinoamericana," *Concilium*, January 1981, for a critique of the persistence of authoritarianism in supposedly "progressive" church structures.

6. The issue of class and the need for historically specific analysis and reflection were major themes of debate at the Third General Conference of Latin American Bishops, held in Puebla, Mexico, in early 1979. Official preparatory documents for the conference took secularization as the dominant problem of Latin American society and attributed social conflict primarily to the "strains" of "modernization." This position was challenged and ultimately modified by those insisting on a more structural analysis of inequality, conflict, and injustice. On Puebla see above all Phillip Berryman, "What Happened at Puebla," in Levine, ed., *Churches and Politics.*

7. Catholicism has traditionally insisted on maintaining an appeal to all classes, nations, and social conditions. The centrality of this position to the church's social and political stance is stressed particularly in Smith, *Church and Politics in Chile.*

8. Cf. Xavier Gorostiaga, ed., *Para entender America Latina aporte colectivo de los científicos sociales en Puebla* (Panama: CEASPA, 1979), pp. 147, 161ff., and passim. There are clearly echoes of classical populism here, above all in the belief that "the people" embody uniquely valid insights and that identifying with the people is a necessary step to valid and authentic political commitment.

9. On evolving debates in Latin America, see Berryman, "What Happened at Puebla"; Bruneau, *Church and Politics in Brazil*; and Levine, *Religion and Politics.*

10. One recent analysis that stresses these points in a discussion of rural violence in Colombia is G. Sánchez and D. Meertens, *Bandoleros, gamonales y campesinos el caso de la violencia en Colombia* (Bogotá: El Ancora Editores, 1983).

11. On violence in Colombia see Daniel H. Levine and Alexander W. Wilde, "The Catholic Church, 'Politics,' and Violence: The Colombian Case," *Review of Politics* 39 (April 1977): 220–39, and the sources cited there.

12. Jean-Guy Vaillancourt makes a similar point in discussing the Vatican's consistent policy of restricting the autonomy of lay groups: "The Vatican could not tolerate real grass-roots autonomy because any form of autonomy and participation on the part of an independent laity was seen as leading to the gradual disintegration of the Church as an ideological and organizational force" (*Papal Power: A Study of Vatican Control over Lay Catholic Elites* [Berkeley and Los Angeles: University of California Press, 1980]). On this point see also Gianfranco Poggi, *Catholic Action in Italy: The*

Sociology of a Sponsored Organization (Stanford: Stanford University Press, 1967). On the fear that underlies this position, see Segundo, *Hidden Motives*.

13. For a detailed account of the evolution of these positions in Colombia, see my *Religion and Politics*, esp. chaps. 3–6. See also my "Continuities in Colombia," *Journal of Latin American Studies*, November 1985.

14. Conferencia Episcopal de Colombia, *La iglesia ante el cambio* (Bogotá, 1969).

15. Ibid., par. 335, pp. 128–29.

16. See particularly Conferencia Episcopal de Colombia, *Identidad cristiana en la acción por la justicia* (Bogotá: SPEC, 1976). For a detailed account, see Levine, *Religion and Politics*, pp. 91–95.

17. On these issues, see Peter Hebblethwaite, *The Runaway Church: Post-Conciliar Growth or Decline* (New York: Seabury Press, 1975), and his penetrating article, "La Iglesia polaca ¿Modelo para la iglesia universal?" *Concilium*, January 1981. See also Vaillancourt, *Papal Power*, Mainwaring, *Catholic Church*, and for a detailed account of papal intervention in the Dutch church, John Coleman, *The Evolution of Dutch Catholicism* (Berkeley and Los Angeles: University of California Press, 1978).

18. These are collected in CELAM, *Aportes de las Conferencias Episcopales, Libro Auxiliar 3* (Bogotá: CELAM, 1978).

19. "Aporte de la Conferencia Episcopal de Colombia," in ibid., pp. 77–354.

20. Ibid., pp. 161–62.

21. Alfonso López Trujillo, *Opciones e Interpretaciones a la Luz de Puebla* (Bogotá, n.d.), pp. 32–33.

22. *Religion and Politics*, esp. chaps. 4–6.

23. On the meaning and implications of Christendom, see ibid., chap. 10.

24. For a detailed account of the history of Catholic organization in Colombia see ibid., chap. 7. See also Kenneth Medhurst, *The Church and Labour in Colombia* (Manchester, England: University of Manchester Press, 1984).

25. This periodization is similar to that used in the training materials for lay leaders issued by the Bishops' Conference. See "Lección No. 9, La Pastoral Social en Colombia," in Secretariado Nacional de Pastoral Social, SNPS, "Curso de Pastoral Social" (mimeo, Bogotá, n.d.).

26. "Lección No. 10, Compromiso Político del Cristiano," in ibid., p. 519. The lesson goes on to list coherence between faith and political options as a necessary complementary criterion.

27. I discuss the ambiguities and contradictions of this position in great detail in *Religion and Politics*, passim. See also Michael Dodson, "The Christian Left in Latin America," in Levine, ed., *Churches and Politics*, for a good statement of the "radical" critique of this position.

28. López Trujillo, *Opciones e interpretaciones*, p. 21.

29. This is visible throughout the correspondence courses. A good example is the discussion of church and politics in "Lección No. 10," p. 483.

30. Secretariado Permanente del Episcopado Colombiano, SPEC, *Agentes de Comunión y Participación Diáconos Permanentes y Ministros Laicos* (Bogotá: SPEC, 1979), p. 15.

31. Such claims are laid out, for example, in the "Mensaje de la Asamblea Plenaria de la Conferencia Episcopal de Colombia," published in SPEC, *Documentación*

(Bogotá, 1980). A recent official publication claims more than six thousand CEBs (SNPS, *Aproximación a la Realidad Colombiana* [Bogotá: SPEC, 1981], p. 109). I discuss the bishops' tendency to rename old groups in *Religion and Politics*, chap. 7.

32. This interpretation is apparent in "Las comunidades eclesiales de base y la Parroquia," *Revista de Miscones* (Bogotá), May–June 1981, and in Ivan Marín, "Experiencia de Ministerios en Colombia," in Conferencia Episcopal de Colombia, *Renovación pastoral y nuevos ministerios* (Bogotá: SPEC, 1975), esp. pp. 104–6. For a critical perspective on the meaning of "base," see Dussel, "La 'base' en la teologia."

33. The eight constitutive traits are listed in SPEC, *Vivamos la iglesia comunidad eclesial* (Bogotá: SPEC, 1981), p. 30. The bishops' view of CEBs draws heavily on the work of CELAM-sponsored institutes. A good example is CELAM, *Las comunidades eclesiales de base en America Latina* (Bogotá: CELAM, 1977). The writings of the Brazilian José Marins have been particularly influential.

34. "Aporte de la Conferencia Episcopal de Colombia," p. 179.

35. See, for example, the experiences recounted in Lernoux, *Cry of the People*, or Torres and Eagleson, eds., *Challenge*.

36. Interview, 23 July 1981.

37. Most articles are published anonymously, to protect the authors against reprisals.

38. "Desde la perspectiva de la Iglesia de los pobres," *Solidaridad* (Bogotá), June 1979, p. 35.

39. See, for example, the documents collected in *SAL Un compromiso sacerdotal en la lucha de clases, documentos, 1972–1978* (Bogotá: SAL, 1978). SAL (Sacerdotes para America Latina, Priests for Latin America) was a national organization of radical clergy and religious in Colombia. Mainwaring reports a similar withdrawal from confrontation in Brazil in *Catholic Church*, p. 214.

40. Interview, 23 July 1981.

41. Interview, 20 July 1981.

42. Conferencia Episcopal de Colombia, *Mensaje Pastoral* (Bogotá: SPEC, XXXVI Asamblea Plenaria, 1981), p. 31.

43. For background on Facatativá and Cali, see my earlier account in *Religion and Politics*, chap. 9.

44. Interview, 21 October 1982.

45. Ibid.

46. Interview, 15 January 1983.

47. Interview, 20 March 1983.

48. Interview, 13 May 1983.

49. Interview, 28 May 1983.

50. Problems may well increase for the groups. In May 1983 a new archbishop was named for Cali. He will apparently seek to end the drift in the archdiocese by unifying church activities and bringing scattered initiatives together.

51. This is a speculative judgment, but initial analysis of related fieldwork in Venezuela suggests that it may be valid. In Venezuela during 1983, I studied the development of peasant cooperatives in one of the most traditionally Catholic areas of the country (a group of mountain villages near the city of Barquisimeto). These groups arose out of a network of local branches of the Legion of Mary (a very traditional group) founded in the peasant village on the initiative of a foreign priest.

The experience of these groups and the human solidarity they provided were the concrete basis for initial organization of a cooperative of small coffee producers. The cooperative has quickly grown into an economically viable, self-sustaining, and independent organization. Common religious belief and experience still provides a base of motivation and commitment to cooperative effort, but the group per se is remarkably independent of clerical control and is beginning to produce a series of autonomous leaders and organizational spinoffs that suggest continued vigorous growth. Karl Mannheim makes a similar point in his discussion of the construction of utopias. In his view, individuals alone can never turn utopian dreams into reality: "Only when the utopian conception of the individual seizes upon currents already present in society and gives expression to them, when in this form it flows back into the outlook of the whole group, and is translated into action by it, only then can the existing order be challenged by the striving for another order of existence" (*Ideology and Utopia* [New York: Harcourt, Brace, and World, 1936], p. 207).

10

Bolivia: Continuity and Conflict in Religious Discourse

Susan Rosales Nelson

Popular Religion, Ritual, and Change

Traditional observances of major religious fiestas in Latin America have drawn fire in recent years from progressive leaders within the Catholic church on the grounds that they reinforce unequal and exploitive relations between social classes and ethnic groups. Several years ago, in an attempt to discourage these practices, a group of Bolivian religious leaders decided to ban the mass from traditional religious celebrations in their diocese. In so doing, they condemned these practices for secular excesses, a pervasive sense of despair, and the absence of salvific referents.

How are we to understand such a radical attack on popular religious expression by the institutional church? What has been the impact of this decision? What can we learn from it about the meaning and uses of ritual under changing social conditions?

To answer these questions, let us begin with the concept of popular religion that has informed the attitudes of theologians and social scientists alike. Students of ritual commonly divide Latin American religious festivities into two general categories, both represented in the Catholic liturgical calendar. The first includes rites and ceremonies officially sanctioned by secular or religious authorities during which the power of the church and state is displayed. By invoking traditional cultural values, norms, taboos, and morals, official festivals consecrate the immutability of the social order. In contrast, the popular or comic celebration springs from the circumstances of daily life, frequently offering satirical or profane comments on political and social exigencies. Whereas official fiestas are restrained, formal, often dignified occasions, popular festivals are frequently characterized by obscene, scatological, licentious, and grotesquely exaggerated behavior.[1]

In many ways, Holy Week exemplifies the official fiesta, representing as it does the most sacred event in Christian history. Latin American Holy Week celebrations, unlike those in North America and Europe, are usually somber events replete with images of suffering and death and practically devoid of symbols of resurrection and salvation. This is in keeping with the picture of Jesus that evolved in Latin America: a relatively weak figure who proved unable to overcome his enemies and save himself, but nevertheless is respected for the dignity and forbearance with which he endured persecution and defeat. Unlike saints who possessed miraculous powers, Jesus represents weakness, pain, even emasculation. He symbolizes not triumph and salvation but patience and resignation.[2]

The epitome of popular religious observances is undoubtedly Carnival. During this pre-Lenten festival a "second world" or "second life" is created,[3] and the particularistic details of everyday life are abandoned in favor of a universalistic idiom more appropriate for considering transcendental matters such as sin, death, and salvation. In many places, Lenten celebrations are an opportunity for the exuberant public exhibition of behavior normally limited to private release. Drinking, pranks, and sexual license become the order of the day, along with dancing and nonstop merrymaking in streets and public places.[4] The general suspension of customary norms results in a brief liminal interval during which an undifferentiated community of equals temporarily replaces the usual social groupings.[5]

Although useful in some contexts, this division into official and popular forms of religious expression tends to limit inquiry into the meaning of ritual by focusing on typologies.[6] Elsewhere, it has been criticized for its elitist implications and misleading assumptions about the direction and source of religious innovation.[7] A further objection is that the concept of official fiestas that conform the individual to society and popular festivals in which social conflicts are allowed limited expression rests ultimately upon a functionalist view of society in which stability is achieved through redressive balancing of social forces.

By way of avoiding some of the problems associated with popular religion, and perhaps thereby illuminating it from another angle, I shall examine instead the nature of religious ritual, its presence within a specific social context, and the meanings assigned to it by its creators. I suggest that in Latin America, religious ritual is a key element in the contest between individuals and groups vying for influence and self-determination. It can be seen both as an issue framing conflict between social classes and ethnic groups and also as an arena in which these conflicts are arrayed. According to this perspective, rituals, whether popular or official, are neither static nor uncritical reflections of the social order. Time, place, performers, audience, and historical circumstances of ritual vary, as do the conditions they portray. The correspondence between ritual and reality is not simple, especially in extreme situations of dominance and subordination common in the Andes. Each type of fiesta provides opportunities for participants to reaffirm important relationships while commenting on existing conditions. Thus religious rituals not only offer a vision of reality and conform individuals to it; they may also attract and direct opposition to the dominant order. In this way, ritual may serve as a reservoir for symbols capable of innovative, even revolutionary, significance.[8]

To investigate these aspects of ritual, let us look at two contrasting modes of religious discourse present in Latin America today. Traditionally, Catholicism has emphasized what might be termed *liturgical discourse*, that is, symbolic manifestations of cosmic and social order. Throughout Latin America and especially in the Andes, procession, music, dance, and costume are employed in religious festivities to integrate spatially and socially disparate units of the universe. In contrast, liberation theologians have increasingly emphasized *evangelical discourse*—defined here as the exchange of ideas generated by the text, meaning, and ideology of the message of the gospels— along with its translation into praxis, or programs for action. An outgrowth of Vatican II and subsequent bishops' conferences, evangelical discourse has signified a revitalization of the teachings of Christianity to reflect political and economic realities of the Third World.

This distinction between liturgical and evangelical discourse allows us to examine directly questions of change in meaning and form by focusing on the dynamic, processual aspects of ritual. Liturgical discourse can be seen as one means of protecting and extending structural continuity among individuals and groups. Most commonly, it involves a public display of actual and mythic relationships encompassing past, present, and future visions of social and cosmic arrangements. In contrast, the use of evangelical discourse implies a rupture with tradition by highlighting the revolutionary message of the "Good News" of the gospel. Neither mode of discourse is the exclusive domain of contrasting segments of Latin American society such as clergy and laity, elites and masses, or specific ethnic groups and social classes. By focusing on the context and uses of ritual, I hope to provide an alternative method of investigating questions of status, power, and meaning.

The following discussion will center on the social, political, and religious implications of two major Catholic fiestas widely observed in the Andes. This analysis is based on fieldwork[9] conducted in Escoma, a small town located an hour's walk from Lake Titicaca in the Bolivian highlands. Throughout Bolivia, numerous towns and villages like Escoma have recently established or widened ties to La Paz and regional centers through expanded market networks and migration. Although the Bolivian revolution and land reform of 1952–53 eliminated large estates from the rural landscape, many traditional social and economic institutions linking Indians and mestizos have persisted relatively unchanged.[10] Much of the worst poverty in the country is to be found in rural peasant communities that typically lack electricity, potable water, adequate facilities for health care and education, and sufficient arable land to provide a secure existence for cultivators.

Highland Society in Bolivia

Today, as in the past, rural Andean society is characterized by two main themes. The first is a persistent inequality between Indian peasants and mestizo town residents. Besides their economic differences, townsfolk and peasants are also separated by divergent perceptions of society and their place in it. At the same time, however, mestizos and Indians share a preeminently ritualistic world view that continues to order and integrate human behavior and its cosmic implications. As a result of these two somewhat contradictory factors, social life in rural Bolivian towns, as elsewhere in the Andes, is composed of an intricate web of relationships that has stubbornly defied modification.

It is precisely in such remote areas that progressive forces within the Catholic church have concentrated their efforts at ecclesiastical and social reform. In its attempt to minister to a widely scattered, predominantly Indian population, the Bolivian church has supplemented the activities of foreign and national clergy with a large number of lay religious facilitators. Although few of them aspire to ordination, their presence has intensified the participation of laity in rural parishes. In addition, because most religious facilitators come from peasant backgrounds and are native speakers of the local Indian language, they have been valuable adjuncts in formulating and carrying out church programs.[11]

As elsewhere in Latin America, ecclesiastical and social reform are increasingly controversial within the Bolivian church as well as the wider society. Meetings to plan church policies are often marked by deep disagreements over the direction and speed reforms should take. As we shall see, the response of rural residents to church-initiated changes is equally divided.

Like many Andean towns, Escoma is inhabited principally by mestizo *vecinos*, as town residents are known, while Indian *campesinos*, or peasants, live in small, scattered hamlets surrounding the town. With expanded education in recent years, many campesinos speak some Spanish in addition to their native language of Aymara, whereas vecinos are at ease in both languages. Campesinos are predominantly small-scale cultivators, producing a variety of tubers and other crops for consumption and sale. Vecinos, on the other hand, avoid manual labor whenever possible, preferring to manage small shops in town and act as marketing middlemen between the agricultural hinterland and the capital city of La Paz, some five hours away by truck. Since land reform in the 1950s, Indians are no longer obliged to provide labor and other services to an estate. In the absence of hacienda owners, town residents have come to constitute a rural elite that exercises considerable dominance over peasants. Through institutions such as baptism and marriage, fictive kin ties of godparenthood are established between mestizos and Indians, thereby perpetuating the economic subservience of the latter. To fulfill their ritual obligations, peasants till the agricultural land owned by their vecino godparents, freeing the latter to engage in more prestigious and lucrative commercial ventures. Indian godchildren also supply casual labor in many mestizo households and are expected to provide produce and animals for sale to their godparents at reduced rates.

Before the revolution, town residents took advantage of religious fiestas to extend their sway over nearby Indian hamlets. Although peasants occasionally constructed their own chapels to worship local saints, they were also obliged to participate in the major fiestas celebrated in town. Eleven Indian hamlets would send dance ensembles to the town plaza for Carnival, and the remaining eleven communities danced in Escoma's patronal fiesta of Santa Catalina. The following year, the dance groups would alternate. Peasant leaders were responsible for organizing dance ensembles from their hamlets under threat of punishment from town authorities. In this way, public rituals reinforced the economic and social hegemony of mestizos over local Indians. Today coercion is no longer an acceptable means of ensuring campesino participation, with the result that usually no more than three or four hamlets send dancers to Escoma's religious festivals.

The church's ban against ecclesiastical participation in rural fiestas was issued in 1978. Since then, saints' days and other religious observances have been conducted in the absence of priests and nuns, although the church doors are usually left unlocked for fiesta celebrants to enter as they desire. Because Escoma's fiestas are now totally under the control of local laity, they provide a unique opportunity to observe how ritual can be employed to transmit a variety of messages, religious as well as secular.

Carnival and Holy Week are two of the most important festivals in the annual calendar of fiestas observed in Escoma. One measure of their importance is size. Hundreds of dancers and musicians and thousands of spectators fill the town plaza for these events, even though they coincide with the busy harvest period. Liturgically, the two observances constitute a single, prolonged sequence: a brief explosion of sensual pleasures and excesses that gives way to an extended period of repentance and preparation, followed by the commemoration of the central events of Christianity, Jesus' passion, death, and resurrection.

In Escoma, Holy Week, unlike Carnival, is presided over by a sponsor who becomes the focus of many of the activities. Despite this difference, both fiestas provide opportunities for individuals, families, and larger hamlet-based groups to attain prestige and power along with divine blessings. Both festivals are highly structured celebrations that require detailed preparation, extensive rehearsals, and elaborate costumes, music, and dances. At the same time, elements of antistructure—such as drunkenness, violence, and sexual license—are present, suggesting that the fiesta's formal aspects permit considerable latitude for behavioral spontaneity that in nonritual contexts would be considered disruptive. Only by examining in detail the symbolic elements and acts that make up fiesta rituals can we hope to understand the discursive mode and messages transmitted on these occasions.

Carnival and Holy Week

Carnival

Carnival observances in Escoma can best be understood as a series of symbolic depictions of the social order, revealed through the ritual of the *ch'alla* and the dance known as the *ch'uta*.

The ch'alla encompasses a range of ritual acts that are commonplace in the Andes. No important enterprise is initiated without a ch'alla. The sale or purchase of a parcel of land, truck, or large animal such as a cow calls for a ch'alla, as does the construction, purchase, or occupation of a new house. The ch'alla is also an integral part of ceremonies of transition, such as baptism, *ratucha*—traditional hair-cutting—weddings, and the conclusion of a period of mourning. The simplest ch'alla consists of pouring a portion of alcoholic drink from one's glass onto the ground before downing the rest. Alcohol and coca are then usually shared with those present. These offerings acknowledge the primacy of the Pachamama, or Aymara earth deity, requesting her blessings for the forthcoming transaction. Coca and alcohol are sacred substances present at all Aymara rituals. Structurally, they mediate between humans and supernatural forces, as well as among humans to reinforce social and cosmic bonds. In some places, coca is referred to as bread or the communion host, making explicit the similarity between the ritual of coca chewing and the Christian Eucharist.[12] When alcohol is added to the ritualistic consumption of coca, the analogy is further strengthened.

During Carnival, three types of bonds are renewed by the ch'alla: those between the living and the dead, between family members, and between fictive kin established through ritual godparenthood. In Escoma, the living venerate their deceased relatives by cleaning and decorating their graves. On Monday of Shrovetide, family groups visit the cemetery to tidy up the graves, which usually have been neglected since All Saints' Day five months earlier. The ch'alla consists of adorning the tombs with confetti and candies, colored streamers, and fresh flowers, while firecrackers are lit in a noisy salutation.

The following day, Shrove Tuesday, the dwellings of the living are similarly attended. First, they are stripped of the old decorations that had been left to gather dust from the previous Carnival. New ones are hung, confetti and candies are thrown onto the roof, firecrackers ignited, and an offering made to the Pachamama. As on the previous day, alcohol, coca, and cigarettes are distributed, and a meal is served to those present. Like the ch'alla in the cemetery, this household ritual is repeated each year during Carnival to renew the bonds among the members of the household as well as those with the deities.

Formerly, the bond of ritual godparenthood was repledged by a special ch'alla called a *taripacu*. Though infrequently observed in Escoma today, in prereform times Indian peasants were annually expected to bring a sheep to their mestizo godparents, who in return provided alcohol and confetti. The two families toasted each other and danced together around the plaza, accompanied by a band of Indian musicians. Nowadays, the taripacu is largely ignored because few campesinos are willing to bear the expense of a costly ritual that so obviously symbolizes their subservience to town residents.

As these descriptions suggest, the ch'alla links individuals to wider networks of living, dead, and fictive kin. Participation in the ch'uta dance, on the other hand, is based on residential ties. Ensembles are usually composed of single young adults from the same hamlet whose families assist them financially to rent costumes and hire musicians. Hamlets vie with one another for the best rendition of a single, standardized dance. The participants perform in the plaza on Sunday and Monday preceding Ash Wednesday, with a reprise the following weekend. Beginning around noon, the performances continue until dark, with each ensemble occupying locations in the plaza assigned by tradition to their community.

Ch'uta dancers perform in couples, though it is not unusual for a man to have two women as partners simultaneously, one on each arm. Men dress in red, wide-legged pants and short jackets with wide lapels, both sewn with small mirrors and fancifully embroidered in colored animal designs. Women wear *polleras*—traditional full skirts—in vivid hues and either shawls or ruffled overblouses of a contrasting color, topped with a bowler hat, the ubiquitous feminine headgear. Incorporating elements of fashion past and present, the dancers' costumes present a stylized version of peasant garb. In this way, dress becomes an integral element in the symbolic representation of an earlier era of subservience:

> The Ch'uta . . . has its origin in the ancient costume of the . . . *pongo*, an hispanicized Aymara word that derives from *puncu*, which in Aymara means door. It is the name of an Indian who fulfilled an obligation without recompense to the owner of a hacienda. He had to arrive at the patron's house [in the city] on Saturday and reside there one week in the office of gatekeeper. He was something less than a servant within the oligarchical organization of Bolivia. He slept on the floor, covered with rags, and was fed on garbage like a dog. He guarded the door to the street, day and night; and received in payment cuffs and kicks from his patrons, the landlords.[13]

The ch'uta dance is performed in the town plaza by campesinos who were never estate peons. In each hamlet, dancers too young to have experienced the prereform period eagerly join dance ensembles and take pride in executing the simple yet exhausting steps. Nevertheless, the display of elements from an era of former servitude inevitably brings to mind the historically inferior position of Escoma's peasants. Rituals like the ch'alla that ostensibly establish bonds between individuals and groups simultaneously acknowledge the gulf between them that cannot be bridged except symbolically. In both the ch'alla and the ch'uta dance, Carnival participants and spectators are reminded of present-day inequalities that persist between Escoma's mestizo and Indian populations.

Holy Week

Holy Week, held forty days after Carnival, is a boisterous occasion marked by a veritable campesino takeover of the town. Unlike most Escoma fiestas, Holy Week has not one but two sponsors. The main sponsor is the *misti capitán*, literally, mestizo leader. He is assisted in meeting fiesta expenses by a *padrino*, or godfather. In the past, both positions were held by vecinos. Recent Holy Week sponsors, however, have been peasants. Nonetheless, mestizo patronage remained a key feature of the fiesta. Both the misti capitán and his padrino could claim financial assistance from their actual godparents, prominent Escoma shopkeepers, during the year-long preparations for the festivities.

In decided contrast to the antic revelry and merrymaking common to many Andean fiestas, Holy Week takes place in a relatively somber atmosphere befitting its emphasis on Jesus' death. In Escoma the misti capitán, here given the fictitious name of Benancio Quispe, and his padrino, Dionicio Mamani, formally inaugurated Holy Week observances on Maundy Thursday amid considerable pomp and solemnity. Heralded by a series of dynamite blasts set off at dusk in the pueblo's soccer field, a procession of perhaps one hundred campesinos slowly marched into town, completing a thirty-minute walk from Quispe's hamlet. The group was accompanied by a small brass band that played a stately, almost dirgelike air that was to become the signature music for the next three days.

Led by the misti capitán, who carried a Bolivian flag, the assemblage slowly proceeded around the plaza, watched but not joined by clusters of vecinos who remained in the doorways of their shops. At each corner of the plaza, the music shifted gears into a more sprightly tune known as "la diana," customarily played to announce the presentation of a gift of alcohol, money, or both to a fiesta sponsor. Quispe genuflected, dipped the flag, and slowly waved it back and forth several times. After this brief homage was completed, the procession resumed its course around the plaza until reaching the rented house that served as headquarters during the fiesta. There the misti capitán provided alcohol and an evening meal for his peasant followers.

Throughout the next day, Good Friday, Quispe and Mamani entertained visitors in their rented headquarters. Although the sounds of the band were audible, there was no dancing in keeping with the solemn atmosphere of the day of Jesus' death. Occasionally Quispe would sally forth from his house, attired in his best suit and a sash in the tricolors of the Bolivian flag. Brandishing a cane—the *bastón de poder*, or staff of authority, carried in prereform times by peasant leaders—he strutted around the plaza by himself, somewhat inebriated. He rarely addressed vecinos directly, and most of them studiously ignored his presence.

Although the diocesan decree forbade services on Easter itself, a mass marking Jesus' crucifixion was held in the church at midafternoon. Meanwhile, outside, several members of leading vecino families decorated a statue of Our Lady of Sorrows, which had been moved to the church courtyard for the occasion. This activity attracted the misti capitán on his rounds. Approaching the gathering, he harangued them to leave their work and come to his house to drink. When they persisted in snubbing him, he entered the church, interrupting the service with the same loud, unceremonious invitation. Anticipating an unpleasant scene, the priest cut short the mass, omitting communion, and led the small congregation outside to conduct the adoration and stations of the cross in the church courtyard. Finally, Quispe abandoned the attempt to persuade vecinos to celebrate with him, and he left alone.

Saturday morning Quispe and his padrino, Mamani, accompanied by the small band, made the rounds of the entire town to pay their formal respects. As he approached each doorway, Quispe bent one knee to the ground and waved his flag from side to side. When the owner appeared, he or she sprinkled the misti capitán with confetti, and the two embraced and exchanged drinks of alcohol and beer to the sounds of "la diana." Occasionally, the band broke into a popular dance tune, and the little group would dance for a few minutes, much to the amusement of vecino onlookers across the plaza.

Several prominent town residents attempted to evade the misti capitán's visit by hiding behind closed doors or sending a younger family member to receive the callers. One vecino muttered that she did not like "those kind of people," as she disappeared inside her shop. Even before the fiesta, mestizos had complained about Quispe's behavior, commenting that pride in sponsoring a major town fiesta had made him and his wife arrogant and even abusive. Many Escoma residents cited Quispe's failure to issue printed invitations to his open house as an example of campesino ignorance of proper fiesta etiquette. As a result, few vecinos responded to his verbal requests to pass by his headquarters. Beyond making critical asides to each other, most vecinos tried to ignore the misti capitán and his fellow celebrants as much as possible during the first two days of the fiesta.

On Easter Sunday, however, it was impossible to remain indifferent to the campesino presence in town. Every shop was doing a brisk business in beer and confetti, but the weekly market was smaller than usual in anticipation of events to come. Quispe and his wife set up a table in the plaza directly in front of the gates to the church, where, surrounded by followers, they invited all to partake of alcohol and beer. Several vecino women joined a group of campesino women drinking together on a blanket near the misti capitán's table. But for the most part, mestizos drank among themselves, apart from the crowd of Indian peasants monopolizing the area in front of the church.

Shortly before noon, two groups totaling several dozen campesinos entered the plaza mounted on horseback. Each group was led by a capitán from one of the hamlets and accompanied by a small brass band playing the now-familiar dirgelike tune of Holy Week. Horses and riders galloped around the plaza several times with little regard for the market vendors, who hastened to remove their wares from the horses' path. Meanwhile, the campesino capitáns and their wives paid a formal visit to Quispe's table, bringing presents of beer and money.

After several hours during which horses and riders continued their circuit of the plaza, stopping only briefly to rest and down a beer or two, the town council, composed of leading vecinos, held a short ceremony in front of the church to present several new *awyllus*—colorfully woven carrying cloths—to those riders adjudged the best. At least one horseman felt himself unjustly passed over and argued in vain for several minutes with the president of the council. The recipients fastened their prizes around their shoulders like capes and, accompanied by their fellows, resumed circling the plaza until evening.

Throughout the day, the general mood of peasants and townsfolk alike was one of vague disquietude. Because the influx of Indian peasants temporarily suspended normal social relations, the ambience of Holy Week was noticeably more tense than that of Carnival. Several times fist-fights erupted between campesinos or rival band members but were quickly broken up by bystanders. Between vecinos, too, tempers quickened with increased alcohol consumption. For the most part, open clashes occurred between members of the same social stratum, that is, between peasants or townsfolk, rather than between an Indian and a mestizo. On several occasions an inebriated vecino insulted a campesino, but each time the latter withdrew, surrounded by companions, rather than provoke a more serious incident.

Time, Space, Power, and Conflict in the Fiestas

The absence of ecclesiastical sanction has thus far had little impact on the tone, content, and size of the festivities associated with Carnival and Holy Week in Escoma. According to vecino informants, church participation before the ban consisted primarily of blessing the sponsors and offering mass on the principal days of Lent and Holy Week. The dancing and ch'alla described above for Carnival have probably changed little since the revolution of 1952. In contrast, Holy Week, once dominated by vecinos, has been taken over almost completely by campesinos in recent years. A number of the rituals associated with both fiestas are, in fact, not directly dependent on the church's presence. These more secular elements have been criticized by progressive clergy as helping to perpetuate mestizo domination over rural Indians. Peasants, however, continue to participate avidly in these events. To understand why, let us examine the meanings conveyed through the liturgical discourse of these rituals.

Significantly, time and space assume special dimensions during these fiestas. Thus the social perception of time is suspended completely for limited periods, such as during the performances of peasant dance ensembles at Carnival and the horse races of Holy Week. These activities last as long as participants have strength to continue. After brief respites dictated by the need to eat and sleep, dancing resumes only to proceed once more to exhaustion. This pattern is repeated for the duration of the fiesta. At such moments when normal time is arrested, feelings of communitas[14] run high as performers and spectators alike become swept up in the relentless music, unflagging performances, and incessant demands to consume great quantities of alcohol.

In a similar vein, festal occasions bring about a symbolic redefinition of public space, especially the plaza, which at ordinary times represents the civilized essence of the town. During fiestas, the plaza becomes the site of the principal events: the ch'uta dancers and the taripacu between ritual godparents and godchildren during Carnival; the hosting by the misti capitán from a table in front of the church; and the processions and horse races of Holy Week. At these times, the center of town is preempted by festival dancers, musicians, and their audience, along with market vendors and customers, becoming impassable to motor vehicles and even bicycles.

The transformation of the plaza, normally the quintessential representation of vecino culture, into the scene of abandoned, almost riotous behavior during these liminal periods speaks of a reversion from "civilization" to a "wilder" state dominated by Indians. The countryside has literally invaded and overwhelmed the town with music, dancing, drunkenness, and weight of numbers. The subservient, domesticated Indian of Carnival emerges during Holy Week as a defiant, unpredictable figure proudly astride a horse—symbol of conquest and civilization—yet behaving in a manner clearly antithetical to more cultured mestizo ideals. This symbolic invasion by the savage only strengthens vecinos' resolve to fortify their civilized world against the peasant onslaught. At the same time, the desire is inflamed among Indians to achieve a degree of self-determination congruent with the fleeting freedom they experience on horseback.

The interaction between townsfolk and peasants during Holy Week is potentially volatile. For four days, campesinos assert themselves in town to a degree not witnessed on any other secular or religious occasion. As the campesino sponsor of a major town fiesta, the misti capitán is especially visible. In a town where few peasants have established residences or businesses, the presence of an Indian holding open house has the potential to aggravate existing tensions between campesinos and town residents. During the Easter Sunday horse races, the misti capitán's table was situated directly in front of the church in the very spot reserved for pueblo dance ensembles, tacitly giving notice of usurpation. In a similar fashion, the invasion of mounted campesinos is an emotionally charged reversal of roles that inevitably recalls actual Indian raids and massacres of mestizo towns, infamous throughout Andean history[15] and still feared by vecinos at moments of political upheaval. By construing the event as a demonstration of horsemanship rather than a veiled threat, the municipal council attempted to diffuse tensions and reassert control over the Indian presence in town. Similarly, although the misti capitán's visit to each vecino residence connotes obeisance, it also forces vecinos to acknowledge, through the ritual exchange of alcohol and dancing, the potential strength of the campesino presence.

Both Carnival and Holy Week are occasions for individuals and groups to assert and reorder their positions relative to one another. During Holy Week, individual actors such as the misti capitán and his padrino garner much of the attention. At Carnival, family clusters are reinforced by the ch'alla. Residential linkages are important during both festivals, as demonstrated by the bonds of endurance forged among ch'uta dancers and the troops of horsemen from nearby hamlets. These activities underscore the economic and ethnic divisions characterizing rural society. Especially for campesinos, these rituals strengthen familial, regional, and ethnic solidarity, each of which challenges mestizo hegemony.

At the same time, examples exist of other rituals that have been discarded, new features introduced, and traditional meanings transformed. The taripacu, formerly associated with Indian inferiority, has all but disappeared, and conciliatory elements have been introduced such as awarding awyllus as prizes. For the younger generation of peasant dancers, the prestige derived from performing the ch'uta in the town plaza far outweighs the symbols of servitude clinging to their colorful costumes.

The Position of the Institutional Church

Given this context of tension and potential interethnic conflict, what is the significance of the withdrawal of ecclesiastical sanction from traditional fiestas? Vecinos are angry about the lack of church participation, which they see as the latest in an ecclesiastical campaign to undermine vecino-campesino relations. They fear the loss of prestige derived from hosting impressive religious festivals that attract spectators from the entire region. More important is the sizable revenue from the huge market attracted by the three- or four-day events. As a result, relations between local clergy and mestizos have been severely strained. Most vecinos dislike the town's senior priest and harbor deep suspicions about the motives underlying current church policies.

Indian peasants are likewise unhappy with the church's ban but for different reasons. Though hesitant to criticize the actions of clergy, who they see as socially superior, a number of peasants are confused and ambivalent about the church's desire to reduce the importance of events like Carnival and Holy Week. Most campesinos are receptive to reducing their economic and political dependence on town residents but are less eager to discard the few rituals that provide traditional avenues for advancement. Fiesta sponsorship and participation in hamlet dance ensembles continue to be key channels through which peasants accord status and redistribute economic surplus. Interhamlet relations are cemented, or at times disrupted, by joint fiesta participation. Rival dance ensembles may compete during their public performances, but ethnic identity and the integration of each hamlet into the region as a whole are heightened by public rituals. Finally, sexual maturity is often validated by participation in festal events, which frequently signal the initiation of courtship.[16]

In addition to these social and political considerations, the religious side of fiestas is important to both campesinos and vecinos, although in different ways. Carnival and Holy Week are major events in which popular religious beliefs are given expression through public dance and musical performances and the ritual exchange of alcohol, food, and coca. Peasants are generally more consistent in observing these religious occasions than are vecinos. They take on ritual obligations to participate in a dance ensemble or sponsor a fiesta in return for a bountiful harvest or the recovery from serious illness. Keeping their side of an agreement with supernatural forces is crucial to assure continued blessings. For peasants around Escoma, liturgical discourse continues to be the predominant form of religious expression.

Although vecinos take little part in religious activities such as major fiestas or even ordinary weekly church attendance they, too, attach considerable significance to the rituals of Carnival and Holy Week. For mestizo townsfolk, Catholicism is one of the most important elements distinguishing civilized white culture from aboriginal society, which they regard as primitive. Escoma's mestizos look upon their tiny town with the church at its center as an outpost of Christianity, surrounded by heathen Indians still immersed in barbaric customs. The historic domination of ecclesiastical and secular authorities over the peasantry has left town residents with the feeling that the church belongs to them, despite recent evidence to the contrary. To vecinos, the observance of traditional ritual forms, even when carried out by peasant sponsors, helps preserve their self-image as guardians of the dominant tradition.

The Catholic church's current attempt to discourage liturgical discourse and thereby reform rural social relations has been resisted by mestizos and Indian peasants alike. By withdrawing from fiestas, the church has challenged not only vecinos' economic hegemony but their self-perceived cultural superiority as well. At the same time, the lack of church presence at fiestas threatens peasants' mechanisms for achieving positions of leadership and social status. Although ecclesiastical emphasis on evangelical discourse, or the gospel message, undoubtedly provides a framework for peasants to address their social and economic problems, it supplies little comfort to those who fear the erosion of traditional social institutions.

The contemporary church views Escoma's Lenten festivals as a direct contradiction of its program of evangelical discourse. In contrast to the fatalism of traditional Latin American observances of Easter, contemporary Liberation Theology offers a new commitment to the poor in this life. Church reformers condemn liturgical discourse for its emphasis on social and ritual order and promote instead the establishment of the Kingdom of God on earth through teaching and praxis. Most priests and nuns working in the diocese believe the church is acting appropriately by attempting to reform traditional rituals associated with fiestas. Their evangelical efforts are directed primarily toward the peasantry, for whom they provide literacy programs, vocational and leadership training, Bible study, nutritional information, and health care. They tend to ignore the majority of the town's mestizo residents, regarding them as recalcitrant obstacles to social reform.

During local fiestas, most clergy prudently leave their parishes to avoid persistent requests for a mass to sanctify the festival. Ecclesiastical leaders concede that the absence of religious sanction from these fiestas is unlikely to eliminate altogether their more objectionable secular components such as drinking, brawls, and extravagant spending. Nevertheless, they express the hope that traditional fiestas will gradually diminish in popularity now that the church has withdrawn its approval.

Conventional analysis views Carnival as simply a momentary outlet for popular aspirations, whereas Holy Week represents the reimposition of authority. But as we have seen, ritual does more than simply reflect the organization of society. Ritual acts, particularly symbolic inversions of power and status, may also strengthen group solidarity, provide unifying images around which rebellion may crystallize, or indicate potential avenues of innovation. Through religious ritual, existing social institutions can be reorganized in such a way as to allow celebrants to form new networks of interaction. This is especially true during liminal periods of ritual, when normal social time is suspended.[17]

Public ritual can be a sensitive index of social and political relations as well as religious belief. Religious festivals such as Carnival and Holy Week are singularly appropriate arenas for the expression of these issues. Their biblical and historical referents establish a ritual framework within which actors and spectators can explore the profound eternal and transcendental relations between humans and cosmos. At the same time, their social context permits direct, immediate consideration of political, ethnic, and class conflicts.

Most clergy committed to social transformation interpret traditional Catholic ritualism as simply recapitulating the status quo and offering little in the way of social options. Thus liberation theologians have tended to see liturgical and evangelical discourse as mutually exclusive aspects of religious expression. As an alternative, I suggest they might better be seen as complementary, rather than contradictory. Evangelical discourse, with its emphasis on biblical exegesis and Christian praxis, represents a clear response to changing social conditions. As we have seen, the same holds for the rituals of popular liturgy, rich with expression and experience. Viewed in this light, liturgical discourse appears more flexible and responsive to social exigencies than usually assumed by critics of churchly ritualism and popular religion. Neither Carnival nor Holy Week in Escoma bears much resemblance to the traditional meaning of these events found in Catholic teaching. Rather, they are best understood as ritual explorations of the places of campesinos and vecinos within a social and cosmic order undergoing constant, subtle revision. For Escoma vecinos and campesinos, eliminating traditional ritual is tantamount to severing, not simply reordering, this connection. Traditional Christian symbols of eternal salvation may not be a feature of Escoma's Lenten fiestas, but vecinos and campesinos have found a means of expressing through ritual their own beliefs about the present and hopes for the future.

Notes

1. For a discussion of official and popular fiestas in Latin America, see Roberto Da Matta, "Constraint and License: A Preliminary Study of Two Brazilian National Rituals," in S. F. Moore and B. Myerhoff, eds., *Secular Ritual* (Amsterdam: Van Gorcum, 1977), pp. 244–64.

2. This accent on suffering and endurance found adherents among Latin American peasants who were vanquished and forcibly converted. For more extended treatment of the Latin American image of Jesus, see John A. MacKay, *The Other Spanish Christ* (New York: Macmillan, 1933); Emile Pin, *Elementos para una Sociología del Catolicismo Latinoamericano* (Fribourg: FERES, 1963); June Nash, "The Passion Play in Maya Indian Communities," *Comparative Studies in Society and History* 10 (1968): 318–27; Miles Richardson, Marta Eugenio Pardo, and Barbara Bode, "The Image of Christ in Spanish America as a Model for Suffering: An Explanatory Note," *Journal of Interamerican Studies and World Affairs* 8 (1971): 246–57; and Stephen Gudeman, "Saints, Symbols, and Ceremonies," *American Ethnologist* 3 (1976): 709–30.

3. See Mikhail M. Bakhtin, *Rabelais and His World* (Cambridge, Mass.: MIT Press, 1968).

4. See, for example, Julio Caro Baroja, *El Carnaval* (Madrid: Taurus Ediciones, 1965); and Roger Abrahams, "Patterns of Performance in the British West Indies," in Norman E. Whitten, Jr., and John F. Szwed, eds., *Afro-American Anthropology: Contemporary Perspectives* (New York: Free Press, 1970).

5. See Victor Turner, *The Ritual Process* (Chicago: Aldine, 1969).

6. For example, see Thales de Azevedo, "Popular Catholicism in Brazil: Typology and Function," in Raymond S. Sayers, ed., *Portugal and Brazil in Transition* (Minneapolis: University of Minnesota Press, 1968), pp. 175–81.

7. See, for example, Natalie Zemon Davis, "Some Tasks and Themes in the Study of Popular Religion," in Charles Trinkaus and Heiko Obermann, eds., *The Pursuit of*

Holiness in Late Medieval and Renaissance Religion (Leiden: E. J. Brill, 1974), pp. 307–36.

8. Examples of the innovative use of symbols can be found in Natalie Zemon Davis, *Society and Culture in Early Modern France* (Stanford: Stanford University Press, 1975); and Victor Turner, "Variations on a Theme of Liminality," in Moore and Myerhoff, eds., *Secular Rituals*, pp. 36–52.

9. Anthropological fieldwork in Bolivia from October 1979 until August 1981 was made possible by grants from the Grace and Henry Doherty Foundation, Princeton, New Jersey, and the Horace H. Rackham School of Graduate Studies, University of Michigan, Ann Arbor.

10. On the effects of the Bolivian revolution on rural society, see Melvin Burke, "Land Reform in the Lake Titicaca Region," in J. M. Malloy and R. S. Thorn, eds., *Beyond the Revolution: Bolivia since 1952* (Pittsburgh: University of Pittsburgh Press, 1971), pp. 301–40; William E. Carter, *Aymara Communities and the Bolivian Agrarian Reform* (Gainesville: University of Florida Press, 1965); Jonathan Kelley and Herbert S. Klein, *Revolution and the Rebirth of Inequality* (Berkeley and Los Angeles: University of California Press, 1981).

11. See, for example, Gregorio Iriarte, "El Movimiento 'Iglesia-Aymara': Caracteristicas y Opciones Pastorales," *Busqueda Pastoral* 45, pp. 56–65; and Enrique Jorda, Juan Gorski, and Roger Aubary, "Pastoral Indigenista en Bolivia: Algunas Experiencias," ibid., pp. 37–54.

12. See Catherine J. Allen, "To Be Quechua: The Symbolism of Coca Chewing in Highland Peru," *American Ethnologist* (1980): 157–71.

13. Antonio Paredes Candia, "Fiestas Folkloricas del Departamento de La Paz," in *Monografia de Bolivia* (La Paz: Biblioteca del Susquicentenario de la República, 1975), 2: 267.

14. A more complete discussion of communitas can be found in Turner, *Ritual Process*.

15. For an account of peasant uprisings in the Escoma region, see Javier Albo, *Achacachi: Medio siglo de lucha campesina* (La Paz: Ediciones CIPCA, 1979).

16. Other studies of Andean rituals and fiesta cycles include Alfred Metraux, *Religion et magies indiennes Amerique du Sud* (Paris: Gallimard, 1967); Joseph W. Bastien, *Mountain of the Condor: Metaphor and Ritual in an Andean Ayllu* (St. Paul: West, 1978); Billie Jean Isbell, *To Defend Ourselves: Ecology and Ritual in an Andean Village* (Austin: University of Texas Press, 1978); and Hans C. Buechler, *The Masked Media: Aymara Fiestas and Social Interaction in the Bolivian Highlands* (The Hague: Mouton, 1980).

17. See, for example, David Gilmore, "Carnival in Funenmayor: Class Conflict and Social Cohesion in an Andalusian Town," *Journal of Anthropological Research* 31 (1975): 331–49; Peter McPhee, "Popular Culture, Symbolism, and Rural Radicalism in Nineteenth-Century France," *Journal of Peasant Studies* 5 (1978): 238–53; and M. J. Sallnow, "Communitas Reconsidered: The Sociology of Andean Pilgrimage," *Man* 16 (1980): 163–82.

11

Conflict and Renewal

Daniel H. Levine

The relation between religion and politics in Latin America today turns now as never before on questions of democracy and democratization. Democracy refers to the inauguration, legitimation, support, and survival of free, pluralistic, and relatively open institutions in national life. Democratization addresses the creation of greater equality and participation within major institutions, including the church. Democracy is the simpler task: Catholic leaders and activists turn their energies to the promotion of human rights, political liberties, and minimal notions of equity and justice. Democratization is harder, for it calls church elites and rank-and-file Catholics to legitimate new concepts of equality and to implement new models of democratic governance in the heart of traditionally hierarchical and authoritarian institutions. Democratization thus means building and sustaining spaces within these institutions in which the practice of democracy can be valued, nurtured, and expressed in day-to-day affairs.

In this concluding chapter, I argue that the conjunction of democracy and democratization is expressed most notably for Latin American Catholicism in the issue of the church's relation to "the popular": popular culture, popular religion, popular classes, and popular organizations of all kinds. As the essays collected here show, the pervasive struggle to define and control the popular in Latin American Catholicism today provides a central axis giving new and as yet not fully understood content to the relation between religion and politics.

It may be well to begin with a definition or two. When we speak of "politics" and "religion" it is important to be specific and to pinpoint insofar as possible the different social spaces in which these two spheres converge. At the very least, three levels of reality are at issue: the relation of institutions (for example, church and state); the articulation of ideologies, norms, and values providing a ground of legitimacy for specific structures, policies, and behaviors; and the creation of organizations and the development of consistent, routine patterns of action and expectation.

Here, religion refers not only to formal church organizations, rituals, and practices but also to groups sponsored and inspired by the church and to the general models of proper behavior and the good society that help organize and explain everyday life. The meaning of politics also expands. In broad terms, politics refers not only to formal political institutions but also to relations of power and equity in any organized setting. This perspective highlights questions of legitimacy at all levels: what makes any activity seem good and proper; what calls group members and citizens to obedience; what gives authority to power.

Posing the issue in these terms is particularly appropriate now, for at this time Latin America faces a wave of democracy (and of pressures for democracy) much like the wave of authoritarianism so notable in recent decades.[1] The transformations in Catholicism considered here are closely linked to this turn in the political cycle. They respond to and gain strength from these changes in society and politics, while at the same time their own inner dynamic clearly promotes and sustains further change in these areas. In the main body of this essay, I shall argue that the church's stance toward democratization is critical to the substance and durability of its contribution to democracy. For beyond legitimating the growth of free and just political institutions, acceptance of democratization in the church has the potential of building what might be called a "democracy of everyday life" and in the process creating a vigorous net of secondary associations that can play a major role in sustaining a pluralist political order.

Or to put the matter from the opposite perspective, if people are not treated as adults in the organized relations of daily life, if the structures of work, family, and culture remain authoritarian in spirit and practice, how deep can we expect their commitment (not to mention the commitment of their leaders) to be toward democracy? At bottom, these debates turn on how to understand and legitimate authority: legitimacy is the thread linking the process in the churches to that in society and politics as a whole. Issues of legitimacy cut through these debates because legitimacy involves more than ideas and slogans. Ideas are never simply "in the mind": they are carried by institutions and expressed in the roles and expectations of daily life. To be effective, then, ideas need carriers, women and men with a regular, acknowledged, and legitimate place in the social order.

In what follows, I argue that growing concern in the Catholic hierarchy at national and international levels over the implications of democratization within the church have led to attempts to withdraw from politics that undercut the church's capacity to assume a forthright, critical, public stance as an institution on issues of central political importance. I begin with an overview of the issues of religion and politics as understood in contemporary Latin American discussions. I pay particular attention to the shifting axes of debate and to the link between changes within the churches and transformations in the general political context. The next section takes up the meaning of the popular in greater detail, with special concern for understanding the ways in which the institutional church's relation to the popular shapes its more general stance in society and politics. A concluding section restates the issues in more general terms and explores briefly the implications of different stances on the popular for the future impact and inner life of the church.

Religion and Politics: Spaces and Issues

The changing relation between religion and politics in Latin America has received considerable attention in recent years, and I do not want to go over that familiar ground here.[2] Instead, in this section I will outline a few of the most salient points to bear in mind in any discussion of the question. Briefly, these are three: changing definitions of religion and politics and hence of the relation between them; the link of this relation to shifts in the overall political context in the region; and the shifting axis of this relation, as visible in the succession of issues central to public debate and concern in the church.

As a start, it is worth restating the obvious: religion and politics have never been separate in Latin America. They have been closely joined ever since the Conquest, bound together in relations of mutual affirmation and accommodation. The historical legacy of these ties was a virtual identification of religion with society and culture and a close alliance of the church as an institution with dominant forces in state and civil society. It became commonplace to consider religion and the church as "pillars" of the established order. But over the last fifty years,[3] Catholicism has witnessed a gradual and often difficult process of change and disengagement from this order. The process is rooted in deep transformation in both politics and religion. I will consider politics first.

Politics has changed profoundly in a number of ways. First, participation has expanded as hitherto unorganized and unrepresented social classes have come forward to press demands and seek redress of grievances. At the same time (and partly in response), the apparatus of the state has been reinforced, and its leaders have pressed broad and more effective claims for control. Finally, as a result of these changes, the classic issues of politics—power, legitimacy, and equity—are now raised openly in every part of every society. The growth of participation, the expansion of the state's claims to control, and the new scope and salience of legitimacy issues together make for a politics that is everywhere and ever-present: there are no sheltered corners left.

At the same time, religion, as expressed in the structures and guiding ideas of Catholicism, has changed. The sources are many. In part, change arises from the well-known dynamics of Catholicism as a whole since Vatican II, carried forward in Latin America at the 1968 Medellín meetings and after.[4] Change also arises from each particular church's attempt to respond in some way to the changing circumstances of the society in which it lives. These internal and external elements intersect in complex ways. Let us take a closer look.

The general transformations in Catholicism since Vatican II have made it possible for the church to break free of traditional ties. In this process, the recognition of historical change as normal (and even desirable) was of fundamental importance. If all social arrangements are historically contingent, then no particular form is necessarily correct and the church is freed (at least potentially) from its previous identification with the established order and its conservative supporters. Moreover, the revival of more communitarian models of the church (epitomized in the notion of the church as Pilgrim People of God) helped move it away from long-established concerns with juridically defined rank and hierarchy and toward an appreciation of solidarity and shared experience as sources of authority and models for action. This new emphasis is decisive. The stress on experience encouraged a broad reevaluation of nonclerical roles—laity and women religious took on new status and took up new tasks.[5] At the same time, legitimating authority with reference to testimony and witness through common experience calls the holders of authority to action as a necessary expression of their religious roles. The notable reassertion of "prophetic" roles in the Latin American church finds nourishment here.[6]

These issues have always been the province of specialists: theologians, bishops, clergy. But, as we have seen, in Latin America the popular impact of such new perspectives has been vastly magnified by what may at first glance seem to be two mundane matters: the translation of ritual and liturgy into Spanish and Portuguese and the growing scarcity of clergy. It is difficult to exaggerate the impact on average believers of technical and linguistic innovations in the church. The priest now faces the people, the mass is understandable, average people participate and comment. They also read the Bible, hear it read, and discuss it. They express opinions and make connections with daily life: it is important that these are mostly people who were always given to understand that their opinions had no value. If these changes are combined with organizational innovations pulling lay men and women into active roles in church life, the effect is tremendous.

The scarcity of clergy in itself is nothing new. The church's traditional response was to import priests, to campaign for more religious vocations, and in the meanwhile to spread resources as far as possible. Thus a priest would periodically visit remote or otherwise unattended areas to celebrate the sacraments and attend to the most basic spiritual needs of the population. But recent stress on the value of informed and aware participation has made this solution deeply dissatisfying, both to clergy and to their clientele.[7] One notable response has been the growing incorporation of women religious and lay people as group organizers and leaders, with special emphasis on deepening religious awareness through prayer, Bible study, and the building of community. In many cases, the experience of getting together for prayer and reflection has been closely tied to the development of a new critical awareness of society and to the organization and legitimation of movements for change.[8]

These transformations within Catholicism intersect with the church's attempt to respond to social and political change in obvious ways. Church leaders want to deliver the gospel message in the most effective way possible. Doing so requires reaching a population that lives in rapidly changing (and often worsening) circumstances and also competing in a hitherto unnecessary way with the bearers of other messages: Protestants, spiritists, socialists, communists, and a variety of mass media. Moreover, as the church's new social awareness and expanding organizational efforts meet the state's broadened claims to authority and control, clashes are inevitable. The problem is not that church leaders necessarily seek political roles and confrontations. With rare exceptions they do not. Rather, their pursuit of redefined religious goals and activities now seems subversive to shaky and fearful authoritarian regimes as diverse as those in El Salvador and Chile.

Religion and politics thus remain linked, but the substance of the tie is different. Church and state are no longer unquestioned allies; religion and politics can no longer be counted on for mutual support. I distinguish "church and state" from "religion and politics" here to stress the scope of the changes involved. Institutions and the relations between them have changed. Ideologies and public legitimations have changed. And finally, the implicit messages which politics and religion together give to the culture of everyday life—messages about hierarchy, deference to established authority, and passivity—have all, at the very least, been thrown into question.[9]

All this is clearly a lot of change in a very little time. To assess the impact and durability of these changes, the difficult matter of sources must be addressed. In other words, does change stem primarily from inner sources or is it primarily a matter of tactics, as church leaders seek to hold their own in changing societies? Phrased in this way the question is unanswerable. Precision is elusive, and in any case the mix of internal and external sources clearly varies with the context and issues at hand. Despite these cautionary words, I would like to stress here that for change to be meaningful and durable, a significant dose of inner transformation is indispensable.

Simply stated, if the changes so visible in Latin American Catholicism are mostly a response to the pressures of authoritarian governments (as in Chile or Brazil) or to the exigencies of particularly brutal civil wars (as in El Salvador), then one might reasonably expect such innovations to wither and decay once circumstances change and external pressures fade. But if they grow out of new understandings of the tasks religious faith requires, and if these understandings are effectively built into reinforcing structures of community and participation with an explicitly legitimate place in the church's normative order, then it seems likely that they will outlive any particular historical conjunction, providing a continuously new and creative basis for expressing religious commitment in daily life. I advance three arguments to support this position: first, the extreme variability of the stance of religion to politics; second, the strong international campaign now under way in the church to limit political involvement while reinforcing traditional values of hierarchy; and third, the changing succession of key issues in Latin American Catholicism, culminating in current debates over the popular, which, as noted earlier, bring the separate threads of this discussion together.

Even the most casual glance at the current Latin American scene reveals that there is no simple unilinear relation between external social and political conditions and the emergence of critical stances and more open structures within the church. Injustice abounds, and authoritarian regimes hold grimly to power throughout the region. In cases like Brazil, Chile, Nicaragua, and El Salvador, church leaders and base groups have married their response to political oppression and social injustice to the vigorous creation of spaces that allow democracy to be practiced and nurtured within the churches. But in the equally repressive and fearful conditions of Argentina, Uruguay, and Bolivia, with isolated exceptions the churches have remained silent, and there has been little internal change. At the same time, relatively open societies like Venezuela and Colombia, where challenges to the church are minimal, have witnessed notable (if isolated) pressures from within to have the church take on a socially critical and innovative role.[10]

This confusing picture takes on order if we consider the relation between religion and politics as a set of tasks of increasing difficulty. The easiest task for church leaders is to deplore violence, denounce injustice, and call for greater equity and democracy. Of course, such tasks are not really easy, but they are surely less difficult than is the job of taking the general commitments laid out in speeches and documents and using them to create new carriers of the message: lay leaders and pastoral agents working with the protection and approval of the ecclesiastical institution. This task is harder, for it draws the institutional churches into new areas and may commit them to defending the actions of motivated laity, who may well take the general ideas advanced by theologians or bishops and carry them far beyond the areas originally intended for application.[11] But as difficult (and often dangerous) as these tasks may be, they are less demanding than is the challenge of sharing power and yielding authority (even in small measure) to set the agenda of religiously legitimate ideas and organizational commitments. The latter course requires incorporating new ideas about authority and new models of organization into the church's own structures.

This is the hardest task of all. It throws long-established routines and expectations into question. Moreover, no matter how warmly such innovations may be welcomed within a particular community, group, religious order, or diocese, they quickly run up against strong international opposition, as expressed most notably today by Pope John Paul II and in Latin America through the orientations of the staff and leadership of the Latin American Bishops' Conference, CELAM. I will explore these oppositions more fully in the next section. Here it suffices to note that opposition typically rests on an explicit link between withdrawal from political involvement by the church and reassertion of authority and unity within the church. Authority here is conceived primarily as hierarchy; unity is built around bishops and clergy. Clerical control and episcopal supervision are stressed; any talk of a "popular church" is violently rejected.[12] This is the pattern in Colombia; and as

Dodson and Smith make clear, the Colombian experience foreshadows developments and conflicts in other areas.

These considerations help make sense of the succession of issues that have provided an organizing axis to debates over politics and religion in recent Latin American experience. In roughly chronological order, these have been secularization and liberalism, Marxism and communism, violence, politics, human rights and the national security state, and the popular. Each has taken center stage because it speaks to the deeply held concerns of church leaders and expresses most directly their understandings of both religion and politics. Let us consider them in turn.

The linked threats of secularization and liberalism absorbed Catholic attention in Latin America for many years. By the postwar period, the church's response had crystallized in many countries in a strategy combining the affirmation of orthodox doctrine and hierarchical authority with the development of Catholic Action movements as "arms" of the church to carry the struggle forward among workers, peasants, professionals, students, and similar groups and to shield them from ideological contamination. The threat of leftist influences drew a similar response, and in many cases there was heated competition between Marxist and Catholic elements in trade unions and political circles. The early push of Christian Democracy in Latin America dates from this period. But by the 1960s, traditional fears of liberalism and leftist influence began to fade, and many hierarchies sought to withdraw from partisan entanglements and thus, in their view, to get out of politics.

At the same time, new concerns arose in the churches over the implications of violence and politics. But violence and politics now differed, this time stemming from two sources: the expanding claims of the authoritarian state and the demands of scattered groups of theologians and grass-roots organizations. The first, embodied in doctrines of national security, called for order, discipline, and a tremendous growth of the state vis-à-vis civil society. Politics was to be curtailed and repression extended throughout the society. The second source, which soon crystallized under the general heading of Liberation Theology, called the church to politics through the denunciation of injustice and the organization for liberation. From this perspective, politics as legitimacy, power, and equity was to replace politics as partisan identification.[13]

Responses were mixed. In some cases, the ideas of Liberation Theology gradually assumed a central role in pastoral planning and in the public positions of the church.[14] Berryman shows this process clearly for El Salvador, and the analyses of Chile and Brazil in this volume confirm the trend. The impact of these ideas was surely magnified by the abuses of the national security state. But the more common response was to reject the notion of political activism for the church and to push for more centrally controlled and delimited pastoral programs. To combine this stance with an often courageous defense of human rights and denunciation of the national security state required that the bishops push for restoration of traditional lines of authority within the church and thus appear as sole leaders and legitimate spokesmen for a united institution. All these issues make sense in a relatively clear sequence of threat and response. But why the popular?

The next section discusses the meaning of the popular in some detail. Here I wish only to stress one distinctive trait that sets the popular off from earlier axes of debate. Whatever else the word may stand for in Latin American Catholicism, "popular" necessarily denotes activity by large numbers of mostly poor people within church structures. Moreover, "popular" carries a claim to self-governance and to greater involvement by group members in managing group business, setting the agenda of group concerns, and explicating the religious significance of all this. In contrast, Catholic Action movements everywhere stress subordination to the hierarchy and operate under firm and continuous clerical supervision.[15]

As Kselman points out in his contribution to this volume, popular religion is both a terrain and an object, embracing the practices of certain groups and a form of religious belief or action. The distinction he draws helps make sense of current debates over the popular in Latin American Catholicism. Clearly, these debates combine a dispute over the proper definition of popular religion, a struggle to control the institutional church's links to popular practice, and a conflict over the significance of class and power relations within the church as well as between it and other social institutions. But despite its claims to address popular aspirations and to arise in some sense out of the experience of the poor, Liberation Theology remains a set of ideas created and advanced mostly by intellectuals.[16] But in contemporary Latin America, grass-roots "popular" Catholic organizations stress social criticism and democratic self-governance precisely because they address both the church's general role in society and the proper organization of authority and responsibility within its formal bounds.[17]

In my research on grass-roots Christian communities, I asked group members if they thought the church had become more open to lay participation.[18] Here is one answer, which shows what the bishops are up against. The speaker is a woman from a slum community on the margins of a major Colombian city.

> But which church? Because look, what I see is that there are parts of the church which do this, because according to the hierarchy . . . the hierarchical church will never let priests get involved in these things. We see that they issue statements about not getting involved in politics, but politics means that they speak about hunger and that they let the people speak about injustice, poverty, and all that. They say we shouldn't slide over into other areas, but what are they really doing? What they are doing is denying the gospels. Because if you read the gospels I tell you I am a Christian and I have a Bible. But I hardly know any of those Biblical citations. I only know one, which is Isaiah 58, which talks about the offerings He wants, and it is to loosen the chains and break the yoke.
>
> They will tell you that yes, they accept that, but only in a nice way, through lots of prayer [lit.: *a punta de padre nuestros*], to who knows what kind of solutions. But in any case, there are parts of the church where people have become aware, and we don't care that much about church hierarchies. What we see is that commitment with the people is more important than being more or less OK with them. So we go on, continuing with the real Christian commitment we have.[19]

This woman's comments make it clear that although leaders of the institutional church seek to define and control the "spaces" of religion and politics, activists and group members do so as well. They bring an understanding of their own urgent needs to the space religion and politics define and look to the church for inspiration, legitimation, and material help. These considerations reinforce the point that we should not and cannot assume that grassroots groups are simply passive recipients of messages from the institution. They see the church and its agents in ways that make sense in the context of their lives.[20] Once the norm of unquestioned obedience is set aside, people come to the arenas of religion and politics with projects of their own. The institutional church and the popular thus cut across one another in complex and often unexpected ways, and the struggle to define and control the popular becomes even more critical. With these considerations in mind, the next section looks more closely at the meanings of the popular and at the opposition it faces in Latin America today.

The Popular as an Organizing Concept

Politics clearly has a double meaning for the church: politics as partisan involvement and public stances and politics as struggles over power and authority within the ecclesiastical institution. Politics in this twin sense is crystallized today in the issue of the church's proper relation to the popular, an issue that turns above all on the meanings given to authority and to class in church discourse. Here, both theology and sociology play a role. Theological debate centers on the nature of the church and hence on the meaning of authority within it. Different senses of the popular clearly arise from different models of the church (as institution, as community, or as People of God),[21] which set contrasting projects for the church, most notably through the sense of unity and belonging on which they rest. The first grounds unity in links to ecclesiastical structures: hierarchy is stressed, with members in a distinct and subordinate relation to clergy, clergy subject to bishops, and so on.[22] The second finds its unity in the solidarity of community and shared experience. Unity here rests on social unity, and hence the need for clerical mediation and control declines.

The sociological debate is parallel and has crystallized in struggles over the meaning and place (if any) of Marxism and Marxist categories of analysis in the church's understanding of social and political change. The process began with Vatican II, which by legitimating the notion of change stimulated a massive borrowing of concepts and models from the social sciences. The intention was to build an explanation for change while preparing the church and its agents to deal more effectively with its consequences. There was brief flirtation with Marxist categories of analysis and sporadic experimentation with various Marxist-Christian alliances.

In the Latin American church, interest in Marxism peaked soon after the 1968 Medellín meetings, with strong reaction developing throughout the region over the dangers of an "oversociologization" of the church and its mission.[23] The bishops feared becoming identified with class conflict and warned repeatedly against the dangers of bringing notions of class into the church. They particularly condemned the transformation of gospel terms into sociological categories—the poor into the proletariat, for example. In their view, this wave of change ran the risk of emptying the church of spiritual content and removing the transcendental element from its message. Without an explicitly religious dimension, the church would become just one more pressure group.

The rejection of Marxism has been powerful, but the church still needed analytical tools to help make sense of the patterns of change going on around it. The gap was filled by a form of sociology that leans heavily on notions of modernization. From this perspective, injustice, conflict, violence, and the like arise primarily out of the transition from traditional rural to modern urban society. Problems are attributed to the strains and tensions of rapid change. This point of view has no place for structurally rooted ties of domination or inequality as causes. There is no hint of class as an organizing perspective.[24]

Throughout the 1970s and into the present decade, these debates over theology and sociology, organization and strategy have been played out in often bitter struggles in religious orders, seminaries, training institutes, schools, parishes, dioceses, and myriad Catholic groups. At issue is the control of such specific items as textbooks and curricula, teaching and training programs for laity, sisters, and clergy, and more broadly, the capacity to set the agenda for Catholic discussions at all levels and for the future social projection of the church.

A brief review of the evidence on CEBs highlights the ambiguities of the process. As we have seen, a great deal has been written about CEBs in recent years, and many observers have stressed that they combine smallness of scale and social homogeneity with internal democratization. Great weight has been given to their class composition and to the convergence of a deepened spiritual life with a critical social and political stance in CEB experience. But much of this writing has been theoretical or at best grounded in a collection of relatively extreme and spectacular cases. As the essays collected here show, the evidence is scattered and contradictory.[25] Very diverse groups take the name of "base community" in Latin America today. They are distinguished by the way they fit into the understandings of church and society that guide the ecclesiastical hierarchy[26] and, further, by the way social pressures magnify group initiatives and dispositions.

All CEBs stress spiritual values and Bible study, but the lessons they draw from the Bible and the way they link spiritual understandings and group life to social and political issues range across the entire gamut of alternatives. At one extreme, CEBs have been closely associated with revolutionary movements in Nicaragua and El Salvador, providing motivation, organized support, and a recruitment ground for more general political movements. In the middle are experiences like Chile or Brazil, where CEBs, strongly promoted and protected by the churches, have spurred religious renewal while sustaining alternative spaces for democracy in heavily authoritarian societies. The other extreme is taken by cases like Colombia, where CEBs are often organized in authoritarian and clerically controlled patterns.

These experiences fit well along a continuum built on political and religious dimensions: both the external element of threat and urgent base concerns and the internal element of different prevailing ideas about church and society contribute to setting the inner life and social projection of the CEBs. In Nicaragua and El Salvador, for example, social conditions worsened rapidly and political struggle turned into civil war, forcing choices on many groups. At the same time, bishops such as Msgr. Romero and key elements of the Nicaraguan hierarchy welcomed the development of CEBs and openly aligned the church against dictatorship and repressive rule. But with the Sandinista triumph in Nicaragua and the murder of Archbishop Romero there has been a pullback.

In part this withdrawal stems from changed political circumstances, but international pressures, reinforcing domestic fears of democratization and overpoliticization in the church, have played a major role. The Pope's 1983 visit to Central America exemplified the pressures and conflicts and has intensified the struggle over the church in these countries. In Chile, there is less polarization, for since the early 1970s church leaders have struggled to reaffirm spiritual values and reinforce internal lines of authority while retaining an independent and critical stance in society. These efforts were spurred by the successive threats of Christians for Socialism and the pretensions of the national security state of General Pinochet. Each in different ways posed a clear threat to the inner life of the church and to the organization of its mission in society, and each has been resisted firmly by church leaders. Finally, in Colombia, the bishops' commitment to traditional models of the church moves them to build CEBs in a highly controlled and authoritarian way. Indeed, as noted in the chapter on Colombia, their attack on popular groups is so bitter and vehement that one suspects the bishops see here a basic challenge to the church as they know it.

Debate and struggle over these issues came to a head in the events surrounding the Third General Conference of Latin American Bishops held at Puebla, Mexico, in 1979. Puebla witnessed a major contest between the points of view outlined here, and debates converged with particular force on issues of class, conflict, commitment, and, of course, the popular. The short-term outcome was a stalemate, but succeeding years have been marked by growing pressures within the church (pushed strongly by the Vatican) to rein in popular groups, delimit the bounds of legitimate political action for church-linked organizations, and rebuild unity and reinforce authority within the church.[27] At issue most specifically has been the revival of older notions of the church as institution and the reaffirmation of its central role in society, culture, and politics. The two go together in complex ways. Authority seen as hierarchy is the core (once again) of an institution whose unity is built and legitimized around the leadership of the church's official agents: bishops and clergy. Vertical ties are stressed and laity made subordinate once again. With this base, the church *as an institution* can then go out to society providing authoritative orientation and guidance. What is not acceptable in this scheme is grass-roots autonomy. Democracy may well be the bishops' sincere public goal, but democratization has no place in their view.

The genie is out of the bottle in Latin America. Its escape and the many attempts to put it safely back inside give form and substance to the links between religion and politics throughout the region. The genie is the people: in the terms used here, "the popular," particularly as expressed in the drive for autonomous, class-based organizations in the church as in society and politics as a whole. To continue the metaphor, the "bottle" in this case is the institutionality of the church, as understood and defended by its leaders and built into the agenda and operative norms of its central institutions.

One way to grasp just why current struggles over religion and politics in the Latin American churches have become so polarized over the popular is to appreciate the weight of continuities in the church. In recent years we have become so conditioned to expect change in the church that significant continuities have been overlooked. As suggested here, one such continuity is the church's own institutionality and particularly the continued attractiveness for many church leaders of notions of Christendom, according to which the good society is founded upon, guided by, and suffused with Christian principles. These principles are defined exclusively by official church leaders, who work not from sociological analysis but rather from a stock of authoritative doctrine.

Despite the many changes recent years have seen, notions of Christendom clearly continue to undergird the mentalities and structural patterns most characteristic of the institutional church. In a sense, they define a comfortable "home" to which church leaders can return after a period of stressful and dangerous innovation.

The weight Christendom assigns to hierarchy, authority, and unity stands in sharp contrast to the popular. The cutting edge of the difference lies in the significance of class. For those promoting popular groups and advancing the notion of a popular church, a stress on class implies recognizing class as a basis for social division and assuming a commitment to take sides in class conflict. Moreover, as we have seen, defining the church's own base in class terms calls conventional structures and lines of leadership and authority into question. In a sense, the popular holds a mirror to the institutional church: egalitarianism is opposed to hierarchy; testimony and shared experience are set against juridically defined rank and role; power sharing is contrasted with the concentration of power; and political commitment takes the place of studied neutrality.

The popular is a salient issue in Latin American Catholicism because it expresses fully the hopes and fears of key groups. It expresses the hopes of many rank-and-file Catholics, poor people seeking greater recognition and responsibility within the church along with support for the active promotion of change in the social and political order. At the same time, the popular stirs the hierarchy's deepest fears. Earlier in this essay, I noted the various degrees of difficulty which the tasks of politics pose to the church. In conclusion, I take up this issue again, posing it now in terms of fear.

Those who control the central institutions of Latin American Catholicism (mostly bishops) have many fears relevant to our considerations. These may be placed in rank order. First, they fear being drawn into potentially dangerous political confrontations through the activities of popular groups identified in some way with the church. This is not a major concern, but rather an inconvenience to be avoided if possible. Second, they fear that the growing salience of class-based groups and demands in the church may dilute its spiritual and religious mission, turning it into just another ephemeral pressure group. Third, they fear the consequences of defining a religiously legitimate space for such groups, which would endanger established understandings of authority and undercut the central role of bishops and clergy. Finally, the bishops fear that redefinition of the church's base in class terms effectively precludes appealing to all social groups and bringing all social classes a message of salvation. These fears are understandable. They grow out of the bishops' role as leaders of a large, heterogeneous institution and rest on their concept of the church's core structure and social mission.

But understandable or not, such fears and the organizations and strategies they generate run up against many obstacles. The genie is indeed out of the bottle, and forceful attempts to reassert control run the risk of alienating the membership and sacrificing the new-found commitment of popular classes to the church. Moreover, significant implications arise for the church's long-term impact on society and for the quality of its own inner life.

A major innovation of recent years has been the creation of spaces within the church that allow democracy to be protected and practiced. In societies where organizational membership and democratic practice are traditionally suspect and limited in the best of circumstances, these innovations laid the groundwork for change far beyond the boundaries of religion as conventionally understood. The struggles over the popular that give flesh and blood to the relations between religion and politics in Latin America today are, in a deeper sense, struggles over how much democratization is needed to make democracy more than just a word.

Notes

An earlier, longer version of this essay was published as "Religion and Politics: Dimensions of Renewal," *Thought* 59 (June 1984). *Thought* is published by Fordham University Press.

1. A recent, highly influential collection of essays on this topic is David Collier, ed., *The New Authoritarianism in Latin America* (Princeton: Princeton University Press, 1979). Unfortunately, democracy and democratization have, until recently, received less attention in studies of Latin America. Kalman Silvert's description of a seminar titled "Democracy, Authoritarianism, and Development in the Hemisphere" remains appropriate: "It is amazing how the group can talk endlessly about authoritarianism, endlessly about development, but cannot find five sentences to say about democracy" (Silvert, *Essays in Understanding Latin America* [Philadelphia, 1977], p. 4).

2. I have discussed these issues extensively in two books: *Churches and Politics in Latin America* (Beverly Hills: Sage, 1980) and *Religion and Politics in Latin America: The Catholic Church in Venezuela and Colombia* (Princeton: Princeton University Press, 1981). Two other recent works are Brian H. Smith, *The Church and Politics in Chile: Challenges to Modern Catholicism* (Princeton: Princeton University Press, 1982), and Thomas Bruneau, *The Church in Brazil: The Politics of Religion* (Austin: University of Texas Press, 1982). For a more polemical statement, see Penny Lernoux, *Cry of the People* (New York: Penguin, 1982). I review recent debates and contributions in my "Religion, Society, and Politics: States of the Art," *Latin American Research Review* 16 (Fall 1981): 185–209.

3. The timing of change obviously varies from case to case, but most observers agree that the interwar period marks the beginning of reconsideration in many nations.

4. In addition to the sources already cited, see Peter Hebblethwaite, *The Runaway Church: Post-Conciliar Growth or Decline* (New York: Seabury Press, 1975), and his article, "La iglesia polaca, ¿modelo para la iglesia universal?," *Concilium*, January 1981.

5. For an illuminating discussion of the impact of such changes on sisters, see Katherine Ann Gilfeather, "Women Religious, the Poor, and the Institutional Church in Chile," in Levine, ed., *Churches and Politics*, pp. 198–224.

6. I discuss this issue in some detail in *Religion and Politics*, especially chapters 3 and 5. Michael Dodson and Thomas Bruneau have made important contributions to the understanding of this question. See Dodson, "The Christian Left in Latin American Politics," in Levine, ed., *Churches and Politics*, pp. 111–34, and Bruneau, *The Political Transformation of the Brazilian Catholic Church* (New York: Cambridge University Press, 1974).

7. In any case, fewer clergy are available to import; traditional sources such as Spain and Portugal have largely dried up.

8. One example that has received great attention has been the experience of base communities. I review these experiences briefly in the next section. Bruneau's *Church in Brazil* has a rich discussion and extensive bibliography on this topic. Sergio Torres and John Eagleson, eds., *The Challenge of Basic Christian Communities* (Maryknoll: Orbis Books, 1981), provides a range of recent statements.

9. This last point is given an original and illuminating discussion in Juan Luis Segundo, *The Hidden Motives of Pastoral Action: Latin American Reflections* (Maryknoll: Orbis Books, 1978).

10. In addition to the essays in this volume, relevant sources are as follows: for Brazil, the two books by Bruneau already cited, as well as Scott Mainwaring, *The Catholic Church and Politics in Brazil, 1916–1985* (Stanford: Stanford University Press, 1985); for Chile, Smith, *Church and Politics*; for Central America, Phillip Berryman, *The Religious Roots of Rebellion: Christians in Central American Revolutions* (Maryknoll: Orbis Books, 1984), and Michael Dodson and Tommie Sue Montgomery, "The Churches in the Nicaraguan Revolution," in Thomas W. Walker, ed., *Nicaragua in Revolution* (New York: Praeger, 1981), pp. 161–80; for Venezuela and Colombia, Levine, *Religion and Politics*. I discuss Colombia in detail in two articles: "Popular Organizations and the Church: Thoughts from Colombia," *Journal of Inter-American Studies and World Affairs* 26 (February 1984): 137–42, and "Continuities in Colombia," *Journal of Latin American Studies*, November 1985. For an insightful and comprehensive general review of developments in the Southern Cone countries of Argentina, Brazil, Chile, Uruguay, Paraguay, and Bolivia, see Brian H. Smith, "Churches and Human Rights: Recent Trends on the Sub-Continent," in Levine, ed., *Churches and Politics*, pp. 155–93.

11. This has clearly been the case of many base communities in Central America.

12. In his 1983 visit to Central America, the Pope stressed these themes. His arguments have resonated strongly in the Nicaraguan hierarchy, now engaged in growing conflict with the Sandinista regime. See Dodson's analysis in this volume and also the recent statement by the head of Nicaragua's Episcopal Conference, Msgr. Vega Mantilla, to the effect that "what is called the 'popular church' is neither popular nor a church. It is not a church because it does not lead to God, and it is not popular because it is allied with power instead of man" (*New York Times*, 18 December 1983).

13. The literature on both the national security state and Liberation Theology is vast. The following provide a useful introduction. On the national security state, José Comblin, *The Church and the National Security State* (Maryknoll: Orbis Books, 1979). On Liberation Theology, see my "Religion, Society and Politics" and the studies reviewed there. A particularly instructive account of the relation between theology,

organization, and action is Brian H. Smith and T. H. Sanks, "Liberation Ecclesiology: Praxis, Theory, Praxis," *Theological Studies* 38 (March 1977): 3–38.

14. The many programs advanced by the Jesuits in Latin America provide a good example.

15. On Catholic Action, see Gianfranco Poggi, *Catholic Action in Italy: The Sociology of a Sponsored Organization* (Stanford: Stanford University Press, 1967). Jean Guy Vallaincourt provides considerable insight into characteristic Vatican attitudes to lay groups in his *Papal Power: A Study of Vatican Control over Lay Catholic Elites* (Berkeley and Los Angeles: University of California Press, 1980).

16. The ideas of educator Paulo Freire on the need for a genuinely liberating education get more lip service than genuine implementation. His advocacy of nondirective leadership and expanded participation is only rarely recognized in practice. A good summary of Freire's views is his *Pedagogy of the Oppressed* (New York: Seabury, 1968) and *Education for a Critical Consciousness* (New York: Seabury, 1974).

17. This is not to suggest that such groups retain no links to the institutional church. Rather, it is the nature of such links that is at issue. Neither side welcomes a break.

18. The full text of the question was "Do you believe that at the present time the church gives more participation to lay people?"

19. Interview, 13 April 1983. Here is the actual text of Isaiah 58:6–8 (King James version):

6. Is this not the fast that I have chosen? To loose the bonds of wickedness, to undo the heavy burdens, and to let the oppressed go free, and that ye break every bond?

7. Is it not to deal thy bread to the hungry, and that thou bring the poor that are cast out to thy house? When thou seest the naked, that thou cover him; and that thou hide thyself not from thine own flesh?

8. Then shall thy light break forth as the morning and thine health shall spring forth speedily; and thy righteousness shall go before thee. The glory of the Lord shall be thy reward.

20. This point has been stressed forcefully and well in a growing literature on the history of popular religion, especially in Western Europe. Relevant sources include Natalie Zemon Davis, "Some Tasks and Themes in the Study of Popular Religion," in Charles Trinkaus and Heiko Obermann, eds., *The Pursuit of Holiness in Late Medieval and Renaissance Religion* (Leiden: E. J. Brill, 1974), pp. 307–36; Carlo Ginzburg, *The Cheese and the Worms: The Cosmos of a Sixteenth-Century Miller* (New York: Penguin, 1980); Carlo Ginzburg, *The Night Battles: Witchcraft and Agrarian Cults in the Sixteenth and Seventeenth Centuries* (New York: Penguin, 1985); and some of the essays collected in James Obelkevich, ed., *Religion and the People, 800–1700* (Chapel Hill: University of North Carolina Press, 1979). Natalie Davis's essays *Society and Culture in Early Modern France* (Stanford: Stanford University Press, 1975) are also important. A very useful account that stresses the church's drive to control popular religion is Thomas Kselman's *Miracles and Prophecies in Nineteenth-Century France* (New Brunswick: Rutgers University Press, 1983).

Recent studies in Latin America include Ralph Della Cava, *Miracle at Joaseiro* (New

York: Columbia University Press, 1970); Ricardo Falla, *Quiche Rebelde* (Guatemala City: Editorial Universitaria de Guatemala, 1978); Douglas Brintnall, *Revolt against the Dead: The Modernization of a Mayan Community in the Highlands of Guatemala* (New York: Gordon and Breach, 1979); Kay Warren, *The Symbolism of Subordination: Indian Identity in a Guatemalan Town* (Austin: University of Texas Press, 1978); and Michael Taussig, *The Devil and Commodity Fetishism in South America* (Chapel Hill: University of North Carolina Press, 1980).

For related analyses on African material, see Karen Fields, *Revival and Rebellion in Colonial Central Africa* (Princeton: Princeton University Press, 1985), and Jean Comaroff, *Body of Power, Spirit of Resistance* (Chicago: University of Chicago Press, 1985). A very useful recent study is R. C. Ileto, *Pasyon and Revolution: Popular Movements in the Philippines, 1840–1910* (Quezon City: Ateneo de Manila University Press, 1979). Comaroff and Ileto stress the need to recapture and reconstruct popular experience in terms meaningful to the actors themselves, which requires careful, systematic, and respectful attention to what popular groups actually say and do, avoiding the temptation to reduce their beliefs and actions to the categories of an externally imposed logic.

21. I discuss these alternatives in detail in *Religion and Politics*, especially in chapter 5. A fundamental contribution to these questions remains Avery Dulles, *Models of the Church* (New York: Doubleday, 1974).

22. Alberto Gruson has neatly summarized the practice to which this point of view leads: "There is a kind of catechism whose goal seems to be to convince the student that he knows nothing, that the catechist knows more (but not much), that who really knows is the sister; who knows more than the sister is the priest; he in turn is subject to the superior knowledge of the theologian controlled by the bishops; and episcopal declarations frequently cite the Pope. The caricature is probably less extreme than it seems: theological faculties are for the clergy but the average priests studied in seminaries; sisters have special institutes just for them; members of lay organizations have study circles; and the average faithful have Sunday preaching, and send their children to listen to the catechist. The important thing to underline here is not (happily) the possibility of some kind of graduated learning, but rather a practically static stratification, like a caste system, based on learning more in its transmission than in its elaboration" (Gruson, "Religiosidad y Pastoral," *Nuevo Mundo* [Caracas], May–June, 1980, p. 233).

23. Smith provides an excellent discussion of the church's relation to Marxism in Chile, distinguishing the relations the church maintained with Marxist groups and governments from its attitude toward the incorporation of Marxist ideas and organizational principles within church structures. The first was most cordial, the second unremittingly hostile. See Smith, *Church and Politics*.

24. Debates at Puebla accentuated the difference between these alternatives. The early working papers and predocument for the conference drew heavily on modernization sociology; the challenge of more structural and class-based views was incorporated into the final document.

25. In addition to the sources cited in notes 8 and 10, above, this discussion draws on the following: for El Salvador, Plácido Erdozain, *Archbishop Romero, Martyr of Salvador* (Maryknoll: Orbis Books, 1981); and for Brazil, Rowan Ireland, "Catholic

Base Communities, Spiritist Groups, and the Deepening of Democracy in Brazil," Working Paper 131, Latin American Program (Washington, D.C.: Wilson Center, 1983), and two articles by Thomas Bruneau—"Basic Christian Communities in Latin America: Their Nature and Significance (Especially in Brazil)," in Levine, ed., *Churches and Politics*, pp. 225–37, and "The Catholic Church and Development in Latin America: The Role of Christian Base Communities," *World Development* 8 (1980): 535–44.

26. It is important never to lose sight of this link. After all, without exception CEBs spring from the institutional church and maintain ties to it. They are ecclesial base communities, and all three parts of the name count: "ecclesial" for religious and church-linked, "base" for basic, and "community" for sharing and solidarity. "Official" church programs, such as those sponsored by CELAM, not surprisingly stress the ecclesial dimension more than the other two. See CELAM, *Las comunidades eclesiales de base en America Latina* (Bogotá: CELAM, 1977). The work of the Brazilian José Marins has been especially influential here.

27. As I note elsewhere in this volume, Msgr. Alfonso López Trujillo has played a central role in this campaign. López Trujillo was for many years general secretary and then president of CELAM. He is now cardinal archbishop of Medellín and is widely regarded as a leading spokesman for Vatican positions in Latin America. His interpretation of the process leading up to Puebla can be found in his *De Medellín a Puebla* (Madrid: Biblioteca de Autores Cristianos, 1980). He discusses the implications of Puebla in great (and often polemical) detail in *Opciones e interpretaciones a la luz de Puebla* (Bogotá, n.d.).

Select Bibliography

Abbot, Walter M., ed. *The Documents of Vatican II*. New York: Association Press and American Press, 1966.

Bastide, Roger. *The African Religions of Brazil*. Baltimore: Johns Hopkins University Press, 1978.

Berryman, Phillip. *The Religious Roots of Rebellion: Christians in the Central American Revolutions*. Maryknoll: Orbis Books, 1984.

————. "What Happened at Puebla." In Daniel H. Levine, ed., *Churches and Politics in Latin America*, pp. 55–86. Beverly Hills: Sage, 1980.

Bricker, Victoria. *The Indian Christ, the Indian King*. Austin: University of Texas Press, 1981.

Brintnall, Douglas. *Revolt against the Dead: The Modernization of a Mayan Community in the Highlands of Guatemala*. New York: Gordon and Breach, 1979.

Broderick, Walter. *Camilo Torres*. Garden City: Doubleday, 1975.

Bruneau, Thomas C. "The Catholic Church and Development in Latin America: The Role of the Christian Base Communities." *World Development* 7 and 8 (1980): 535–44.

————. "Church and Politics in Brazil: The Genesis of Change." *Journal of Latin American Studies* (November 1985).

————. *The Church in Brazil: The Politics of Religion*. Austin: University of Texas Press, 1982.

————. *The Political Transformation of the Brazilian Catholic Church*. New York: Cambridge University Press, 1974.

————, and Faucher, Philippe, eds. *Authoritarian Capitalism: Brazil's Contemporary Economic and Political Development*. Boulder, Colo.: Westview Press, 1981.

————, Mooney, Mary, and Gabriel, Chester, eds. *The Catholic Church and Religions in Latin America*. Montreal: Centre for Developing Area Studies, 1985.

Buechler, Hans C. *The Masked Media: Aymara Fiestas and Social Interaction in the Bolivian Highlands*. The Hague: Mouton, 1980.

Canovan, Margaret. *Populism*. New York: Harcourt Brace Jovanovich, 1981.

Cardenal, Ernesto. *The Gospel in Solentiname*. 4 vols. Maryknoll: Orbis Books, 1976–82.

CELAM. *The Church in the Present Day Transformation of Latin America in the Light of the Council*. 2 vols. Bogotá: CELAM, 1970.

257

Christian, William, Jr. *Apparitions in Late Medieval and Renaissance Spain*. Princeton: Princeton University Press, 1981.

———. *Local Religion in Sixteenth Century Spain*. Princeton: Princeton University Press, 1981.

Comaroff, Jean. *Body of Power, Spirit of Resistance*. Chicago: University of Chicago Press, 1985.

Comblin, José. *The Church and the National Security State*. Maryknoll: Orbis Books, 1979.

Davis, Natalie Zemon. *Society and Culture in Early Modern France*. Stanford: Stanford University Press, 1975.

———. "Some Tasks and Some Themes in the Study of Popular Religion." In Charles Trinkaus and Heiko Obermann, eds., *The Pursuit of Holiness in Late Medieval and Renaissance Religion*, pp. 307–36. Leiden: E. J. Brill, 1974.

DeKadt, Emannuel. *Catholic Radicals in Brazil*. New York: Oxford University Press, 1970.

Della Cava, Ralph. "Brazilian Messianism and National Institutions: A Reappraisal of Canudos and Joaseiro." *Hispanic American Historical Review* 48 (1968): 402–20.

———. "Catholicism and Society in Twentieth Century Brazil." *Latin American Research Review* 11 (1976): 7–50.

———. *Miracle at Joaseiro*. New York: Columbia University Press, 1970.

Dodson, Michael. "The Christian Left in Latin American Politics." In Daniel H. Levine, ed., *Churches and Politics in Latin America*, pp. 111–34. Beverly Hills: Sage, 1980.

———, and Montgomery, Tommie Sue. "The Churches in the Nicaraguan Revolution." In Thomas W. Walker, ed., *Nicaragua in Revolution*, pp. 161–80. New York: Praeger, 1982.

Eagleson, John, ed. *Christians and Socialism: Documentation of the Christians for Socialism Movement in Latin America*. Maryknoll: Orbis Books, 1975.

———, and Scharper, Phillip, eds. *Puebla and Beyond*. Maryknoll: Orbis Books, 1980.

Falla, Ricardo. *Quiche Rebelde*. Guatemala City: Editorial Universitaria de Guatemala, 1978.

Fields, Karen. *Revival and Rebellion in Colonial Central Africa*. Princeton: Princeton University Press, 1985.

Gheerbrant, Alain, ed. *The Rebel Church in Latin America*. New York: Penguin, 1974.

Gilfeather, Katherine Ann, M.M. "Women Religious, the Poor, and the Institutional Church in Chile." In Daniel H. Levine, ed., *Churches and Politics in Latin America*, pp. 198–224. Beverly Hills: Sage, 1980.

Ginzburg, Carlo. *The Cheese and the Worms: The Cosmos of a Sixteenth-Century Miller*. New York: Penguin, 1980.

———. *The Night Battles: Witchcraft and Agrarian Cults in the Sixteenth and Seventeenth Centuries*. New York: Penguin, 1984.

Goodwyn, Lawrence. *Democratic Promise: The Populist Movement in America*. New York: Oxford University Press, 1976.

Gremillion, Joseph, ed. *The Gospel of Peace and Justice: Catholic Social Teaching since*

Pope John. Maryknoll: Orbis Books, 1976.

Gutierrez, Gustavo. *A Theology of Liberation: History, Politics, and Salvation*. Maryknoll: Orbis Books, 1973.

Hebblethwaite, Peter. *The Runaway Church: Post-Conciliar Growth or Decline*. New York: Seabury Press, 1975.

Hill, Christopher. *The Century of Revolution, 1603–1714*. New York: W. W. Norton, 1982.

————. *The World Turned Upside Down: Radical Ideas during the English Revolution*. New York: Penguin, 1982.

Ileto, Reynaldo. *Pasyon and Revolution: Popular Movements in the Philippines, 1840–1910*. Quezon City: Ateneo de Manila University Press, 1979.

Ireland, Rowan. "Catholic Base Communities, Spiritist Groups, and the Deepening of Democracy in Brazil." Working Paper 131, Latin American Program. Wilson Center, Washington, D.C., 1983.

Kselman, Thomas A. *Miracles and Prophecies in Nineteenth-Century France*. New Brunswick: Rutgers University Press, 1983.

Lernoux, Penny. *Cry of the People*. New York: Penguin, 1982.

Levine, Daniel H. "Authority in Church and Society: Latin American Models." *Comparative Studies in Society and History* 20 (October 1978): 517–44.

————. "Continuities in Colombia." *Journal of Latin American Studies*, November 1985.

————. "Popular Organizations and the Church: Thoughts from Colombia." *Journal of Inter-American Studies and World Affairs* 26 (February 1984): 137–42.

————. "Religion and Politics: Drawing Lines, Understanding Change." *Latin American Research Review* 20 (1985): 185–201.

————. *Religion and Politics in Latin America: The Catholic Church in Venezuela and Colombia*. Princeton: Princeton University Press, 1981.

————. "Religion, Society, and Politics: States of the Art." *Latin American Research Review* 16 (1981): 185–209.

————, ed. *Churches and Politics in Latin America*. Beverly Hills: Sage, 1980.

————, and Wilde, Alexander W. "The Catholic Church, 'Politics,' and Violence: The Colombian Case." *Review of Politics* 39 (April 1977): 220–39.

MacKay, John A. *The Other Spanish Christ*. New York: Macmillan, 1933.

McPhee, Peter. "Popular Culture, Symbolism, and Rural Radicalism in Nineteenth Century France." *Journal of Peasant Studies* 5 (1978): 238–53.

Mainwaring, Scott. *The Catholic Church and Politics in Brazil, 1916–1985*. Stanford: Stanford University Press, 1985.

————. "The Catholic Church, Popular Education, and Political Change in Brazil." *Journal of Inter-American Studies and World Affairs* 26 (February 1984): 97–124.

Nash, June. "The Passion Play in Maya Indian Communities." *Comparative Studies in Society and History* 10 (1968): 318–27.

Obelkevich, James, ed. *Religion and the People, 800–1700*. Chapel Hill: University of North Carolina Press, 1979.

Sanders, Thomas G. "Catholicism and Authoritarianism in Chile." *Thought* 69 (June 1984): 229–43.

_____. "Popular Religion, Pastoral Renewal, and National Reconciliation in Chilean Catholicism." *American Universities Field Staff Reports*, South America Series, no. 16 (1981), pp. 1–12.

Segundo, Juan Luis. *The Hidden Motives of Pastoral Action: Latin American Reflections.* Maryknoll: Orbis Books, 1978.

_____. *The Liberation of Theology.* Maryknoll: Orbis Books, 1976.

Smith, Brian H. *The Church and Politics in Chile: Challenges to Modern Catholicism.* Princeton: Princeton University Press, 1982.

_____. "Churches and Human Rights in Latin America: Recent Trends on the Subcontinent." In Daniel H. Levine, ed., *Churches and Politics in Latin America*, pp. 155–93. Beverly Hills: Sage, 1980.

_____, and Sanks, T. H. "Liberation Ecclesiology: Praxis, Theory, Praxis." *Theological Studies* 38 (March 1977): 3–38.

Stern, Steve. *Peru's Indian Peoples and the Challenge of Spanish Conquest: Huamango to 1640.* Madison: University of Wisconsin Press, 1982.

Taussig, Michael. *The Devil and Commodity Fetishism in South America.* Chapel Hill: University of North Carolina Press, 1980.

Thomas, Keith. *Religion and the Decline of Magic.* New York: Scribner's, 1971.

Torres, Camilo. *Father Camilo Torres: Revolutionary Writings.* New York: Harper & Row, 1972.

Torres, Sergio, and Eagleson, John, eds. *The Challenge of Basic Christian Communities.* Maryknoll: Orbis Books, 1981.

Turner, Victor. *Dramas, Fields, and Metaphors: Symbolic Action in Human Society.* Ithaca: Cornell University Press, 1974.

Warren, Kay. *The Symbolism of Subordination: Indian Identity in a Guatemalan Town.* Austin: University of Texas Press, 1978.

Wilson, Bryan. *Magic and the Millennium: A Sociological Study of Religious Movements of Protest among Tribal and Third World People.* London: Heinemann, 1973.

Contributors

Phillip Berryman was the American Friends Service Committee Central America representative from 1976 to 1980. In addition to numerous articles and chapters, he has recently published *The Religious Roots of Rebellion: Christians in the Central American Revolutions.*

Thomas C. Bruneau is Professor of Political Science at McGill University. His research deals with politics in Brazil, the church in Brazil, and the political transition in Portugal and Brazil. His most recent books are *The Church in Brazil: The Politics of Religion* and *Politics and Nationhood: Post-Revolutionary Portugal.* He is currently working on the Brazilian transition in comparative perspective.

Michael Dodson is Professor of Political Science at Texas Christian University. He is the author of numerous works on politics and religion in Latin America.

Thomas A. Kselman is in the Department of History at the University of Notre Dame. He is the author of *Miracles and Prophecies in Nineteenth-Century France.*

Daniel H. Levine is Professor of Political Science at the University of Michigan. His most recent books are *Churches and Politics in Latin America* (ed.) and *Religion and Politics in Latin America: The Catholic Church in Venezuela and Colombia.*

Scott Mainwaring is in the Department of Political Science and the Kellogg Institute of International Studies at the University of Notre Dame. He is the author of *The Catholic Church and Politics in Brazil, 1916–1985.*

Susan Rosales Nelson recently completed the Ph.D. in anthropology at the University of Michigan. Her current research focuses on religious and social change among peasants in Latin America.

Charles A. Reilly is Research Director at the Center for U.S.-Mexican Studies of the University of California, San Diego. He is the author of numerous articles on development and political change in Latin America. He coedited *Religión y política en México.*

261

Brian H. Smith is Associate Professor of Political Science at the Massachusetts Institute of Technology. He is the author of *The Church and Politics in Chile: Challenges to Modern Catholicism*, as well as of numerous articles and chapters. He is currently working on the role of nongovernmental organizations in development in Latin America.

Index